W9-CNS-005

the pregnancy quiz

Try the quiz at the start of your pregnancy and then again at the end, and see how far you've come.

1 Colostrum is:

a) a very attractive ruin in Rome

b) stuff that comes out of your bosoms before you breastfeed

c) that strange blue goo that newborn babies are covered in

d) a thrash-trance band from near Dubbo

2 Can you retain fluid and be dehydrated at the same time?

a) don't be ridiculous

b) oh, lordy, yes

c) it depends on what star sign you are

3 Should you try to get time off before the baby arrives, rather than work until the due date?

a) yes

b) uh-huh

c) ooh, yeah

d) damn straight

4 Which is the most relaxing birth support team:

a) a midwife and your partner, sister or friend

b) a film crew, a live-on-the-Internet technical support team, a stills photographer, your children, parents and second cousins, all the girls from work and somebody called Arthur who took a wrong turn on the way to the canteen

c) nobody at all

5 Inducement is:

a) a very large diamond ring and a holiday in the Bahamas

b) an artificial medical process to stimulate labour

c) holding a Tim Tam at the end of the vagina to coax the baby out

d) a technical term for the placement of the placenta

▶

6 Braxton Hicks is:

a) that lantern-jawed bloke who slept with his aunty on 'The Bold and the Beautiful'

b) a term coined by NASA astronauts for a false alarm, named after an over-excited engineer on the Apollo 12 mission

c) practice labour contractions

d) a combination of the two most popular baby names in Kentucky in 1897

7 Palpation is:

a) what happens to your cervix when you have an orgasm

b) a pretentious word for 'having a feel'

c) the medical term for the faster heart rate you attain towards the end of a pregnancy

d) the opposite of temptation or craving: something that makes you nauseated

8 Placenta is:

a) the most popular girl's name after Sarah, Rebecca and Madison

b) the geographical location where you have your baby

c) a big gloopy item that looks like a liver and keeps the baby alive with nutrients and oxygen

d) a terrific marketing opportunity if you put it through a blender, whack it in a moisturiser and give it a French name

9 The easiest way of giving birth is by:

a) taking all the drugs you can get your hands on and shouting a lot at random

b) imagining you're in a perfectly charming wheat field having sex with Brad Pitt

c) having a general anaesthetic and paying someone to look after the baby for the first ten years

d) whatever means are necessary at the time

e) just like they do it in the movies

10 Women who say childbirth doesn't really hurt are:
a) lucky
b) deluded
c) insane
d) men

11 A primigravida is:
a) one of those ballerinas who doesn't eat enough
b) a woman giving birth for the first time
c) the first time you feel the baby move inside you

12 Living with a newborn baby is:
a) just like a lovely holiday
b) exhausting
c) what was the question again?

13 If you don't have a husband, you can:
a) get help from relatives and friends
b) just go straight to hell, you flaunty Miss Jezebel person
c) claim benefits and be involved in special re-employment and study programs provided by the federal government

14 Post-partum means after the birth. Antenatal means:
a) prenatal, or before the birth
b) you're against the whole idea of pregnancy, or being in any way slightly natal
c) another word for childbirth

15 Sex is:
a) really a tremendously heightened sensual experience all through pregnancy
b) just asking for trouble
c) apparently something that single, childless people do in their spare time

MRS FANNY BRAXTON HICKS

KAZ COOKE

The **real** guide to pregnancy

DUFF

VIKING
an imprint of
PENGUIN BOOKS

While every care has been taken in researching and compiling the medical information in this book, it is in no way intended to replace or supersede professional medical advice. Neither the author nor the publisher may be held responsible for any action or claim howsoever resulting from the use of this book or any information contained in it. Readers must obtain their own professional medical advice before relying on or otherwise making use of the medical information contained in this book.

VIKING

Published by the Penguin Group
Penguin Group (Australia)
250 Camberwell Road, Camberwell, Victoria 3124, Australia
(a division of Pearson Australia Group Pty Ltd)
Penguin Group (USA) Inc.
375 Hudson Street, New York, New York 10014, USA
Penguin Group (Canada)
90 Eglinton Avenue East, Suite 700, Toronto ON M4P 2Y3, Canada
(a division of Pearson Penguin Canada Inc.)
Penguin Books Ltd
80 Strand, London WC2R 0RL, England
Penguin Ireland
25 St Stephen's Green, Dublin 2, Ireland
(a division of Penguin Books Ltd)
Penguin Books India Pvt Ltd
11 Community Centre, Panchsheel Park, New Delhi – 110 017, India
Penguin Group (NZ)
67 Apollo Drive, Mairangi Bay, Auckland 1310, New Zealand
(a division of Pearson New Zealand Ltd)
Penguin Books (South Africa) (Pty) Ltd
24 Sturdee Avenue, Rosebank, Johannesburg 2196, South Africa

Penguin Books Ltd, Registered Offices: 80 Strand, London WC2R 0RL, England

First published by Penguin Books Australia Ltd 1999

26 25 24 23 22 21 20 19 18 17

Text and illustrations copyright © Kaz Cooke 1999

All rights reserved. Without limiting the rights under copyright reserved above, no part of this publication may be reproduced, stored in or introduced into a retrieval system, or transmitted, in any form or by any means (electronic, mechanical, photocopying, recording or otherwise), without the prior written permission of both the copyright owner and the above publisher of this book.

Designed by Sandy Cull and Leonie Stott © Penguin Group (Australia)
Typeset in Shannon and Minion 11.5pt by Alena Jencik
Printed and bound in Hong Kong through Bookbuilders

National Library of Australia
Cataloguing-in-Publication data:

Cooke, Kaz, 1962– .
    Up the duff : the real guide to pregnancy.

    Includes index.
    ISBN-13: 978 0 670 88289 2.
    ISBN-10: 0 670 88289 5.

    1. Pregnancy – Popular works. 2. Motherhood – Humor.
    3. Pregnancy – Humor. 4. Pregnant women – Physiology.
    5. Pregnancy – Psychological aspects. I. Title.

618.24

www.penguin.com.au

for Oofty Goofty

♡ ♡

Dearest Lui & Renato,
Congrats on your
wonderful news.
We hope you enjoy
reading this book as
much as we did.

♡ Rach Ant
Zara ☺

contents

'VERTICAL STRIPES FLATTER
THE MATERNAL FIGURE' - SALES ASSISTANT

Intro

Why did I write this book? Aren't there enough pregnancy gurus? For a start the last thing you need when you're pregnant is a bossy-boots insisting you 'should' feel this and 'must' do that. Who wants to have, or be, a guru? Not me. Okay, so first, I got up the duff. Then realised I had no idea what I was in for.

I bought a squillion pregnancy books and discovered they often contradicted each other on key points; they're only relevant in Idaho or Shropshire; or they're written by rich women who think you should get a sink installed in your child's bedroom (I ask you), or by people pushing their own personal theory, which may or may not involve giving birth in a wading pool full of lavender water and the dog.

The other thing pregnancy books tend to do is describe the size of the developing foetus in comparison with food. One week it's a brazil nut, then a plum, then an eggplant. At one point I became convinced I was going to give birth to a giant muesli.

And most of the books finish at exactly week 40 when the baby is due. In real life, while you're pregnant, you can't think any further than the birth. But the very minute you have a baby you can hardly remember a thing about the pregnancy. It's suddenly entirely irrelevant and you have to deal IMMEDIATELY with a tiny person who depends on you completely (and also do stuff with your bosoms they don't even ask from exotic dancers).

For some reason I had always imagined that being pregnant would just be like being me with a big bump out the front. It hadn't occurred to me that the reality of being pregnant eventually would be felt constantly in every physical part of my body, and in every recess of what I fondly used to call my mind. Even though I had heard about nausea and fluid retention and vagueness and a ferzillion other things, for some dumb reason I thought they were part of an old-fashioned pregnancy, relegated to history along with the concept of 'confinement' and Mrs Spinoza's mechanical home-perm-and-gherkin-bottling machine.

I'm a career woman, I thought. I'm over 30. I've always pretended to be in control of my life, and that doesn't have to stop just because I'm pregnant. I'll just live my life the way it has always been (without getting shickered and having a few fags at the weekend). Work will go on as normal, life at home will be just the same, only I'll need bigger shirts at some point. My life will only completely change once the baby comes out.

WELL.

Apparently not.

I had not bargained on the body taking control of itself. The power of the mind? Pah, and furthermore, snorty snonking sound. As far as my body was concerned, its major priority was growing a healthy baby. Several times I felt my legs going off along the corridor for a lie down when I thought my torso should have been elsewhere. I woke up in the middle of the night compelled to eat banana sandwiches and drink glasses of soy milk. I had become a host organ.

My first thoughts every morning and my last thoughts at night were about being pregnant, and there was a fair whack of it in between. (This is as well as the other stuff you usually have to be on top of in your normal life.) Would I be a good mother? What if something went wrong? Was it too late to have second thoughts? Should I feel guilty about having second thoughts? Where do we stand on third and subsequent thoughts? Where the hell are my keys? Why is the Vegemite in the freezer? Did I do that? What the hell has happened to my HAIR? What's that weird bump forming on my gums? Do stretch marks stay that fetching shade of royal purple forever? Will I ever want to have sex again? What do people mean when they say 'pregnancy hormones'? Is it true some aromatherapy can make you have a miscarriage? Is it any wonder they keep making horror movies about motherhood and creatures inside us? Isn't this miraculous? Isn't this uncomfortable? Isn't this terrifying, and wonderful, and fascinating, and boring as batshit, all at the same time? Am I supposed to feel serene, or just seasick? If you don't do your pelvic-floor exercises will your fanny fall out? Why can't I feel the baby move yet? Could the baby stop

moving for a while and give me a rest? What about those cigarettes I had before I realised I was pregnant? Will I ever be able to
be alone again? How can I tell people I don't want my career
back? How can I get my career back? When does a foetus become
a baby? Does that mean if it's born then it will survive? Could I get
any fatter? What's pre-eclampsia and how do you get it? What can
you see on an ultrasound screen? What if labour goes on forever
and nothing comes out? Could somebody get me a cup of tea?

And then when I had a baby the questions *really* started.

So to find out what's what, I wrote *Up the Duff*. The researchers
and I went to work, and then experts checked everything written
about their special area and suggested new bits, and then the
editor asked a gadzillion questions and in the normal course of
events I would have had a huge tantrum but I was too tired
because by that time I'd had a baby, so instead we checked it all over
again and took bits out and put bits in and waved it all about, and
now here it is.

If you read everything in the book you might think pregnancy
is a terrible minefield of bizarre health complaints. Don't freak
out: lots of the pregnancy problems are rare – they're included
'just in case'. If you do have a special interest or problem, though,
this book will give you the basics. And if there's something you
need to know more about, you can find an organisation or book
that will point you in the right direction recommended in the
'Help' section (that's the bit at the back).

— Kaz

PS: Oh, yeah. The Diary of Hermoine the Modern Girl's pregnancy includes many aspects of my own experience, with a few
stories from other people thrown in and the odd embellishment.
It is not quite my story. A girl has to try to cling to some sense of
mystery (especially when she's got baby vomit up her nose).
(Don't ask.)

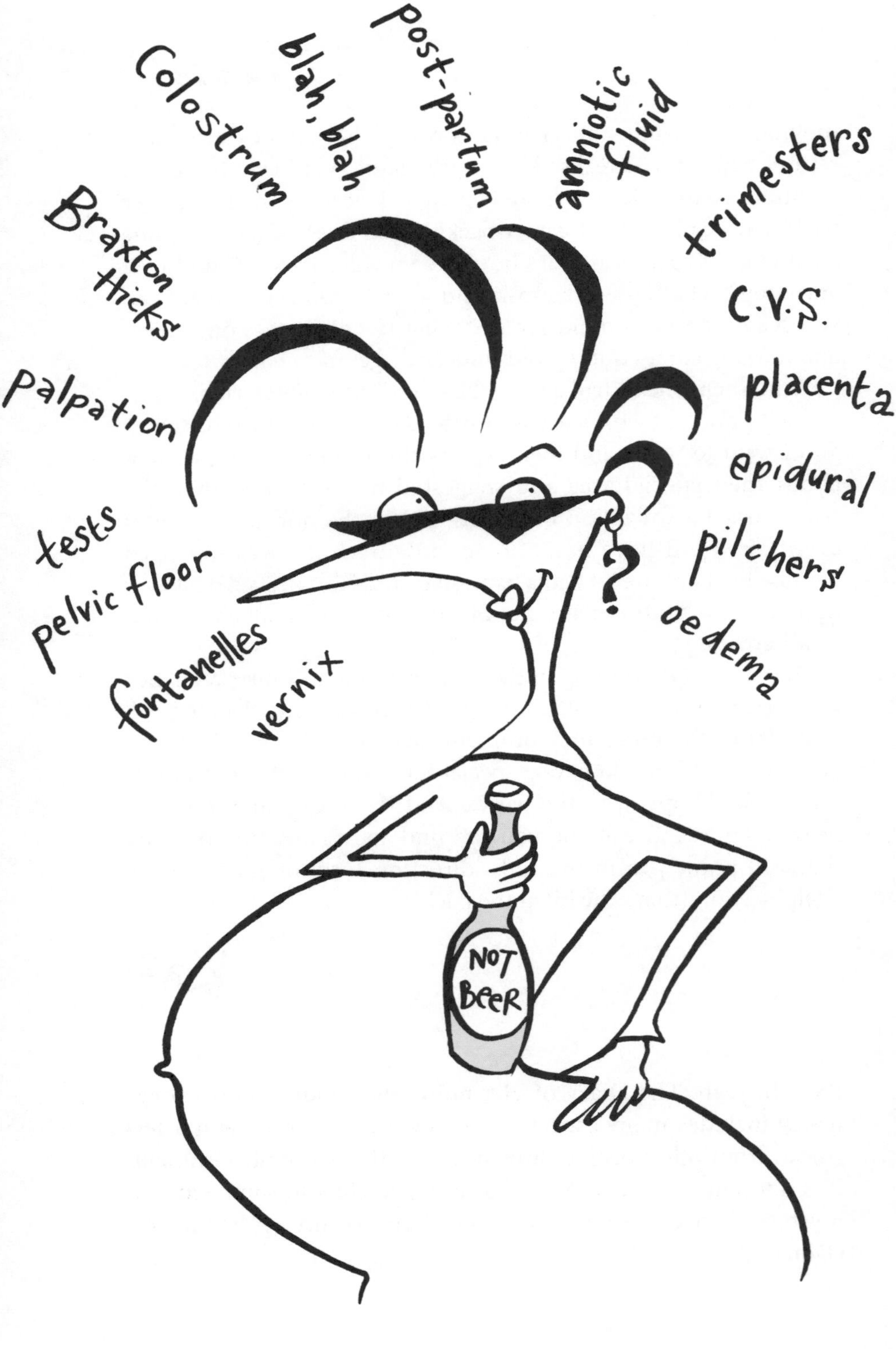
Colostrum
blah, blah
post-partum
amniotic fluid
trimesters
Braxton Hicks
C.V.S.
placenta
palpation
epidural
tests
pilchers
pelvic floor
oedema
fontanelles
vernix
NOT BEER

TERMS of ENDEARMENT

From conception we call the developing baby an EMBRYO, even in its earliest, cell-dividing days. At ten weeks, the embryo becomes a FOETUS, although you'll find that the term is often used for the unborn baby at all stages from conception to birth. All its organ systems are formed by then, and it's ready to expend most of its energy on maturing and growing.

At twenty-eight weeks the foetus becomes a BABY, even though a lot of medical staff still call it a foetus right up until it's born. We've called it a baby from week 28 because most premature babies born at this stage are likely to survive with modern, teaching-hospital care. (Many babies survive an earlier birth, although very premature babies often have continuing health problems.)

PREGNANCY SPEAK

The trimesters
'Trimester' means three months, so:

◎ the first trimester is up to the end of week 13

◎ the second trimester is week 14 to the end of week 26

◎ the third trimester is week 27 until birth.

Dates
This book, like most doctors, counts a pregnancy from the first day of your last period. So even if technically you conceived two weeks ago, you're 'four weeks pregnant'.

what's going on

Not much. By the end of the week, you've just finished the last period you'll have for a while. You're into the 'follicular' phase of the menstrual cycle, which means the egg-making and dispatch phase ('follicle' is the name for the tiny sac in which the egg matures). One of your two ovaries is deciding which of the eggs developing in this menstrual cycle will be the one to go forth. (An egg is also known as an ovum, if you want to get all Latin about it.) Your ovaries release 400–500 mature eggs during your 'fertile' years. It only takes one to get pregnant.

Your body is going about its usual hormonal carry-on. Lots of oestrogen (actually several oestrogens, just called 'oestrogen' as an umbrella term) is being produced by your ovaries. This stimulates the uterus to grow more lining, called the endometrium, to replace the lining that has just left as your last period. This new endometrium is the welcoming surface for the egg if it's fertilised. The egg is extremely weeny: about a tenth of a millimetre in diameter).

DiARY

I took an inventory of my life recently, and wrote it down with an eyebrow pencil on the back of a brown paper bag that used to have a muffin in it. It pretty much came out this way:

⁎ Hermoine Harridan.

⁎ Age: 32.

⁎ Unglamorous fashion designer for small struggling rag trade company, Real Gorgeous Pty Ltd (we make the Real Women Wear label, sizes 8–18).

⁎ Sagittarius (tactless and jovial).

⁎ Hobbies: eating, sleeping, buying shoes.

⁎ Accoutrements: perfectly decent boyfriend called Des, who works in a garden shop. Part of a house, mortgaged. Nice couch. Some ageing white goods. $3,500 in the bank.

⁎ Shape: not unlike the fruit known colloquially as a pear. With legs. Unusually fat knees. Never mind. Rest of self reasonably overweight, but nothing that a lot of exercise and a little less reliance on chocolate and cheese wouldn't cure.

⁎ Medical history: long tussle with endometriosis, a menstrual condition that often causes infertility, which I have controlled by taking the Pill full-time without a break. Haven't had a period for four years.

⁎ Doctor's advice last time I went: if you want to get pregnant, come off the Pill and start bonking like a rabbit (or words to that effect).

So Des and I had a talk. Six months before, I'd said I wanted to have kids and he'd said it was too soon (he's only 31, my toyboy). This time though, he'd thought about it and was as ready as he'd ever be, particularly since I told him that, given my medical history, nothing at all might happen, or it might take two years to get everything working again. I told Des there were a few things to sort out: like what would we do if a test during pregnancy showed that the baby had Down syndrome? And how would he feel if the kid grew up to be a gay man?

Des put his head on the side and thought for a moment. 'As long as he barracked for Footscray I can't see the problem.'

We each made a list of stuff we'd have to do before I got pregnant. Mine said:

✳ Go off Pill, and see Beck (that's my herbalist and medical adviser and fellow champagne admirer) about what else I should be on instead.

✳ Lose weight.

✳ Get fit.

✳ Lotto ticket.

✳ Stop smoking.

✳ Stop drinking.

✳ Get driver's licence.

✳ Don't roll about in pesticide-soaked paddocks, stop eating junk food, cook magnificently cunning little low-fat dishes from primary food sources, stop saying 'fuck' so much, get legs waxed, organise the sanding of the floor of our new house without actually breathing in any of that polyurethane topcoat. (The sanders, who breathe it in all day long, seem to have the IQ of somebody called Igor in a lab coat.)

I gaffer-taped the list of things to do onto the fridge. Then I took it off and replaced it with a note on a small piece of the muffin bag saying, 'Change entire life immediately', and threw my packet of Pills in the bin in a rather melodramatic fashion.

There was absolutely nothing on Des's list except:

✳ Buy milk and bread.

✳ Have sex.

info

getting ready for pregnancy

This is the time – before you get pregnant – to tackle any relationship problems or sort out any mixed feelings you have about life, and pregnancy. Why do you want to have a baby? Do you want a toddler and a teenager (that's what babies become)? Have you talked it all out with your partner, if you have one? Will the father be involved after the baby is born? How can you protect yourself from sexually transmitted diseases while trying to get pregnant? Is pregnancy going to spoil your chances of getting that part in *Bikini Busters: The Sequel*?

Some people think that having a baby will bring them closer together. These people should take a powder and lie down. Having a baby is probably the most stressful thing you'll ever do. Everyone quotes Nora Ephron: 'A baby is a hand grenade thrown into a marriage'. And there's all the practical stuff to think about *before* you get up the duff:

⑥ Are you really ready to make the transition from ready-for-anything-at-a-moment's-notice to 'slave-to-baby'-Mummy-who-hasn't-had-time-to-shower-in-two-days-and-whose-every-outing-must-be-planned-with-a-military-precision-that-needs-to-be-

totally-flexible-if-the-baby-wakes-up/won't-wake-up/cries/vomits/
needs-feeding/poos-on-the-mobile-phone? If you postpone the
decision, does that mean you might later be trying to get pregnant
when your fertility is declining rapidly?

◉ If you have a partner, this is a very fine time to share your
ideas about parenting, to avoid heartache further down the track.
Do you need to move in together? Are you both going to stop
smoking during the pregnancy? What are your views on prenatal
(also referred to as 'antenatal') testing? What would you do if you
found out your child had a severe abnormality or a disabling
condition? How would you cope with the idea of terminating the
pregnancy, or living with a baby who will grow up always having
special needs? Will the baby be part of a religious group? If it's a
boy, will you have him circumcised? (Many of these issues are
explored in this book and you can look up topics such as prenatal
testing and circumcision in the Index.)

◉ What child-care arrangements do you see as ideal? What's
going to be possible, or affordable? How about education? Who
does most of the housework and other unpaid jobs around the
house, and would that need to change? Do you share the same
feelings about the possibility of your child growing up to be gay,
or a stockbroker? What are your views on discipline and the issue
of hitting children? Do you have a good support network of
family and friends? Have any of them had recent experience with
babies? Do you have Plan B for any of this stuff?

◉ Do you need to take out private health insurance? If you want
private obstetric and hospital care and to choose your own
obstetrician, you do need insurance. Insurance funds have waiting
periods, usually of about twelve months, before you can claim for
pregnancy-related costs. Make sure you check exactly what they'll
pay for. Many only cover some in-hospital expenses, and no out-
of-hospital bills.

◉ See your doctor and natural therapist and announce that
you've decided you're going to try to get pregnant. They can give
you a clean bill of health to start with, and will probably

recommend that you start taking a special pre-pregnancy multi-vitamin supplement that includes zinc and folate and excludes vitamin A, which can harm an unborn baby. The doses will have to be modified once you are pregnant because your baby will have different needs. Pregnant women are often deficient in zinc, which is important for the baby's development. Folate, or folic acid, can reduce your risk of having a baby with spina bifida or a related problem. You need to *start* taking a folate supplement for at least a month before conception. As with any supplements, check with your doctor that folate is compatible with any other drugs you are taking. (See Eating and Supplements in 'Week 2' for more info on zinc and folate.)

◎ If you don't have immunity to it, get vaccinated against rubella (German measles), which can harm an unborn baby. Be careful not to conceive until three months after the shot. You may also need new vaccinations or booster shots for diseases such as tetanus or hepatitis B. (And if you think you could already be pregnant, check with your doctor about vaccinations as some can cause damage to an unborn baby.)

◎ If you suffer from a chronic health problem (for example, asthma, heart disease, liver problems, thyroid disease, diabetes, epilepsy, multiple sclerosis or mental illness), you should discuss medications and the management of your condition during pregnancy before you conceive.

◎ If you or your partner has a family history of hereditary disorders, speak to your doctor about seeing a genetic counsellor before conceiving (see Genetic Counselling in 'Week 10').

◎ Family planning clinics (see that section in 'Help'), like your doctor, can advise you on all sorts of things, from termination to where to get support throughout your pregnancy, at the birth and afterwards.

◎ The fitter and healthier you are going into conception and pregnancy, the better. Growing another human being is a huge workload and it's a job that goes on twenty-four hours a day for about nine months. If you're trying to get up the duff, the following are important: eat healthy food and take the right supplements, after consulting your doctor (see Eating and Supplements in 'Week 2'); exercise; stop smoking, drinking and taking recreational drugs, subject to your doctor's advice (see Looking After Your Embryo and Foetus in 'Week 4'); tell your doctor or pharmacist you are trying to become, or may be, pregnant before you buy any prescription, over-the-counter drug, or vitamin, mineral or herbal supplement; don't take any painkillers based on ibuprofen or aspirin (under various brand names); don't take anything on anybody's advice until you have asked a medical professional with up-to-date knowledge; aim to increase or decrease your weight so it's within the recommended range for your height and build (this is not the weight your Aunty Verna or *Cosmopolitan* magazine thinks you should be – ask your doctor about it). Some women's hospitals have special programs for overweight or underweight women to increase their fertility (see Women's Hospitals in 'Help' for phone numbers).

⑥ If you have a partner, encourage him to adopt a healthy diet and lifestyle so he will be producing healthy sperm when you conceive (in other words, try not to have unprotected sex with a drug fiend who won't eat his greens).

⑥ Go to the dentist. You may as well get any dental work that includes X-rays, anaesthetics or medication out of the way before conception rather than having to wait until after the birth.

⑥ Check out your entitlement to parental leave with your employer. In a large company you may be able to do this anonymously by phone if you don't want to flag your intentions. And check your entitlements with your union or the relevant government department, as well as your employer. Most women employed in the public sector get thirteen weeks' paid maternity leave and can negotiate when to come back after unpaid leave of up to a year. In the private sector you're entitled to a year's unpaid leave and possibly six to thirteen weeks' paid leave as negotiated. Men can usually take one week's unpaid leave at the time of the birth, and maybe even a year unpaid if they're the primary caregiver.

Some employers offer other benefits worth pursuing, including flexible working arrangements after the baby is born, and work-based child care. If there are two working parents involved, find out whose job offers a better package and child-care arrangements. If you're on contract or a casual employee, you may not have any entitlements.

◎ If one parent is taking time off paid work to look after the baby, how are your family finances going to be reorganised? (How do you spell 'budget'?) How would you feel about a joint account? Or about an automatic transferral of money from the income of the paid partner to the account of the one at home with the bub? Do you need to start a special savings account in case of emergencies? Would it be a good idea to rob a bank at this point?

◎ Make sure all household appliances and painting or renovation processes are foetus-friendly, without fumes or leaks.

◎ Check that your car or proposed car has or can have an anchor point installed for baby and child restraints. Don't buy an SUV or a four-wheel-drive car. (This doesn't apply to all-wheel-drive sedans.) Four-wheel drives are over-represented in accidents where children are hit in their own driveway – and a kid hit by a four-wheel drive is statistically very much more likely to die. (For the same reason remove any bullbar.) Proximity alarms, lenses and video-checking systems are not a guarantee of safety and can promote false confidence, according to car accident authorities. All vehicles have blind spots, especially low to the ground.

◎ Buy a lottery ticket. If you win, buy a great washing machine, a dryer, a fridge with the freezer at the bottom, and a cordless phone you can carry from room to room that has a hands-free speaker function. If your house doesn't have good heating or cooling and you need it in your climate, install it. Book a fully qualified mothercraft nurse through a reputable nanny agency to come and help you in the first couple of weeks at home. If there's any money left over, get yourself a holiday and an emerald tiara.

SPECIAL HINTS FROM A MOTHER
Before you decide to have a baby:
- spend time with friends who already have a baby, or older children, and have a good, hard look at their life
- spend at least a full day from dawn until late with a mother and a small baby; it's impossible to imagine just how much work is involved until you are in the thick of it.

trying to get pregnant

If you're trying to get pregnant, make absolutely sure you know which times of the month are most fertile for you: probably about day 14 if you have a twenty-eight day cycle, counting the first day of your last period as day 1. Your doctor can help you with discussions about ovulation, fertile mucus and the other nitty-gritties.

According to Professor David de Kretzer from the in vitro fertilisation (IVF) team at Monash Medical Centre, you shouldn't 'keep trying' forever. If you're not pregnant after a year of having unprotected sex, get a referral from your local doctor to a medical fertility specialist. If you're approaching 40, don't leave it as long as a year. Generally speaking, your fertility declines steadily after 35 and plunges after 40.

It may be a good idea to see someone even before you start trying. An obstetrician or fertility expert can talk to you about ways to maximise your chances of conception based on your individual situation. (Conception rates for your age group, for example, could be irrelevant to you if you have a medical condition that's preventing conception.)

 If you're having trouble, see Infertility in 'Help', as well as your doctor.

BOOKS FOR PRE-PREGNANCY

The Natural Way to Better Babies: Preconception Health Care for Prospective Parents by Francesca Naish and Janette Roberts, Random House, Sydney, 1996.

Offers natural ways and various theories to improve your health and fitness before getting pregnant. It also aims to improve fertility, but of course this will not work for everyone.

Planning a Baby: How to Prepare for a Healthy Pregnancy and Give Your Baby the Best Possible Start by Dr Sarah Brewer, Vermillion Books, through Random House, Sydney, 1998.

A medical perspective from England, including sections on vitamins, exercise, sexually transmitted diseases, male sexual health, trying to conceive and miscarriage.

REALITY CHICKS

The Mask of Motherhood: How Mothering Changes Everything and Why We Pretend It Doesn't by Susan Maushart, Vintage, Sydney, 1998.

The author is a Western Australian mother and social scientist who talks about the possible negatives of mothering, including the loss of a sense of self, the breastfeeding propaganda war, the chaos and confusion, the pain, the lot. She reminds us that for every woman who says breastfeeding was a wildly erotic and bonding experience, there are others who feel like a milking cow limping from one disaster to the next. And that for every model looking radiant in a magazine with a clean, new baby, there are other women madly trying to juggle offspring, work, a house and relationships.

Life after Birth: What Even Your Friends Won't Tell You About Motherhood by Kate Figes, Viking, Melbourne, 1998.

Despite the intensely unrealistic photo of sunnies-sporting, blonde-bombshell pregnant woman in the nuddy on the front cover, this book is actually about the unglamorous side of things.

The list of contents tells the story, including 'Childbirth: Just the Beginning', 'Emotions', 'Exhaustion', 'Relations with the Father', 'Friends and the Outside World'. Resources are all relevant to England, not Australia.

Motherhood: Making It Work for You by Jo Lamble and Sue Morris, Finch Publishing, Sydney, 1999.

Two Sydney psychologists (and mums) have based this book on their program to help mothers understand that being a mum is individual – there's no one recipe and no room for horrible guilt when you're not a so-called superwoman. Its hopeful message is 'there is joy despite the drudgery'. Contains lots of experiences from real-life mums, and sections on thinking clearly, being in control, overcoming guilt, how relationships change with a partner, expectations versus reality and strategies to deal with these issues. This is a good book to keep if you become a mother.

Motherlove (1995) and **Motherlove 2** (1997) edited by Debra Adelaide, Random House, Sydney.

Stories by well-known Australian writers and mothers about birth and beyond.

A Better Woman by Susan Johnson, Random House, Sydney, 1999.

A true story of the bizarre consequences of childbirth for one woman. While her medical experiences are mercifully rare, Susan Johnson's feelings as a mother are not. She writes of the damage and healing wrought on work and personal relationships, and the truth we all eventually learn: 'I am the good mother and I am the bad mother . . . caught in the same skin'.

Read any of the books about how to care for a baby (see Baby-care Books in 'Week 43'). It will give you a tiny inkling of what you're in for.

your record

Write down your thoughts here and in the other
Your Record sections of the book, so that in the
future you can look back at your pregnancy.

The changes you made to get ready for pregnancy.

Why do you want to have a baby?

What do you imagine looking after a baby
will be like?

How do you think your life will change after the
baby? What do you think you will do about work?

what's going on

By about day 14 (day 1 is the first day of your last period), you've reached the dispatch stage and your body is ready to OVULATE. This means this month's 'dominant' egg is released from one of your ovaries, and 'waved' into the nearby opening of a fallopian tube by tentacly-looking bits on the end of the tube. You have two fallopian tubes, one on each side of the uterus, providing the link between each ovary and the uterus. At the time of ovulation, your vaginal mucus (look, you're going to hear a lot worse words and concepts than vaginal mucus in the next nine months so pull yourself together) will usually look like raw eggwhites, and is known as 'fertile mucus'. And at some point you'll have to get some sperm up there. Most women do this by having sex with a bloke: this is still the easiest method.

After this week, you'll be into the 'proliferative' part of your menstrual cycle. This means the endometrium (the lining of the uterus) is 'proliferating' – growing like mad.

Diary   I decide to blow our savings and take Des away to a Pacific island for a week to ravish him constantly. Before we go I see my herbalist, Beck, who's also had years of experience as a hospital midwife. She gives me a tonic and some vitamins that include something called folate and heaven knows what other baby-friendly stuff, in preparation for Operation Up Duff. Des and I both need a holiday to fortify us anyway, having been working like demons to pay for the new house.

I believe there are many ways you can pinpoint the moment of ovulation, involving thermometers, ropes and pulleys, and other implements. I should have got out the calculator and a protractor and a slide rule and a sextant and a sexton and half a sundial to work out when I might ovulate. (Don't know what a sexton is, but it sounds rather raunchy.) I haven't enough endometrium to have a period, but that's how it is when you come off the Pill after four years on it non-stop. A menstrual chart's about as much use to me as a stuffed aardvark.

Instead I just guess.

So ten days after I've come off the Pill, I am poised for Operation Ravishment. Des keeps looking up from his beach towel and science fiction novel and saying, 'Hello, is it that time again?', when he sees the look in my eye, and manfully trailing me back to the hut. But in between ravishings and drinking champagne, I start to have second thoughts about being pregnant.

This could be a big year for me at work; even the chance of designing my own small range of clothes. I'm in line for promotion to head designer of Real Women Wear (stuff sold to people you or I might know, in things called 'shops', as opposed to what's known rather unkindly in the industry as 'Sluts on Stilts Wear': the flashier end of the collections called 'couture', the mad, show-offy bits that end up only on catwalk models).

I go over and over the decision, obsessing about all the things I couldn't have if I had a baby: independence, a disposable income, velvet shoes, the chance of being able to walk out the door and catch a plane or go to the shops by myself, vomit-free shoulders, bosoms I can call my own. And I know women whose partners say they'll 'help' instead of 'I'll do half', and house husbands (primary caregivers, thank you very much) who play with the kids but don't cook the dinner or do any washing.

I keep double-checking with Des that he really wants to stay home the first year of the baby's life while I go out to work, and that he'll also do the washing. Then I start panicking – as I'm sure most blokes do – that I've got to bring home the bacon and stay employed for the next twenty years. We have long conversations about changing my mind, what it will do to the career, how being childless would be so much easier.

After a particularly well-executed ravishing on the Tuesday morning I lie there looking at the languid ceiling fan with the definite feeling that *that* was exactly the sort of behaviour that would get one pregnant, if one were able to get pregnant. Which of course triggers the decision to go back on the Pill as soon as I get home and postpone the whole thing.

'It's all right, Hermoine,' according to Des the Ravishee. 'Plenty of time. It's up to you.'

Then he says something terribly sensible, which is that there is never an ideal time to have a baby unless you're the sort of person who has nothing to do all day, vats of money and a spare teddy bear. Neither of us falls into this category, but really it could be worse. We're both in work, we've got somewhere to live and a car and neither of us has a conviction for aggravated assault. And even if things were not so good, we'd work it out somehow. Still, it might be better to just wait and see if I get the promotion before I spend any more energy swinging from the chandelier in the nuddy making diverting remarks about likely ovulation days. Metaphorically speaking.

info

eating and supplements

You usually need more than the standard requirements of energy, protein and certain vitamins and minerals when you're pregnant, although you might be getting nearly everything you need already (and no, a whisky and pavlova each day does not keep the doctor away).

Basically, you've got to pay attention to your overall intake of everything to sustain the healthy growth and development of your baby. Not to mention getting through pregnancy without fainting around the joint and being all gaunt and frazzled.

How many kilojoules you need will depend on your age, height, build, weight at the time of conception, current diet, and whether you're a couch potato. Remember that for almost everyone it's important to put on weight during pregnancy. This is no time to go on a weight-loss diet or a fast. Either could be very dangerous for your baby and you.

Although some women won't need to increase their energy intake at all, the average recommended increase is 700 kilojoules a day. You need to add more than this if you were underweight to start with; you're a teenager; or you're carrying more than one baby. Your individual diet should be discussed with your midwife, natural therapist, doctor, obstetrician or the pregnancy dietician at your hospital or health centre.

To keep your weight gain within recommended limits while giving your baby all the goodies it needs, and so you don't get madly hungry, you need to eat quality kilojoules. Fresh, seasonal food provides far more nutrients than highly processed 'convenience' and junk foods.

Most people can get all the nutrients, vitamins and minerals necessary for a healthy pregnancy from a well-planned, balanced and varied diet. And the vitamins and nutrients you eat are always better value than ones in tablets or capsules.

But who always eats a perfectly balanced diet? No one unless they've got a private chef and time, dedication and squillions of dollars. You could be frantically busy and not quite eating what you should. Or throwing up could be leaving you depleted of vital nutrients. Or you might be trying to get through pregnancy on a vegan diet (no animal products), which is just not adequate for foetal development. (You may want to reconsider your vegan status during your pregnancy.) Special recommendations for vegans and vegetarians are scattered throughout this section.

Taking some supplements during pregnancy can be a good way of improving your intake of nutrients if your diet isn't perfect. Remember to talk to your doctor before taking any supplements prescribed for you by somebody else or that you've bought independently. (Early routine blood tests can identify pre-existing deficiencies in iron, vitamin B_{12} and folate.)

Your individual needs for certain supplements and doses will be different from those of anyone else, so talk about them with your hospital or local clinic dietician, midwife, doctor, obstetrician or natural therapist. Some multi-vitamin supplements (BUT NOT ALL, especially ones with vitamin A added) are fine and handy during pregnancy because they combine a lot of your needs in one pill, but read all labels carefully.

warning: vitamin A
Excessive levels of vitamin A are associated with birth defects, including cleft palate and heart malformation. Don't take any

vitamin A supplement while pregnant, and make sure any multi-vitamin you are taking doesn't have vitamin A in it. Sometimes vitamin A turns up in unexpected places such as a B-group vitamin supplement. Avoid eating pâté, liver or fish liver oils (which have high levels of vitamin A).

protein

You'll usually need an extra 6 grams a day on top of your non-pregnant requirement. That means you need a total of 5–6 serves of protein a day: 1 serve could be 1 glass of low-fat milk (unless you need the fat); 30 grams of hard cheese; 150 grams of yoghurt; 100 grams of lean meat; 200 grams of fish; or 1 cup of cooked beans or lentils.

Vegetarians need to be really strict about combining grains with legumes – to maximise the quality of their protein intake. Protein-rich foods include miso, tofu, eggs and dairy foods, seaweeds, nuts and seeds. Vegans will need to pay special attention to their protein requirements.

If you've been vegetarian or vegan and crave meat while you're pregnant, listen to your body and eat meat or fish if it doesn't upset you, or answer the call for extra protein with other foods.

calcium

Your tiny offspring is growing bones and teeth, and will pinch the very calcium out of your bones if you don't step up your intake. This might mean you're more likely to get osteoporosis later in life. Many natural therapists say that calcium deficiency is one known cause of cramp, while many medical doctors say this is a fallacy and there's no scientific proof. If calcium helps your cramps, take it.

You'll probably need to have at least 1,100 milligrams of calcium a day during pregnancy (3 or 4 glasses of low-fat milk or the equivalent yoghurt or cheese). This is about a third more again than your non-pregnant requirement. Teenagers who are still growing themselves will need an especially high calcium allowance during pregnancy. Check with your dietician or doctor.

Some examples of calcium-rich foods are dairy foods (milk,

yoghurt and parmesan cheese in particular), spinach or other leafy green vegetables, broccoli, tofu and tinned fish. Some people want to get all their calcium needs from dairy products, not least because 600 grams of cooked spinach or 1 kilo of cooked broccoli yield the same amount as a glass of milk. (This doesn't mean you can just drink litres of milk and never eat your greens!) But if you want or need to avoid dairy products, your other calcium-packed options include sardines, tinned salmon with the little bones in it, and tahini made from unhulled sesame seeds.

⏀ It's a good idea to maintain a calcium supplement (which ideally contains magnesium and zinc as well) while breastfeeding is making demands on your body's calcium supplies.

magnesium

You need magnesium or you don't get the full effect of the calcium and protein you take in. It's also used in therapeutic doses to combat pre-eclampsia – pregnancy-related high blood pressure (we'll get to that later in the book). Some good sources of magnesium are whole-wheat flour, muesli, wheat germ, beetroot leaves, silverbeet, spinach and raw parsley.

⊘ It's important to have magnesium included in a calcium supplement because of its crucial role in helping to retain calcium in bones and because normal diets are often deficient in magnesium.

vitamin D

You need vitamin D to help you and the baby absorb calcium, and to prevent health problems in the baby. Everyone needs it, with extra if they're pregnant or breastfeeding. The best natural way to make enough vitamin D is to absorb full sunlight five or six days a week (you don't have to take all your kit off, but some exposed skin – face, arms and hands – is necessary.) A person with dark skin needs to spend three to six times as long in the sun to make the same amount of vitamin D as a pale-skinned person. Australian experts recommend more than half an hour in mid-winter sun and six to seven minutes a day of summer sun for pale folk. Anybody who wears a full veil or otherwise keeps most of their body covered should think about finding a private place and time to expose their skin to sunlight.

❋ If you know you can't get enough sun (winter in southern climates being an obvious problem), talk to your doctor about a supplement. Don't buy a vitamin D or multi-vitamin supplement without advice from your doctor or pharmacist about the dose: too much vitamin D can be bad for you and the baby.

zinc

Zinc needs to be increased during pregnancy and lactation (breastfeeding). Zinc is needed for enzyme production, brain and nerve formation and to help build an immune system in the foetus. Proper zinc levels have been linked to safer birth weights and less-premature babies. This mineral is often really low in pregnant women's diets. It's found in wheat bran, wheat germ, dried ginger root, brazil nuts, hazel nuts and peanuts (with lesser levels in other nuts), dried peas and other legumes, red meat, chicken, fish, wholegrains and cheeses, especially parmesan.

❋ A zinc supplement is even more important if you're taking an iron supplement because iron may interfere with the body's absorption of zinc. Vegetarians and vegans especially may need a zinc supplement. A zinc supplement during breastfeeding is also often recommended.

folate (folic acid)

This B-group vitamin is now universally acknowledged as a supplement every woman should take for one month before pregnancy and for three months after conception. It has been proved dramatically effective in reducing neural tube defects by up to 70 per cent. Neural tube defects – the main one is spina bifida – affect one in 600 pregnancies. Although folate is naturally available in green leafy and yellow vegetables and wholegrain cereal, up to half of it can be lost in cooking or storage.

⊘ Just to cover yourself, it's best to take a supplement rather than try to make up the folate requirement in food every day. A daily dose of at least 400 micrograms (µg) – not 400 milligrams (mg), the more common measurement of many supplements – is the recommended daily dose. Higher doses may be recommended if you've already had a pregnancy with a neural tube problem. When you buy the supplement, make sure you get at least 400 micrograms (mostly they come in 500-microgram daily tablets, which is fine). If you're taking a multi-vitamin or mineral supplement that contains folate, check there's at least 400 micrograms of it a day: there usually isn't.

other B-group vitamins
Vegetarians and vegans will need to take vitamin B$_{12}$ supplements or drink plenty of soy milk fortified with B$_{12}$. B$_{12}$ only occurs naturally in animal products and is crucial in developing the baby's nervous system, brain and red blood cells.

⋂ A supplement containing B-group vitamins can be good for keeping up energy levels during pregnancy.

iron
Your iron requirement increases during the pregnancy: up to 20 per cent of pregnant women become iron deficient. Extra blood volume – yours and the baby's – means more iron is needed to make more haemoglobin. The placenta gives first priority to the baby's iron requirements, taking it from your blood, and you risk anaemia if you don't make up for this. You're considered to be at higher risk from iron deficiency if you're having a multiple pregnancy, you've had children quickly one after another, you've been vomiting a lot during pregnancy or you're a vegetarian or vegan.

You need 22–36 milligrams per day during the last six months of pregnancy compared to a non-pregnant requirement of 12–16 milligrams. Iron absorption is helped by vitamin C and hindered by tea, coffee and antacid medicines. Some examples of iron content in 100-gram servings of food are lean beef (3.4 mg);

sardines (2.4 mg); eggs (2 mg); wheat bran (12.9 mg); raw parsley (8 mg); spinach (3.4 mg); lentils (2.4 mg); dried peaches (6.8 mg); dried figs (4.2 mg); and dried apricots (4.1 mg). (If you want a quick boost of iron, have a drink such as Ovaltine or Milo.)

Iron supplements are sometimes recommended from about the thirteenth week of pregnancy to keep up that daily requirement of 22–36 milligrams after the first trimester. Vegetarians who are not careful about their diet, and vegans, will need an iron supplement. Vegetarians will also find it very helpful when they don't feel like eating a mountain of spinach. Supplements may cause constipation, or sometimes diarrhoea, and this should be discussed with your dietician, natural therapist, midwife or obstetrician, who can suggest an alternative form.

fats

You gotta have 'em for proper foetal development, but steer clear of saturated fats. Use mono-unsaturated vegetable oils, such as extra virgin olive oil, for cooking and salad dressings. You also need fatty acids, found in linseeds or linseed oil, pumpkin seeds, walnuts and pecan nuts, and oily fish; and linoleic acid, found in seeds, seed and vegetable oils, nuts and dark green vegetables. Avoid high-fat cooking methods such as frying and roasting in fat: better to grill, steam and stir-fry.

sugar and salt

Going for nine months without any sugar is, of course, deeply weird. But do try to avoid refined sugars where possible, for all the usual reasons. (You probably already know that eating a block of chocolate the size of your head is not considered healthy.)

A completely salt-free diet isn't recommended, but there's enough natural salt in food without shaking on extra.

fluids

Get onto them! You'll have more blood pumping around and the amniotic fluid surrounding the developing baby is constantly being replaced. (Not to mention all that sweating and crying that can go on.) Drinking at least 2 litres of water a day will help you avoid constipation and urinary tract infection. Steer clear of diuretics such as caffeine and alcohol. Diuretic drugs are unsafe during pregnancy, even if you have fluid retention: you could try plain dandelion-leaf tea (this is not the same as dandelion-root coffee substitute: dandelion-leaf tea looks more like a bag of bad marijuana or lawn clippings).

more info on eating and supplements

 Beware of many books on eating in pregnancy that are brought in direct from England or the US with all the recipes in pounds and ounces and sometimes unrecognisable ingredients such as cilantro (coriander) and collard greens (who knows). Others have obsessive average week-by-week weight targets that are best ignored by real individual human beings such as ourselves.

Women's Trouble: Natural and Medical Solutions by Ruth Trickey and Kaz Cooke, Allen and Unwin, Sydney, 1998.

What a woman needs and why (apart from a masseur and a chocolate ice-cream). Covers all sorts of things that can go wrong with the girlie bits from ovarian cysts and period pain to PMS, endometriosis and major surgery. Explores the herbal and medical options for each problem. Contains sensible guidelines on eating for health.

 The dieticians at your hospital, women's health centre or community health clinic will be able to help you. See Women's Hospitals and Women's Information Services in 'Help'.

PREGNANCY BOOKS

 A lot of books are handed to you when you're pregnant. Don't take them. When a friend recommends a book, buy the latest edition of it yourself. Some pregnancy books with out-of-date, even dangerous medical and safety info are passed around. And don't lend yours when you've finished with it. Here's a brief critical look at the main ones in circulation.

What to Expect When You're Expecting by Arlene Eisenberg, Heidi E. Murkoff and Sandee E. Hathaway, Workman, USA, 1997.

Despite the stupid drawing on the front – which shows a woman in a rocking chair who looks like she's recovering from a lobotomy – this hefty paperback is a great pick-up-and-put-down, look-it-up-when-you-need-to pregnancy guide that includes things that can go wrong. Has been adapted by the Childbirth Association of Australia, although it can still be rather too American on occasion. If you've thought about it, developed it, or are worried about it, it's probably in this book somewhere.

New Active Birth: A Concise Guide to Natural Childbirth by Janet Balaskas, Thorsons, UK, 1991.

Janet Balaskas is a long-time activist for the concept of active birth, in which the mother is in control of the labour situation, is able to move about, gives birth in an upright position (such as squatting or kneeling) and prepares for this during pregnancy with yoga and other natural methods. There is a manifesto about why this is so much better for mother's bodies and minds. (In the old days hospitals forced women to give birth on their backs with their legs in the air, working against gravity.) The book is full of yoga exercises demonstrated by women in horizontal-striped outfits, who look like very calm giant bees. There are lots of diagrams and photographs and explanations of active childbirth, and sections on home and hospital births, water births, and post-natal issues and exercises. (Note: make sure your obstetrician agrees with the principles of active birth if you are anticipating using this method. The book does not cover any medical intervention that may be really needed in the end, such as a caesarean. Not being able to have an active birth has nothing to do with you preparing wrongly. It's just the luck of the draw.)

New Natural Pregnancy: Practical Wellbeing from Conception to Birth by Janet Balaskas and Gayle Petersen, Sandstone Books, Sydney, 1999.

Concentrating on the mother, a holistic look at pregnancy with sections on emotions, nutrition, yoga and exercise, massage, natural therapies and holistic healing. Lots of illustrations of exercises, massage techniques and natural remedies for common pregnancy complaints.

The New Pregnancy and Childbirth by Sheila Kitzinger, Doubleday/ Dorling Kindersley, 1997.

Sheila the guru, Sheila the natural birth pioneer, Sheila the psychosexual water birth advocate. This revised edition, from England, is one of the pregnancy 'bibles' that gets handed on. Lots of illustrations of baby in the uterus, yoga, and sex during pregnancy (Good LORD!). Very comprehensive, including the emotional side of pregnancy and birth, the dad's experience, and the newborn's first days. Includes photos of births.

Conception, Pregnancy and Birth by Dr Miriam Stoppard, Viking, Melbourne, 1999.

A large-format book with the best in-uterus photos, although I didn't think much of the text. It has an emphasis on body and beauty concerns as well as the usual pregnancy and birth stuff. Her previous pregnancy book has drawings that make the pregnant woman look like a demented robot having a bad-hair day.

Your Pregnancy Questions and Answers by Glade B. Curtis, consulting editor D. F. Hawkins, Element Books, England, 1997.

Written by a couple of gynaecologists, one English, one American. Hundreds of questions answered, but in a very brief way. Covers pregnancy, single mums, problems, nutrition, tests, childbirth and feeding. Unfortunately, info about laws, entitlements and services are not relevant to Australia. A good one if you're anxious.

 **Pregnancy, Birth and the Early Months: A Complete Guide** by Richard Feinbloom, Addison-Wesley, US, 1993.
An experienced American paediatrician, Feinbloom has written a sensible book with a detailed section on labour, pain relief and things that can go wrong, as well as pregnancy. Some of the information can only be relevant to the US.

Preparing for Birth with Yoga by Janet Balaskas, Element Books, England, 1997.
All the women in the photos look very calm and supple. I say we kill them now.

your record

List the strategies you took to try to get pregnant, such as identifying ovulation. (If you *weren't* trying, why not record your method of contraception for posterity!) How long did you try for?

what's going on

Fertilisation! Inside you your single-cell egg is tootling slowly down the fallopian tube when it is rather suddenly accosted by an insistent sperm, which wriggles inside it. The cell splits in two, then those two new cells split in two, and so on, within a surrounding jellylike coat. This fertilised egg or embryo takes about four days to languidly drift down the tube and into the uterus. A couple of days after arriving it finally sheds its jellylike coating and decides where to park itself, usually in the top, front part of the uterus. By now it's made up of about 200 cells. There's an innie bit that is the embryo; and an outie bit that will become the placenta (which will sustain the developing baby) and the amniotic sac (which contains the nice, warm amniotic fluid 'bath' the growing baby will float around in).

The embryo sends out roots to anchor it in the endometrium surface and draw in goodies from your bloodstream. It's this system that develops into the placenta.

DIARY

We're getting ready to move house. I want everything in its place. Tidy, tidy, tidy. I've been collecting boxes and putting things in them and pretending this means I'm an organised person with a streamlined life. Actually it just means that I'm a disorganised person in possession of a number of boxes.

Des bought a small mini-van to transport his grasstrees, ficuses and, on really tasteful landscaping jobs, small statues of weeing cherubs. This vehicular purchase, along with moving to a larger house, has led to much unseemly speculation. Combine real estate move, larger motor car and a hint of an enigmatic smile, which one cultivates to cover a whirling sense of nothing-to-speak-of going on in the brainish region, and there is an immediate up-the-duffian calculation on the part of bystanders.

Some people, almost always the ones who have their own kids and often plenty of them, bang on about it constantly. 'Are you pregnant yet?', 'When are you going to start a family?', as if a baby's just something you send off for with a stamped, self-addressed envelope.

Luckily we don't have the sort of parents who pressure us, given that Mum died before I could remember her, nobody knows who my Dad was, and Des's parents are usually off studying lichen in the most bio-eccentric mountains of Venezuela, rather than demanding that we have some grandchildren to keep them amused. I am constantly amazed by the parents of friends who think it's their perfect right to insist that their offspring hurry up and 'give them grandchildren'.

I'm sure Aunty Peg, who raised me with the help of Uncle Stan before he ran off with that belly dancer from Dubbo . . . what was her name? Raelene the Magnificent was on the posters, but I'm pretty sure she made the last bit up . . . anyway, I'm sure Aunty Peg would be rapt, but at least she isn't leaning on me. Uncle Stan, who has become a born-again pensioner-feral, would no doubt go all new-age on me. And he ought to know by now I'm not the earth-mother type.

Just for fun, Des and I have been playing parents with a Tamagotchi baby we found at a garage sale – it's one of those tiny

Japanese digital games that look like key rings. We turned the game on, called our electronic-screen baby Fred and pressed Start. There was a button to be pressed when Fred produced what the instructions called 'dung'. And buttons to press to see Fred's weight and age; to play paper, scissors, rock with him; to give him rice or a bottle; and to 'discipline' him. (Unfortunately there seemed to be no Child Protection Unit button.)

Every night Des bounds in from a day of demanding clients saying things like, 'What about a daiquiri fountain on the east lawn?' and 'I've never liked agapanthus' and 'Can't we just concrete that bit?' and 'No, I've changed my mind', and he asks breathlessly and tenderly, 'How's Fred?'.

And each time, flushed with the bloom of mothering a newborn, baby-purple extruded-plastic capsule with digital liquid-crystal output screen thingie, I report, 'Haven't seen him all day. Busy', 'Try the cutlery drawer' or 'I left him in a café.' Or more often, the simply poignant diagnosis, 'Well . . . Fred's dead.' Bloody depressing game, if you ask me.

No, it has to be said: motherhood is the hardest and most honourable job in the world. Oh well. With my medical history it might take years to get pregnant. If at all. Probably just as well. Let's face it, I'm not likely to get a reference from Fred.

I suppose if I'm going to stay off the Pill, I had better find a friend with a baby and spend a day or so with them. I was off wearing miniskirts in foreign parts when Amanda's babies were small, and not that interested really. Now that I am, I realise most of my friends are lesbians or career women who are only just starting to wonder how they might manage it. The only one who's already launched her kayak into the creek is Marg, and she's only four months pregnant. I guess I can practise on her baby when it arrives. I had better find an instructional video called something like 'A New Baby: Which End Up?'.

We just don't live any more in a tribal society surrounded by a million kids of varying ages and great scads of extended families. My second cousin Bazza has six of the blighters, but they live on the other side of the globe so there's not much practising to be had there. There should be some kind of library service.

info

sense of smell

Your sense of smell may be far more acute than usual during pregnancy, especially in the first three months. You may even notice it before you know you're pregnant. Perfumes or food smells that previously seemed downright scrumptious may now send you heaving to the bathroom. What's really annoying is that none of the experts seem to be able to say why. Maybe the nausea is a defence mechanism so you're more likely to identify 'off' foods that could harm you or your baby. Maybe it's to compensate for the last two-thirds of a pregnancy often being accompanied by a blocked nose (due to a general increase in bodily secretions you don't want to have to think about yet). Or maybe it's just a meaningless side effect of one of the 'pregnancy hormones'.

aromatherapy

Aromatherapy, the therapeutic use of essential oils, can make you feel nurtured and relaxed during pregnancy, but some essential oils can harm your unborn baby or bring on labour or even a miscarriage, especially if applied directly to the skin during a bath or massage.

Qualified aromatherapists advise against any aromatherapy applied directly to the skin in this way during pregnancy, especially during the first trimester, without advice from an aromatherapist specialising in pregnancy. Some oils are not even recommended for burning to scent a room when you're pregnant.

Unfortunately some masseurs who use essential oils without being qualified aromatherapists are simply unaware of any risks and will tell you anything they use is quite safe at whatever concentration they feel like squirting on you. And even the oils considered 'safe' for massage or in the bath should be used at half-strength during pregnancy.

It can be confusing for a layperson to decide what is safe. For example, despite spearmint used directly on the skin being in the 'banned during pregnancy' list given below, some pregnancy magazines recommend it to relieve nausea when used as an infusion to breathe in or to scent a room.

Oils generally considered safe for use during pregnancy include lavender, grapefruit, orange, lemon, tangerine, mandarin, neroli, sandalwood, ylang-ylang, geranium (after the fifth month), bergamot, ginger and tea-tree.

Oils that can induce miscarriage (abortifacients) or bring on a period (emmenagogues) must be avoided during pregnancy. They include, but may not be exclusively confined to, yarrow, aniseed, tarragon, caraway, atlas cedarwood, camphor, hyssop, pennyroyal, spearmint, parsley and parsley seed, rosemary, nutmeg, Roman chamomile, German chamomile, myrrh, juniper, lovage, pepper-mint, basil, Spanish marjoram, clary sage, sage, bay, vetiver, pine, thyme, jasmine, wintergreen and angelica.

Remember that you may be supersensitive to smell, but your nose can also be blocked up during pregnancy and therefore *less* sensitive to smell. So always follow the recipes given by a qualified aromatherapist rather than your schnozz. And obviously, for your own comfort, don't use anything that makes you feel queasy.

Here are some safe aromatherapy ideas.

☺ Aches and pains – throw a couple of drops of lavender oil in the bath.

☺ Fatigue – in a burner to send the smell wafting through the room, 2 drops of lavender oil, 1 drop of mandarin oil and 1 drop of ylang-ylang oil; or 1 drop of lavender oil, 1 drop of mandarin oil and 2 drops of ylang-ylang oil.

⑥ Nausea – in a burner, 1–2 drops of lemon oil or lemongrass oil; or make some ginger tea (see Nausea in 'Week 4') – drink the tea and breathe in the aroma as you go.

⑥ Insomnia – put 3 drops of lavender, mandarin or ylang-ylang oil, or a mixture of the three, in the bath; scent your bedroom with 2–3 drops of lavender or ylang-ylang oil, or a mixture of the two.

⑥ Stuffy nose – make an inhalation by adding 2 drops of eucalyptus or tea-tree oil to a bowl of hot water, then stick a towel over your head and breathe in the vapour for a couple of minutes. (You can't use many 'cold remedy' drugs during pregnancy so this is a good one to remember.)

⑥ Bad circulation – in a burner, 2 drops of grapefruit oil, eucalyptus oil or frankincense.

Many women burn lavender oil when giving birth – but wherever there are oxygen tanks a naked flame is banned. Many hospitals provide electric burners for essential oils during labour. Aromatherapy won't actually help with pain relief.

herbal teas

Many herbs can bring on a period, or cause miscarriage or birth defects. Always check with a trained herbalist. (No more than three cups of any kind of herbal tea should be consumed every day as a habit.)

Herbal teas that are generally considered safe during pregnancy include: peppermint, fresh ginger, lemon balm, chamomile, and dandelion leaf (which is a safe diuretic) but not dandelion root. Herbal teas should not be confused with essential oils: an oil extracted from a plant contains very large quantities of components that could be dangerous, whereas a tea made from the plant might not.

medicine and natural therapies

Remember, don't take medicines, herbs or vitamins without consulting a properly trained doctor or herbalist. Just because your friend took something during her pregnancy that she swears by doesn't mean it's safe for you or your baby. Some preparations can be taken at different times during the pregnancy; others are dangerous at different times, or at any stage. Some preparations are safe *except* during pregnancy. Don't assume because something is 'natural' it is 'safe'. And always tell your doctor and natural therapist what the other one has prescribed.

Beware of dippy 'natural therapy' or 'diet' advice. Most diets that involve restriction of certain food types are not suitable for pregnancy, and fasting is compleeeeetely out of the question as it could damage the developing baby or even cause miscarriage. (See Eating and Supplements in 'Week 2' for all the lowdown on eating during pregnancy.)

WEEK 4

what's going on

Your period is due. Maybe you've started going wee, wee, wee all the way home. Perhaps you've gone off the smell of alcohol and cigarettes, and foods that you usually like. Now or in the next few weeks, you might start feeling slightly queasy, which in bad cases results in vomiting. (According to one pregnancy book photo, this is when you will wear a hideous smock and an Alice band, and stare out the window holding a cup and saucer like a demented fool.)

The tiny embryo burrows into the wall of the uterus until it's completely embedded, and keeps getting bigger every day. The ovaries are pumping out the hormone progesterone to make the endometrium tough. The sex of your baby, the colour of its hair and eyes, how tall it can grow and whether it has natural footy talent – all these factors have been genetically programmed from the start, and can't be altered. By the end of this week the embryo's

about a fifth of a millimetre – still too little to see without using

magnifying instruments.

DiARY

Went for a drink with my old pal Juan, whose wife has been at home with the kids for four years and is now dashing her head against a plywood wall trying to get into the workforce again – the restaurant industry wants her to work split shifts for approximately 75 cents a day. He says apart from this whole work problem, and vomit and poo, motherhood is INCREDIBLY GLAMOROUS.

I meet with the boss about becoming head designer of Real Women Wear and agree to a schedule of sacred weekly meetings with the new buyers. I sign on the dotted line for my first range. Off to Paddy's party with the girls and smoke about seven cigarettes – and have two glasses of killer punch. For some reason I don't want to get drunk. Have a bit of a half-hearted dance. I'm feeling kind of tired and out of sorts. Not quite nauseous but squirgly in the tummy.

For some reason I've started being absolutely vile to Des. I don't know why. I'm quite aware I'm doing it but I can't stop myself: I am the Bitch Queen of the Universe. He comes in the front door and I narrow my eyes looking for a fault. I swear if he came in the door with a bunch of mauve roses and tickets to the Bahamas I'd probably say, 'Wipe those filthy boots!', for all the world as if I had suddenly developed a passion for clean floors. I'm really starting to worry. I think I'm turning into a gorgon.

Oh, how could I be so STUPID? It must be PMT. I've just forgotten what it's like after four years on the Pill.

info

nausea

Some people still call it morning sickness, but it isn't, so they shouldn't. It can get you at any time of the day, even all day. Not everybody gets it, but most pregnant women experience some form of nausea, usually in the first trimester, and half will throw up at least once. It can range from a slightly queasy feeling to full-on, head-in-a-bucket, serious vomiting. For some very unlucky women, it persists after the fourteenth week, even all through the pregnancy.

The cause has not been absolutely identified, and may even vary from person to person. The culprits are thought to include any or all of the following: high levels of the hormone HCG; a fall in blood pressure resulting from progesterone-induced relaxation of muscles, which causes dilation of the blood vessels; less efficient digestion due to less stomach acid in the gut; an increase in oestrogen challenging the liver to break it down, so the liver works overtime; and altered senses, which means that some smells and tastes make you feel sick. (For more info see Pregnancy Hormones in 'Week 12'.)

Here are some things that may help.

⊚ Eat small, frequent snacks to avoid an empty tummy or a low blood-sugar level – keep a handbag or briefcase 'pantry' of dried fruit, dry biscuits and raw nuts, fruit or vegetables.

⊚ Have four or five smaller meals a day instead of three biggies (this can also be useful in the third trimester when your tummy is squished up).

⊚ Eat something bland *before* you get out of bed in the morning, such as dry toast or a dry biscuit, or have a small amount of fruit juice.

⊚ Have a snack just before bedtime.

⊚ Avoid the fish market or perfume counter or anything else that makes you feel queasy; this can include fatty or fried foods, cigarette smoke, coffee and alcohol.

⊚ Maintain your intake of protein (chicken soup is good) and complex carbohydrates (potato, rice and pasta).

⊚ Avoid getting tired or stressed.

⊚ Try ginger tea – infuse 1–2 teaspoons of grated fresh ginger (or a piece of ginger, about the size of your little finger and chopped into four or five bits) in a small teapot of boiling water for 5 minutes; strain; add honey or a squeeze of lemon to taste, breathing in the steam as you go.

◉ Sniff a fresh lemon.

◉ If you've been vomiting, drink lots of water so you don't dehydrate.

◉ Try vitamin B$_6$, which may be recommended by natural therapists and doctors for severe sickness.

It's not common for vomiting to be so bad that it needs medical intervention, but if you are vomiting more than once a day for days in a row, or any aspect of your vomiting is distressing, tell your doctor straight away. The main risks are that you'll dehydrate, especially if you can't keep down fluids, or the baby will miss out on nutrients.

Nausea is often said to be a good sign – evidence that the hormones are pumping, indicating a strong, stable pregnancy. Some people claim first-trimester nausea lowers the risk of miscarriage. (Others point out that nausea affects only half of all pregnant women, so it's hardly a prerequisite for a healthy pregnancy.) More severe nausea is associated with a twin or multiple pregnancy because the hormone levels in the bloodstream are higher.

looking after your embryo and foetus

Teratogens are infections, substances or environmental factors that can damage an embryo or foetus at certain stages of development – the biggest danger being in the first three months of pregnancy. (In usual tactless-doctor language, 'teratogen' is derived from the ancient Greek *teras* meaning 'monster'.) The effect of teratogens can range from impaired growth or increased risk of a miscarriage through to serious birth defects.

The impact on the developing baby depends on the teratogen – some are much more dangerous than others – and your level of exposure, as well as what stage of pregnancy you're at when exposed, and individual susceptibility, and luck. (Even if you know somebody who drank vodka like a mad thing through their pregnancy and had a 'normal' baby, it doesn't mean the same will apply for you.)

It's believed that not much damage is likely to be done between conception and when the egg implants itself in the wall of the uterus six to eight days later. The most dangerous time is from implantation to the tenth week after conception, when major organs and limbs are being formed. But some teratogens can affect major parts of the developing baby throughout the whole pregnancy, including the brain, eyes and sex organs.

scary illnesses

Hyperthermia (overheating)   Any illness that causes a high temperature (38.9° Celsius or more) for an extended time, especially in the first three months of pregnancy, can cause damage to an embryo or foetus.

Toxoplasmosis   This illness can be symptomless or feel like mild flu. It's caused by a parasite commonly found in raw or undercooked meat (meat should be cooked to an internal temperature of at least 60° Celsius), including game birds; unpasteurised goat's milk products; and the poo from cats and, more rarely, dogs. The infection can cause brain and eye damage in the foetus, and miscarriage. The greatest period of risk is the third trimester. Many people come into contact with the parasite at some point and develop an immunity to it.

Avoid cats. Wear gloves when gardening. Before eating raw, garden-grown produce, wash it thoroughly with detergent and hot water.

Listeriosis This relatively rare bacterial infection is transmitted through foods. Its symptoms include fever, headache, tiredness, aches and pains. It may cause miscarriage or stillbirth. High-risk foods are raw, insufficiently cooked and prepared, 'ready-to-eat' seafood, such as smoked fish and mussels (but tinned fish should be safe); premixed salad vegetables; precooked meats and pâtés; thickshakes and soft-serve ice-cream; and unpasteurised milk or milk products, especially soft cheeses such as brie, blue vein and camembert.

Rubella (German measles) Rubella can cause such a high incidence of abnormalities in babies (congenital rubella syndrome includes blindness and deafness), particularly when mothers are exposed to it in the first trimester, that routine immunisation is now offered to all girls in Australia. Often you need a booster shot, so before trying to get pregnant it's a good idea to have your doctor organise a blood test to check your immunity. If you need to be vaccinated, wait three months afterwards before trying to conceive, so your system has time to destroy the live virus in the vaccine. Your obstetrician will organise a rubella test for you if you're already pregnant.

Syphilis This increasingly uncommon sexually transmitted disease (STD) can cross the placenta and cause premature birth and stillbirth, or long-term effects in children such as dental abnormalities. It can be detected in routine pregnancy tests and safely treated in early pregnancy. It can also infect the baby during the birth, and the baby can then be cured with drugs.

Gonorrhoea Another STD, gonorrhoea can also infect the baby during the birth, and the baby can then be cured with drugs.

HIV Pregnant women with HIV will not automatically pass it on to their babies. Estimates of transmission range from 14 to 50 per cent. Mothers with HIV must not breastfeed, as transmission rates are much higher. (This is why infant formula is once again being promoted by health workers in Africa.)

Genital herpes An active case can infect the baby during birth. If you have genital herpes, your obstetrician should closely monitor it in the latter part of the pregnancy. If you have an active case at the time of delivery, a caesarean delivery will protect your baby from the chance of possible infection.

Cytomegalovirus The most common infectious cause of mental retardation and congenital deafness, cytomegalovirus is another virus in the herpes group. A blood test can check whether you have already been infected: most cases of foetal damage happen when you are first infected.

Hepatitis C It is believed that very few pregnant women with hep C will have babies who are infected. There are only a few case studies so far, but it is thought that babies are more likely to get hep C if their mum was exposed to it in the third trimester. There is some suggestion that transmission is more likely if the mum has HIV as well.

Other diseases and conditions There are many diseases and conditions that can affect your embryo or foetus. Some of these have 'silent' symptoms so you may not be aware of any risk or problem. Tell your doctor about any high fever, rash, sweats or fluid retention during your pregnancy or any other symptom that worries you.

what goes in: dangerous substances

Just about everything you ingest while you're pregnant will cross the placenta in some form and affect the developing foetus or baby. This includes drugs, alcohol, chips, cheese and air. It may help while you're putting something into yourself to imagine putting it into the baby at the same time (this will remind you: chocolate biscuit okay; four cocktails not so much).

No prescription or over-the-counter drug, herbal or natural remedy or vitamin or mineral supplement should be taken during pregnancy without consulting a doctor who knows you're pregnant. No recreational or street drugs are safe to use during pregnancy. (But it can be even more dangerous to try to quit an addiction to heroin, for example, during the pregnancy – see below.) It's a good idea to get 'clean' before you conceive, and you can get help to stay that way. Many people think that knowing they're having a baby will get them to quit drugs or alcohol, but that's rarely enough. Everyone needs help to quit an addiction, and it's available. Make sure you tell your doctor and obstetrician about any drugs you've used during pregnancy: they're not allowed to tell the police.

Vitamin A Any supplement or acne or skin treatment containing vitamin A should be stopped while you're pregnant, and avoid liver or liver products, including pâté.

Caffeine An intake of three or more cups of tea or coffee a day is associated with low birth weight and may double, some say triple, the risk of miscarriage in the first trimester. The same is true of cola drinks.

Painkillers and other over-the-counter drugs Anti-inflammatory painkillers containing ibuprofen or aspirin (they come under various brand names) should not be taken by pregnant women without medical supervision as they could lower hormone levels vital for a continued pregnancy. Don't buy painkillers (or any other drugs) at a supermarket or other shop without first discussing them with a doctor or pharmacist who knows you're pregnant.

Herbs Many herbs, herbal supplements, herbal teas and juice-bar additives are unsafe for pregnant women and their developing babies (see also Herbal Teas in 'Week 3'). Never assume 'natural' or 'herbal' means that something is okay to take during pregnancy, and seek up-to-date professional advice no matter what you're told by friends.

Alcohol Doctors used to believe that, although an excessive amount of alcohol could cause the serious defects of foetal alcohol syndrome, a few drinks here and there were safe. Experts now say that any amount of alcohol can have a damaging effect on the foetus's development, so all major national and global health organisations recommend that pregnant and breastfeeding women give alcohol a complete miss. I'm often asked rather pleadingly by pregnant women to agree that one drink a day or a couple a week is fine, and it might be for some people, but it's just not possible to say definitely that this is safe. Sorry, ladies, but guaranteeing no effect means saying no grog for the duration.

Cigarettes   Cigarette smoking stunts the growth of the foetus. This has been an 'excuse' for women who keep smoking while pregnant ('It'll be an easier birth if it's a small baby'). But smoking also inhibits the growth of the placenta and is believed to be linked to miscarriage, sudden infant death syndrome (SIDS), childhood asthma and other respiratory traumas for babies and children.

Marijuana and hashish (dope)   Their use is linked to premature birth and low birth weight. There is no known 'safe' amount.

LSD and other hallucinogens   LSD carries the risk of miscarriage and chromosomal damage. There is little research on other hallucinogens but it's safest to assume any amount is dangerous.

Ecstasy   There isn't much detailed research yet on 'newer' recreational drugs – although ecstasy has been associated with increased risk of placental bleeding – but we know they're definitely not a good idea when you're pregnant.

Amphetamines (speed and ice)   These drugs are associated with premature babies, baby heart problems and other complications.

Heroin and methadone   These drugs can cause prematurity, low birth weight, mental problems and stillbirth. Babies share their mother's addiction and so suffer withdrawal symptoms when they are born, although this can be managed by medical staff. Prescribed methadone is preferable to heroin in pregnancy because it provides a regulated dose to the foetus. The baby must be weaned from its methadone addiction after birth. Coming off heroin suddenly while pregnant is a cause of miscarriage: don't stop abruptly without talking to your doctor.

Cocaine   Even a single, one-off dose can damage a foetus.

environmental hazards

If your job or workplace is unsafe during pregnancy, you have the legal right to be given duties that don't expose you to the hazards. Avoid any of the following.

Radiation   X-rays can cause malformations in a foetus. Tell any doctor or dentist who wants to X-ray you that you're pregnant. If you had one before you knew you were pregnant, ask your obstetrician about the risk to the foetus. It's usually not bad news. Low-level radiation emitted by computer visual display units has not been proven to have an effect on pregnancy or a developing baby.

Getting too hot   As with overheating caused by illness, your body temperature should not be above 38.9° Celsius for an extended time.

Poisons and pesticides   There are heaps of potentially harmful substances at home and in the workplace. Read labels and avoid using toxins. Definitely avoid 'fumy' cleaning products, including oven cleaners and drycleaning solvents, most paints, lacquers, thinners, paint strippers, pesticides, herbicides, petrol, glue, many manufacturing chemicals and waste products. Beware of lead in the air in heavy traffic areas and nearby soil, in old house paint and in some water, particularly in houses with old lead pipes or lead-soldered pipes. Lead can also leach into food or drink from very old or handmade china or earthenware pottery.

People in high-risk jobs include health-care workers, farmers, gardeners, factory workers, printing or photographic processing workers, artists, chemists, hairdressers, nail artists, beauty therapists, drycleaners, cleaners, and people who work with petrol. Exposure to air pollution – such as carbon monoxide from car exhausts and smoke from cigarettes – may be a problem if your job involves driving in heavy traffic for much of the day, directing traffic, working at a bus station or at a venue filled with cigarette smoke, such as a pub.

Unfortunately, the list of potentially harmful substances you might come into contact with is extensive. Fortunately, most babies turn out fine anyway. To find out whether substances or practices specific to your circumstances are harmful during pregnancy, make sure you check with your doctor, workplace industrial health and safety officer, your union, or the National Health and Medical Research Council. You mustn't rely on your employer as the only source of information about what's in your workplace and what the risks are to you.

TELL YOUR DOCTOR STRAIGHT AWAY ABOUT ANY:

- bleeding from the vagina
- vomiting, if you can't keep down fluids
- abdominal pain
- fainting
- high temperature
- major fluid retention
- worries
- instruction or information they gave you that you don't fully understand
- really funny baby jokes you've heard.

cm
1
2
3
4
5
6
7
8
9
10
11
12
13
14
15
16
17
18
19
20
21
22

what's going on
Your period hasn't turned up. You might feel premenstrual, with slightly swollen breasts, as well as weeing more often and feeling queasy.

The embryo is still very tiny but starting to form into a tube shape and growing very quickly. The head and tail ends 'become obvious. The heart and blood vessels are only just starting to form so the embryo doesn't have its independent circulation yet. At this stage the placenta consists of lots of 'tentacles' called chorionic villi. Eventually they will grow into the big, temporary organ that runs the exchange between you and your developing baby, which sends in nutrients and oxygen and takes out waste products and carbon dioxide, using the vein and two arteries in the umbilical cord that connects it to the baby. You'll find that pregnancy books disagree on the size of the developing baby, partly because some measure from head to bum, and some from head to feet.

Diary We move house and my thirty-third birthday party on Sunday is conducted amid towers of cardboard boxes and tea-chests full of stuff we didn't even open at the last house. My advice to anyone under 27 is don't blink or you'll be 33 before you know what happened. Kind of like Rumpelstiltskin. (Only your beard isn't usually *quite* that bad.)

People at the party keep asking, 'Hermoine, do you want another drink?', and I keep saying no. Just like that. No, meaning no, I don't want a drink, which means people keep looking at me strangely. Or I say yes and then leave the drink somewhere under a tree.

And it is really flash champagne too, being my birthday and everybody being nice about it. And normally, although I don't smoke – except other people's (oh all right, and those times when I buy a packet for a party . . . yes, and those other times when . . . oh shut up) – I will have the odd puff at a social extravaganza, even one involving tea-chests. But this time I just don't feel like it. Begin to feel quite snappy and restless. All sort of 'It's my party and I'll pout if I want to'.

Then I get scared. I start to think: 33. Thirty-three and I don't want to party any more. It's over. It's been over since Des bought that mini-van. What was I thinking – that I could live in a house with a perfectly nice man who owns a mini-van and has a steady job and earns his own money and doesn't expect me to pay for everything and isn't some kind of frustrated troll of a tortured artiste?

What happened to my life? When did I get sensible? How can I escape? Maybe I should run through the streets in the nicky-noo-nar shooting out streetlights. Or I could just go to bed. I'm a wee bit on the nod and I've been squirgly again. Must be coming down with something. Need a good night's rest, probably. Nightie-night everyone. Please. Don't stop drinking on my account. I'll just zzzzzzzz.

4 a.m. Hang on a minute.

9.10 a.m. Pop down to the chemist. Need some dental floss, some cotton balls, some orange nail polish, naturally, and oh, what the hell, I'll take that $17 home pregnancy test kit on a whim.

Pregnancy tests from the chemist have obviously changed since last I was a careless idiot. You used to have to wee into some sort of container (yoghurt jar, bucket, beer stein with 'Mallacoota Muster' written on the side of it, that kind of thing), and then dip a white plastic magic wand, which was a bit like a flat biro, into it. The most useful instruction was always 'Use the midstream urine for the test'. What that meant was that you did some wee, then you stopped, if you had pelvic-floor muscles like a steel trap, and neatly did a mighty bull's-eye midstream wee into the jar, then stopped (steel trap again), removed the jar and finished the wee.

What always happened was more like sticking a thimble under a waterfall and then snatching it out again and finding that, although you had wee on your hand, the outside of the jar, your hair, the cuffs of your trousers and some articles in another room entirely, you'd managed to miss the jar.

Now you're supposed to hold the magic wand in one hand and – I'm sorry, but basically you just piss on it for a minute or so. This seems such an incredibly male thing to do. I almost feel like trying to write my name in the snow with my own wee. But there is no snow. Only a thin, blue line showing in the 'window', which the instructions say means you're pregnant. And I'm not talking a baby blue, a wimpy sort of a 'We think it's within the realms of possibility that you might conceivably have conceived'. No, it is almost a luminous, pulsating navy blue indicating 'YOU, madam, are *utterly* UP THE DUFF good and proper!'.

I always thought I might cry a tiny tear of feminine, yet sensible joy. Instead, I stare at the wall thinking 'Oh . . . Woo.'

Ring Des and tell him to come straight home from water polo practice, there is something I have to tell him.

'Ooohhhh,' he says, 'Woo,' sounding like he knows what it might be.

I tell him at the front door. He looks pretty shocked. We just start laughing, with tears in our eyes, and then we can't stop laughing. It just seems so ridiculously UNLIKELY. Des says he is happy, and then talks about the finer points of water polo really fast for about 25 minutes. I think he's in shock.

'You told me it would probably take two years to get pregnant,' he says later, quietly.

'Ooops. Woo,' I concur.

Des commences to grin for two days straight, the grin punctuated by an expression of profound bewilderment. I begin to refer to him as the bewilderbeest. Luckily he's an optimist whose most remarkable traits include a 'she'll be right' attitude to almost anything. If you told Des there was a cyclone coming, he'd be dead interested from a meteorological point of view.

info

pregnancy tests

Home pregnancy test kits bought at the chemist work the same way as a test a doctor would do on a sample of your wee. The kits test for the presence of HCG (human chorionic gonadotrophin hormone). The first wee of the day will have the greatest concentration of HCG.

You can do the test as early as fourteen days after conception, about when your period would be due. Results of these tests are almost always accurate, especially if they're positive. A false negative result can happen if the levels of HCG being produced

by a pregnant body are low. So if your period doesn't start, and you still suspect you are pregnant, you can wait a few days and do the test again, or go to the doctor for a blood test, which can measure HCG levels as early as one week after conception.

After a positive home test, or other signs of early pregnancy such as a missed period, tender breasts, nausea, frenzied weeing, a funny metallic taste in your mouth, tiredness or moodiness, you should go to the doctor for a physical examination. The doctor should be able to confirm the pregnancy and see further signs such as an enlarged uterus and the changed texture and colour of the cervix (the small opening, and surrounding tissue, between the uterus and the vagina).

Depending on your medical history your doctor might refer you to an obstetrician (a specialist pregnancy doctor) straight away; or your first visit may be when you're about twelve weeks pregnant.

ectopic pregnancy scan

When the pregnancy is confirmed, an early ultrasound scan might be recommended, especially if you have ever had a miscarriage, you have a medical history that might indicate a blockage in a fallopian tube, or the doctor suspects you have an ectopic pregnancy, which happens when the egg implants itself outside the uterus, usually in a tube. Sadly, an ectopic pregnancy can't be saved and turned into a viable pregnancy. Unless the body naturally aborts the embryo very early, it is a very serious medical problem and must be resolved by surgery as soon as it is diagnosed.

Risk factors include a previous ectopic pregnancy; pelvic inflammatory disease; damage to or scarring of the fallopian tubes caused by infection or surgery; endometriosis; an intra-uterine device (IUD) in place when you conceived; your mum, when she was pregnant with you, took a morning-sickness drug called DES (diethylstilboestrol), which causes malformation of the reproductive organs in some babies.

Symptoms of ectopic pregnancy, which usually occur at about six weeks, may include abdominal pain, either on one side of the abdomen or more generalised, that can come and go; spotting or bleeding; dizziness, faintness, paleness and sweating; nausea and vomiting; sometimes shoulder pain; and sometimes a feeling of pressure in the bum.

Tell your doctor or obstetrician immediately about these symptoms. Early treatment improves your chances of saving the tube and maintaining fertility. (One in ten ectopic pregnancies ends in infertility.) If a fallopian tube bursts, the pain is terrible: go straight to hospital because you'll need emergency surgery. Remember, it's definitely possible to have an ectopic pregnancy even if you think you can't conceive because you're on the Pill or Minipill.

routine tests

If you're seeing your local doctor, they'll do some early, routine tests or refer you to an obstetrician. At your first – and usually the longest – visit to the obstetrician, they'll compile a comprehensive medical history, noting details of your previous illnesses and surgery; your allergies; prescription medications or alternative treatments you're taking; gynaecological and obstetric history, including the pattern of your menstrual cycle; any STDs, past pregnancies, miscarriages or pregnancy terminations (abortions); any family history of twins or genetic disorders; your lifestyle, particularly your diet, smoking, drinking, drugs, work and fitness habits; your family's medical history, and perhaps even your mum's obstetric history. Mind you; most doctors nowadays understand that your mother's obstetric history is neither here nor there. How long your mother was in labour, whether she had nausea, what size you were as a baby, all that stuff is more than likely to be completely irrelevant to your own experience of pregnancy.

The routine tests carried out by your doctor or at your first visit to the obstetrician will probably include:

⊚ an 'internal examination' to confirm the pregnancy and some chat to estimate the due delivery date

⊚ perhaps another wee test to also confirm the pregnancy

◎ weighing and measuring you

◎ a Pap test (in which some tiny cells are collected from your cervix)

◎ basically a bit of an all-round 'physical' – an examination of your heartbeat, lung capacity, blood pressure, pelvis and abdomen

◎ examination of breasts and nipples

◎ urine test for high protein levels that could indicate a potential health problem for you

◎ blood test to establish your blood group, possible anaemia, and immunity to rubella, hepatitis and syphilis. HIV testing is now also offered to all women.

Usually you visit the obstetrician monthly until late in the pregnancy, after which visits become fortnightly, and then weekly close to delivery. Some doctors will ask you to bring a urine sample to each visit to be tested for glucose (which can indicate a blood sugar imbalance) and protein. (Chemists sell small, cheap, plastic specimen jars.)

As a routine at each visit your blood pressure will be checked and your tummy examined to measure the growth of the uterus, and you'll probably be weighed. After about twelve weeks you'll be able to hear the heartbeat when the obstetrician puts a listening device like a stethoscope on your tummy.

It's easy to forget something you've been meaning to ask the obstetrician – list your questions somewhere in your diary as they occur to you, and jot down the answers while you're there, too, because sometimes your head's in a whirl with all the new info and you can't remember them afterwards.

WEEK

would you like a cup of tea?

what's going on

You can consider visiting your GP and dating the pregnancy – meaning: work out when you conceived. (This is different from dating during pregnancy, an activity that is often curtailed, especially in the last few months.) If you haven't already, you may start to feel grumpy or nauseated.

The embryo is growing rapidly and beginning to look tadpoley. The tadpole tail will eventually shrink and the remnants become the baby's coccyx. In the centre of the embryo is the

6 start of the digestive system, lungs and bladder. This is surrounded by a layer that will develop into muscles, skeleton, heart, kidneys and genitals, and this is wrapped up in what will become the skin, nervous system, ears and eyes. Tiny bumps are appearing that will grow into arms. The immature heart starts to beat and pump blood around the embryo and into the chorionic villi (the pre-placenta) and can be clearly seen as a pulsation on an ultrasound screen. Really, the whole thing looks like some tiny thing that might come out if you sneezed.

yeah? You and whose army?

DiARY

Work is hotting up. We sign to produce two new fashion ranges for a couple of big department stores. The spicy earth colours of winter! The divine madness of spring! You know the sort of thing. Will we get it all done before the baby arrives? I can't even tell anyone I'm pregnant yet. The convention is to wait until after thirteen weeks, when they reckon the biggest risk of miscarriage is over.

We tell some close friends of Des's, quietly, at a wedding. They scream. I have to pretend there is a spider down my underpants to explain the kerfuffle.

I now know why horoscopes are a dead loss. You'd think they could warn you: 'This week you'll get put in the pudding club'. No, mine just said: 'Financial difficulties may arise on Tuesday. Your lucky colour is caramel'. Nobody's lucky colour is caramel. It's not even a colour, it's half a meal.

Beck says I need to get my GP to refer me to an obstetrician straight away because of my endometriosis, which can cause an ectopic pregnancy. I ring an obstetrician who she thinks is excellent. She heard this guy had a pretty good attitude. What clinched it for her was seeing him talk on telly the year he was the doctor who had delivered most of the babies born to heroin-addicted mums. A journalist made a disparaging comment about the mothers, and he gently cradled a baby in his arms and said something that displayed general decency and compassion. His name is quite daggy – Herb – which is strangely reassuring also. Maybe I'm becoming conservative in my old age, but I just don't want an obstetrician called Sparky.

I explain my medical history to Dr Herb's receptionist/midwife who is almost certainly called Lorraine. All the sensible women I meet I automatically think of as Lorraines. Lorraines never wear high heels and they always know everything about their specialty, whether it's knitting, delivering babies, running a doctor's surgery, or netball strategy.

Before I get to meet Dr Herb, I have to have an ultrasound to check that the pregnant bit of me is where it should be – in the uterus – instead of ectopic (stuck in a fallopian tube), which can be very dangerous. So I go across the road to discover that my first ultrasound appointment means sitting in the waiting room for approximately 738 HOURS filling in a DAMN FORM.

Who is your family doctor? (Haven't got one.)

Last period? (Well, in my case about four years, but surely that's going to take too long to explain.)

Number of previous pregnancies? (One. Well, therein lies *another* story, but do they really want to hear about the anaesthetist who wanted to get the termination over so he could get to the footy on time? Probably not. Nor, I feel sure, do they want to know about the ex-boyfriend who threw a cheque on the kitchen table in front of house mates and visitors, saying, 'That's for my half of the abortion', and then refused ever to speak to me again. This pregnancy business sure flicks open the clasps on your emotional baggage.)

I look at the posters on the wall of a foetus developing week by week. It was so long ago. I can't remember now whether I terminated at six weeks or eight weeks. So many of us women having babies in our thirties had abortions when we were younger, vowing that we would only become mothers when we could be good at it. I'm glad I waited. I didn't even know who I really was then. But I really don't want to look at that poster.

Previous surgery: how many operations? (Can't remember so compromise by writing 'Heaps'. That should give 'em the general idea.)

Husband's name? (Haven't got one. Well, I have got a boyfriend. Must be worse for Marg when she reads this sort of thing on forms. I mean what is a single girl supposed to write? 'Missing In Action'? 'NA (Not Available)'? 'NOYB (None of Your Business)'? Or just 'Albert Einstein'?)

I go into a small room and lie on a flat, hard, raised couch. The ultrasound operator, Dr Donaldson, sits next to me at about hip level with a screen in front of him and a nurse behind him taking notes on a computer. Yet another screen is mounted high on the wall in front of me so I can see what Dr Donaldson sees.

What I see is a tiny dot on the screen pulsating incredibly quickly and rhythmically. That's the embryo's heartbeat. And it's all in the right spot: the uterus. I feel incredibly relieved. Then Dr Donaldson starts going all avuncular on me and saying I should realise that there might be 'wastage'. It takes me a beat or two until I realise he's warning me that it's very early days and I could have a miscarriage – only he's got a pet word for it. Geez, how sensitive.

I have a quick visit with Dr Herb afterwards.

'Everything's absolutely fine,' he grins.

info

miscarriage

About one in eight confirmed pregnancies ends in miscarriage. It's believed the figure might be one in four of all pregnancies, but many miscarriages occur very early and are mistaken for a period. As you get older your risk increases; you're also more likely to miscarry if you have already had a miscarriage.

About three-quarters of all known miscarriages happen in the first trimester. A miscarriage that happens after week 13 is called a late miscarriage. Loss of a baby after about twenty weeks is called a preterm stillbirth – the date used varies slightly from State to State.

You may hear a doctor refer to a miscarriage by the medical term 'abortion'. As well, when a pregnancy ends in miscarriage because the embryo does not develop, the embryo is often called a 'blighted ovum'. These insensitive medical terms do not help your feelings at the time. Feel free to tell the doctor off for being tactless. They should learn that they're hurting somebody's feelings at the worst possible time, even if to them it's just business as usual.

By far the most common symptom of miscarriage is bleeding from the vagina. If this happens, it is important to contact your obstetrician immediately. You will need to be ready to describe the colour, quantity and time frame of the bleeding. Light spotting might not be a cause for alarm and the doctor might tell you to rest for a couple of days. A heavy flow could mean the doctor will tell you that you need to go straight to hospital.

Vaginal bleeding occurs in about a quarter of pregnant women, but most of them go on to have healthy babies.

After a miscarriage you may need to have a small operation to prevent infection, which makes sure the uterus is free of all the tissue that should come out. The endometrium will grow back as good as new. The operation is known as a curette, or a D and C (dilatation and curettage), and is performed under general anaesthetic in hospital: it's covered by Medicare. If you miscarry before six weeks you probably won't need a D and C.

Don't use a tampon for any bleeding during pregnancy, and keep the pad you do use until you have spoken to your obstetrician. And don't have penetrative sex until the bleeding has been checked by the doctor.

I know this sounds a bit gross and depressing but, if you can, keep any clots and tissue from a miscarriage in a clean plastic bag or container, so they can be examined. This can help your obstetrician decide whether the miscarriage is complete, and help a pathology laboratory work out what caused the miscarriage.

Possible causes of miscarriage include 'nature rejecting a problem with a pregnancy', such as foetal abnormality; exposure to certain chemicals, illnesses or medications; problems with the uterus, placenta, cervix, sperm, immune system or egg implantation; and hormonal imbalances.

An 'incompetent cervix' (another charming medical term) is sometimes diagnosed when miscarriage occurs. It means that the cervix gets over-eager and opens too soon. This is the cause of up to a quarter of miscarriages in the second trimester (week 14 until the end of week 26). Previous gynaecological surgery or laser treatments, abortions or miscarriages could increase your risk of this condition – another reason to give your obstetrician your full medical history. A misbehaving cervix can be stitched closed during your next pregnancy until the baby is ready to come out.

After you've had a miscarriage, get all the information you can from your obstetrician – make sure all your questions are answered – and review the possible risk factors that could be avoided or treated in future pregnancies. If you have more than two miscarriages, you'll usually be tested for uterine problems and hormonal imbalances and have your immune system evaluated.

Miscarriage is no less distressing because it's common. Friends and family can make things worse by well-meaning but insensitive remarks, such as 'Hurry up and have another one', or 'You'll soon get over it'. It's important to allow yourself time to talk over and mourn the loss with your partner, who may grieve differently from you, causing friction. It can be really helpful to find a support group so you can talk to and hear from people who have been through it.

 Contact your local women's or public hospital, women's health information services or a grief counselling service and ask to be put in touch with a support group (see Women's Hospitals, Women's Information Services and Grief and Loss in 'Help').

your record

Do you know exactly where and when you got pregnant? After a party, on holiday, while recreational boating perhaps? Have a guess!

What date did you find out you were pregnant? What mix of emotions did you experience? If you have a partner, how did you break the news?

Average approximate embryo length this week from head to bum

1
2
3
4
5
6
7
8
9
10
11
12
13
14
15
16
17
18
21
22

what's going on

Your breasts may be bigger and more sensitive, and the nipples and surrounding areolae may have started to look bigger and bumpier. (The little bumps on each areola are officially called Montgomery's tubercles but who cares about Montgomery, whoever he was: 'little bumps' sounds a lot cuter.) You could have continuing nausea and need to wee a lot. Foods may taste different, and you may go off the smell of things you previously liked.

Teeny buds that will grow into legs are appearing on the embryo. Everything continues growing at a cracking pace. The heart is going strongly inside a developing chest but the lungs have only just started to form. Embryonic kidneys begin to develop and function (the finished kidneys come later). The head bulge is getting more like the right shape. The chorionic villi are making more and longer tentacles into

WEEK

the uterus. Some books say the embryo is about the size of a brazil nut or an olive ('Shall I compare thee to a cocktail party nibble?'), but we are officially going with coffee bean.

DiARY

I couldn't be less interested in sex if my private parts had been packed away in a shoe box in the back of the wardrobe. This will not do. Where is the surge of lascivious sex-kittenry the books promise and the magazines go on about?

Take the pregnancy special issue of this month's *She* magazine, and I quote: 'In the middle of your pregnancy, your libido soars. You're not too enormous but you're round enough not to be concerned about maintaining the missionary position in the quest for a flat stomach and no chins. You bounce about with abandon.' Oh bollocks.

Apart from the fact that the last thing you want to be thinking about when you're having fun is whether he's thinking about your double chin – and anyway what bloke is thinking anything except 'Whacko!' with a girlie on top of him? – apart from a few pointers on that kind of palaver, I'd just like to know where these magazine writers get off, telling us how we're going to feel. As if everybody is the same as them – that is, wanders around saying things like 'Beige is the new black, essentials this summer include platform pantyliners with a daisy motif, and in the middle of your pregnancy you'll be a bonking fool.'

I've been reflecting on Dr Donaldson at the ultrasound using the appalling word 'wastage' to warn me about a possible miscarriage. It must be his regular spiel to everybody. Anyway it has reminded us again not to tell anyone in case something goes wrong. So we've only told Georgie, Jill, Marg coz she's already pregnant, Beck because, let's face it, she is my medical adviser and I'll probably need a bit of advice, Amanda, Steve and Pina, Janie, Lucinda, Maz, Juanita, Heather, Col and Davo. Less than a hundred people, anyway.

Apart from that I might have to tell some people at work so they don't think I've lost my mind. (I go around with this permanent off-the-air expression, which actually indicates I'm talkin' sales figures and thinkin', 'Creature inside me! Creature inside me! Size of a Tic Tac. I feel seasick right now and I have to pretend I don't! Bleeeeuuurghhh! I beg your pardon, I appear to have thrown up on your shoes', or simply 'I know something YOU don't know.')

We don't want to tell everyone we're 'expecting' and then have to say, 'Oh we lost it', as if we'd been a bit careless in the Safeway car park and left the little bundle in the returned trolleys section by mistake. I heard that one in eight pregnancies ends in miscarriage.

'Oh no, that's not right,' says Beck.

'Thank God I've got you to calm my fears with proper medical facts, Beck,' I say.

'I think it's one in five, or maybe even four,' she explains helpfully.

So much of pregnancy seems to be about odds. It automatically turns you into a gambler. The statistics mean everything and nothing at the same time. One in four is high, even if some of those are miscarriages you wouldn't know about because they would be just like having a period. And if you do have a miscarriage, your own personal chance was 100 per cent. And if you don't have a miscarriage, your individual risk was zero per cent. But you can't help brooding on 'one in four' and every other percentage risk they tell you about.

We go to a birthday barbie at Des's family – we don't tell. The next night, Des's college reunion dinner is full of preggo ladies. Des wants to tell everyone and has to be sternly restrained.

Poor Des. He's got a seasick, exhausted girlfriend who'd rather stick peas up her nose than have sex, and he's going to be a daddy. I think we're both feeling kind of like it's all been a theory and now it's actually going to happen. Well actually, it still feels a bit theoretical. Maybe I'm just in denial.

I know intellectually that I'm pregnant, but it just doesn't feel real. I can't tell by looking, and I don't suddenly feel like knitting bootees or protecting my offspring with the ferocity of a lioness. I have no more idea about raising a child than I did six weeks ago. No sudden illuminated shaft has split the heavens asunder, pierced the top of my noggin and said in a very deep voice, 'You are going to be a mother.' Just as well, really. I'd probably wet my pants.

I am very grumpy indeed. Des has read somewhere that newborn babies look like their father so the father will stick around. I reply that all newborn babies look like the federal treasurer of the day, and what's that got to do with anything? Des wonders why hormones would make you grumpy when surely nature intends you to keep the man happy, to protect you. I refrain from saying that being grumpy is a perfectly bloody natural reaction, and furthermore it is no doubt serving the important purpose of teaching you that if the bloke runs off with a sailor, or proves to be a dead dud at hunter-gathering, you can do it all yourself.

After all, most women with one child and a husband feel like they have two children and anyway why is there a mess in that corner and I believe you forgot to take out the garbage again and WHERE'S MY BLOODY DINNER?

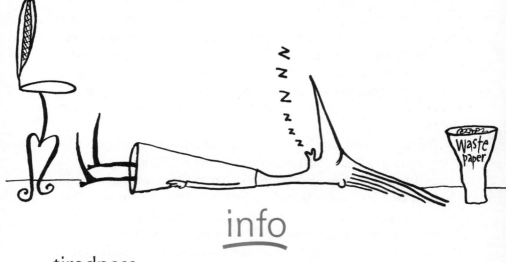

info

tiredness

One of the symptoms of the first trimester can be an incredibly draining exhaustion – which you can't even complain about because most people don't know that you're up the duff.

Here's the weird thing: in the past, if you've been really tired, you have probably pushed through it. With first-trimester pregnancy tiredness, you find yourself following your feet up the hall and getting into bed. You have turned into a robot. Welcome to reality: your body is now running you, rather than the other way around.

A lot of women who go out to work full-time spend the first trimester coming home from their job, going straight to bed, waking up and demanding dinner from their house mate(s) or calling in takeaway for themselves, and then going back to bed.

Most women start to feel perkier and less nauseated by week 14 (but the tiredness comes back in the third trimester).

Here are some of the reasons why you may be so tired:

⊚ the high levels of progesterone in the system during the first trimester can have a sedative effect

⊚ your metabolic rate increases 10–25 per cent to support the developing foetus, and a whole lot of other parts are working overtime, such as your heart

⊚ your body is putting the development of the foetus first – you are making eyelids and bones and sex organs and lungs and a placenta and stuff so for heaven's sake who WOULDN'T need to lie down with all that going on?

⊚ all that extra night-time weeing means you're not getting the deepest, most restful part of sleep

⊚ just being nauseated (see Nausea in 'Week 4') can make you feel exhausted.

Some ways to combat tiredness are:

⊚ win the lottery; quit work; sleep all the time; get a cleaner, a masseur and, oh, hang the expense, a personal chef like Oprah's; live in a posh hotel

⊚ give in to it, don't fight it – your body will win this round anyway, so you may as well not start your life as a mother by being frazzled

⊚ let your doctor, midwife or natural therapist know the extent of your third-trimester tiredness: a non-constipating iron supplement may work wonders

⊚ find a storeroom or sickroom where you can nap if work

commitments mean long days at the office (some Pregnant Ladies we know used to just Lie Down under their desks) – and don't forget to eat lunch at your desk if you use the lunch hour for a kip

☺ nap when you get home if you work away from home

☺ nap when you can if you work at home

☺ meet friends for lunch or on the weekends rather than at night (smoky pubs and nightclubs, and alcohol, are probably making you feel sick at the moment anyway) – you can always come back to daiquiris in a year or so

☺ keep one day, or at least an afternoon on the weekend, completely free; several Pregnant Ladies we know spent All Weekend in bed for the first three months

☺ if you have a partner or flatmate who has not been pulling their weight in the housework department, renegotiate so they see that doing the tasks/chores is about rights and responsibilities rather than about 'helping' you or doing you a favour; alternatively, get used to mess – or both

☺ if you already have little children, give them away to relatives. Sorry. No. Try to nap when (if) they do.

weeing all the time

Weeing all the time is a very common symptom of pregnancy in the first thirteen weeks or so. It's not that you're over-excited, it's just that your uterus is taking up more space, putting pressure on the neighbouring organs, including your bladder. Even more congestion is caused by the extra blood vessels and blood flow developing in the pelvis to sustain the placenta and carry the extra weight.

It may be less of a problem in the second trimester because the uterus 'pops' outwards at the front, making the pelvis temporarily less crowded. But then constant weeing usually comes back in the third trimester when there's a serious space shortage –

at which stage it can feel as if your baby is kicking your bladder, or grabbing it, or generally tossing it around and headbutting it.

You still need to drink lots of water during the day to avoid dehydration, but you can try drinking less in the evenings in an attempt to reduce the number of trips to the toilet during the night. (Experienced mums will grimly inform you that getting up to wee all night long is good training for the interrupted sleep caused by night feeding once the baby is born. I say try not to do it until you have to.)

If you get a burning or stinging sensation when you wee a lot, mention it to your doctor. You may have a urinary tract infection, which you can treat with some simple crystals added to what you're drinking that are available from the chemist. Cranberry juice can also help.

cm

Average approximate embryo length this week from head to bum

1
2
3
4
5
6
7
8
9
10
11
12
13
14
15
16
17
18
19
20
21
22

what's going on

You are continuing to wee more often because your bladder is being crowded by the uterus. A lot of fancy hormonal footwork is going on to keep building the placenta.

You might feel nauseated AND constipated: jackpot! You may be starting to feel tired: your body has a lot to do that is normally not on the agenda. Your hair may be getting thicker, and downstairs there may be more vaginal mucus than normal.

Your embryo has become that classic curled shape, the big fat head with a tail (not a very attractive shape at this point, and similar to a prawn from space, sure, but we all have to start somewhere). It's still so tiny, but it's about a million times bigger than the fertilised cell that started moving and shaking six weeks ago. The external bits of the ears now start to be visible, and the tiny hands are webbed.

EEK 8

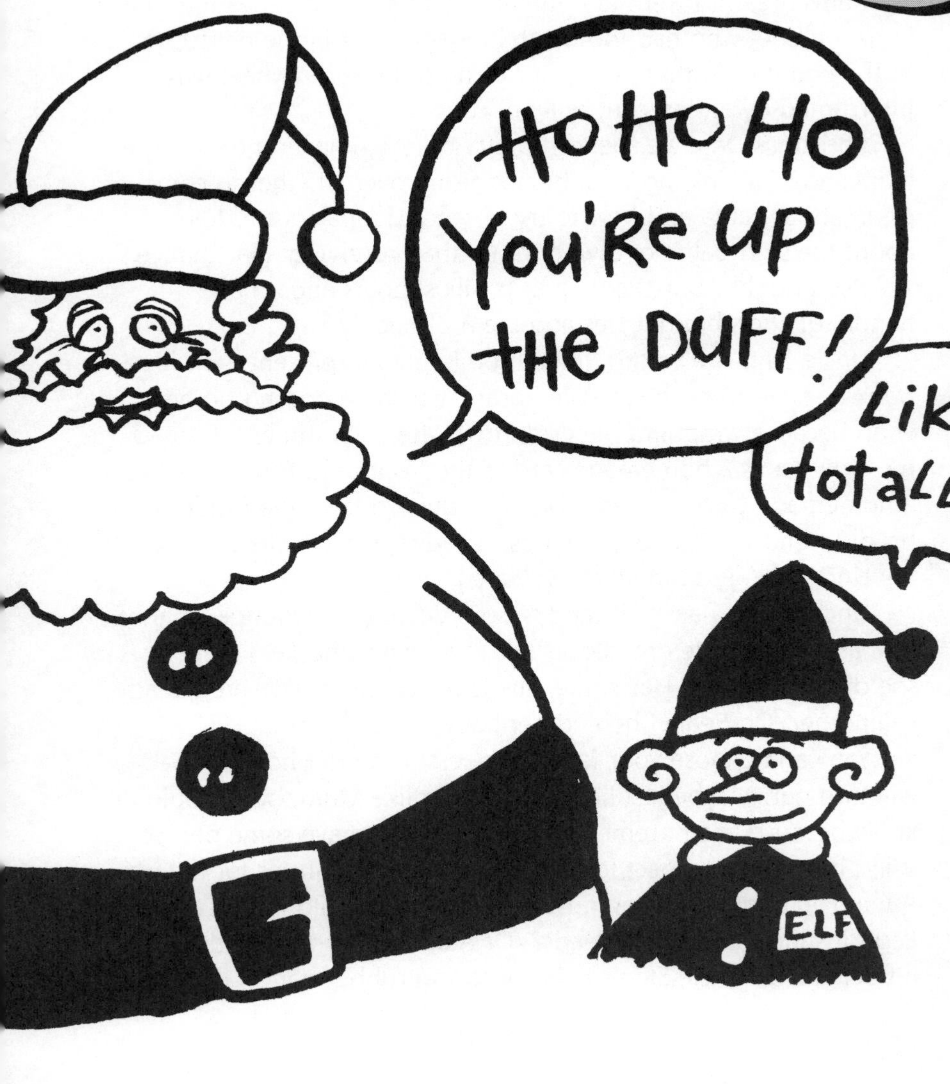

DiARY

I am having strange, vivid dreams. Last night I dreamt that American author Gore Vidal came to afternoon tea and I gave him a Chocolate Crackle on a silver plate and he said, 'How perfectly charming.' I was completely furious that Des woke me up at that precise moment to kiss me goodbye as he went to work.

'But I just gave Gore Vidal a chocolate crackle!' I said accusingly.

'Yes, dear,' he replied, which was probably about the only thing he could have said.

I also dreamt I went to a funfair on a Pacific island with a well-known model who had too much luggage to fit in the helicopter. In the end it didn't matter as our turn on the Ferris wheel was interrupted by an insistent military coup.

Christmas Day. We spend it pretty quietly, knowing that in the twinkling of an inkling we'll be agonising over whether to come clean about Santa and how to try to teach a rapacious toddler about the spirituality of giving rather than receiving. (Fat chance.)

I've bought Aunty Peg a pair of silk slippers and a flash handbag. She's bought Des and me a plastic fly swat.

Uncle Stan (we've got him a mobile phone) presents us with a book he stole from the mobile library, which he doesn't bother to wrap because wrapping paper destroys the environment. Instead he sticky-tapes a homemade card to the front of it. And when I say a homemade card, I mean a bit of cardboard from the inside of his girlfriend's packet of pantyhose. (Re-use, recycle, read my lips: my Uncle Stan is a hippie cheapskate.)

Uncle Stan's new girlfriend is twenty-five years younger than him and has purple dreadlocks and is a total fruitcake. I suspect she drinks hemlock. Her name, allegedly, is Aurelia. We are already calling her 'Oh Really' behind her back.

You can't choose your family, I guess. I wonder how our baby will turn out. Maybe just like Stan. Or just like Mum, but I wouldn't know because I can't remember her. At least I have some photos. Will I have more respect for what she went through, or for the way Aunty Peg and Uncle Stan raised me? Will our child inherit Aunty Peg's instinctive morbid dreads? Or Aurelia's purple dreads? Or be influenced by Uncle Stan's habit of saving rubber bands, rolling them into balls and then trying to sell them to Mormons who come to the door?

Bloody nausea. Queasy isn't the word for it. I am nauseous all the time and desperate for it to stop. Whoever called it 'morning sickness' was a complete maniac. (I keep involuntarily singing 'Get it in the morning, get it in the evening, get it at suppertime'.) Beck thinks it's just too much oestrogen in my system and my liver is having trouble clearing it out.

Aurelia would probably say if I was a Pisces I would accept my pregnancy and wouldn't get 'morning sick' and that it's all in my mind. At least I've got a mind, I could tell her.

'The HCG hormone almost certainly has something to do with it, but we don't really know what causes it,' Dr Herb had said when I asked him about it during my first visit. I seem to have hit upon a non-infuriatingly patriarchal doctor.

Why do the preggo books just say, 'Eat dry crackers before you get out of bed in the morning'? I mean, that's not very informative, is it? They might as well say: 'Sacrifice a chicken and study its entrails. An interestingly shaped spleen means you will continue to have nausea until the thirteenth week.'

Beck says, 'Don't worry, nausea means the baby is hanging on in there. If it stopped suddenly THAT would be a worry because it could mean a miscarriage.'

Nausea stops suddenly for a whole day. Oh my God.

Nausea starts again. Thank God.

Bloody nausea.

I'm also weeing all the time. In some circles this is regarded suspiciously, and one person even starts a rumour that I have such a severe cocaine problem I have to go to the toilet three times during a dinner party. In other circles you get smug looks from mothers who think they're onto you. And one of the models at work asked if I was bulimic and suggested I try laxatives instead. Crikey.

Des and I take a long walk on the beach and decide we don't want to have a baby with Down syndrome because it's not fair to have a child who might need constant medical intervention yet mightn't understand why. And we can't take care of our child

forever: one day we'll be gone. We decide that we would terminate
if we had to. Des says the decision is ultimately mine and he'll
support it. I know that many would disagree with our reasons and
decision: they'd say people with Down syndrome lead full and
happy lives, and that termination is wrong. I reckon it's a really
personal, difficult decision, and the 'right' answer may be different
for different people. It's all very tricky. Beck advises that if it comes
to that, we could always say there was a miscarriage so other
people who knew about the pregnancy didn't judge our decision
to terminate. Sounds like a good idea. The result of all this is we
decide I should have a test that estimates the risk of giving birth
to a baby with Down syndrome.

We've chosen an interim name so we don't have to say 'it' all the
time. Cellsie – as in bunch of cells – is what we're calling the embryo-
baby-offspring-thingie inside me. We'll have to come up with
something else before kindergarten but it'll do for the moment.

info

cravings

You know how you sometimes crave chocolate or pasta, or maybe
red meat, when you're premenstrual? Pregnancy cravings can be
similar. Most pregnant women get a craze for one sort of food or
another for a short period – usually ice-cream or something
sugary. You can go through stages, craving steamed vegies, then
chocolate, then tropical fruit. (You can also go right off a food
that used to be a favourite. This can include strong-smelling foods
and green leafy vegetables that are the slightest bit 'slimy'.) It's best
to keep sugary snacks to a minimum as they don't provide real
energy and can stack on extra weight you won't need.

You might get a funny taste in your mouth that seems kind
of metallic. This is thought to be due to the high level of various hormones in your blood, which can change the taste of
your saliva.

constipation

High progesterone levels are relaxing the muscles in your digestive tract, causing intestinal activity to slow down. This means your poo is going on a slower journey than usual, so it loses water and can become hard, causing constipation. (In the third trimester you can experience even worse constipation as your ginormous uterus squashes the bowel.)

Here are some ways to avoid constipation.

⑥ Drink at least 2 litres of water, spaced out across the day; try some warm water first thing in the morning if it doesn't make you feel nauseated.

⑥ Eat plenty of natural fibre – fresh and lightly cooked root vegetables, fruit, wholegrain breads, high-fibre cereals, such as porridge, and brown rice. Choose whole foods instead of processed foods and pre-prepared breakfast cereals whenever possible. If this is a bulkier load of fibre than your body is used to, have smaller meals more often while you adjust. Remember that the more fibre you eat, the more you need to drink.

⑥ Get plenty of exercise.

⑥ If chemical iron supplements are causing constipation, talk to your doctor or natural therapist about a herbal alternative.

⑥ Constipation can also come with the added discomfort of bloating and farting. This should disappear when the constipation goes. Too much unprocessed bran, and sometimes too much raw food, which is hard to digest, can cause bloating. Lightly steamed vegies are easier to absorb than hard, completely raw ones.

⑥ Don't take any laxative preparation without discussing it first with your doctor – some laxatives, including those that contain senna, can produce violent expulsive actions, causing painful con-tractions of the bowel, which in turn can upset the uterus next door.

more info on constipation

Your herbalist or natural therapist can help you with natural methods of dealing with constipation, especially after the birth.

Women's Trouble by Ruth Trickey and Kaz Cooke (for details and full review see More Info on Eating and Supplements in 'Week 2').
This book gives many hints about dealing naturally with constipation, including a seed mix you can add to cereals or drinks that helps things along.

WHO TO TELL? WHEN TO TELL?

Many people wait until the end of the first trimester (after thirteen weeks) to publicly announce their pregnancy, when the greatest risk of miscarriage is over. This allows you time to adjust to the idea of being pregnant and to share feelings in private. It also delays the moment when relatives go berserk and can't shut up about it. Once they know, your mother, mother-in-law, father and father-in-law (not to mention acquaintances) will descend with advice, horror stories, theories and judgements about your plans to return to work or not return to work. Even totally positive expressions of joy from your extended family can be overwhelming. Maybe you'll want to pick a weekend to break the news so everyone can celebrate together.

Parents often choose not to tell their toddler until the pregnancy is visible because for a littlie it seems like an eternity until something interesting happens. (Well, actually, you don't have to be a toddler.)

Work Exactly when you want to tell your employer will depend on your relationship with them and your position within the organisation, but they should hear the news from you and not on the office grapevine. Your employer should be advised in writing that you are pregnant and when you plan to start your maternity leave. You will probably need to include a doctor's certificate confirming your due date. You might want to give as much notice as possible so your employer can consider how to best cover your job while you are on leave and how you might make a bleary-eyed return. They'll need time to advertise and interview for your position. Many women hide their pregnancy for as long as they can because of possible discrimination. Before you tell your employer, find out your leave rights (see Getting Ready for Pregnancy in 'Week 1'). Legally, you don't need to tell your employer until ten weeks before you plan to stop work, but it's hard to imagine that nobody would have noticed you were pregnant before then. ▶

Friends with pregnancy troubles You may have a friend who wants to be pregnant but it's not possible for them right now. They may be having trouble conceiving, have had a miscarriage or several miscarriages, or they may be on the in vitro fertilisation (IVF) program. You may even have a friend whose baby died. The news that you are pregnant will be bittersweet for them. Here are a few hints that might make it easier.

● Tell your friend about your pregnancy privately, perhaps in her home when nobody else is around. Although she will be happy for you, she may have a cry because your pregnancy reminds her so much of what she wants for herself. Don't tell other friends about her situation if she wants to maintain privacy.

● Let your friend know that you will answer any questions about your pregnancy, but that you'll try not to talk to her about it all the time, and she has your full permission to tell you to shut right up if you get obsessed with baby business.

● It might be a good idea to arrange that your friend first visits you and your new baby at home, away from the hospital, when you won't have other visitors. Don't insist that she hold the baby, or discourage her. Don't be alarmed if she cries when holding the baby. She will find her own way to deal with it in her own time.

● Don't for heaven's sake tell her to 'just relax' and she'll get pregnant, or insist she try some folk remedy you've read about, or suggest that she do whatever you did. She may already know about an infertility support group or counsellor. Often available in both city and rural areas, these services can usually be contacted through community health centres, family planning centres and the nearest women's hospital.

your record

Are you feeling queasy? When?

What smells and/or foods make you feel sick?

What are you doing to combat queasiness?

How have you changed your eating habits during pregnancy?

If you're taking supplements, record them here.

what's going on

Your stomach may not be at all preggie-looking yet. As it grows, your centre of gravity will change and you will become, well, a person with the grace of a hippopotamus rather than a fruit bat. So this is the time to attend to any handy-type problems around the house – loose carpeting, tricky steps, bits of bathroom that get slippery or dangerous or awkward to manoeuvre around. And if there's something you need to get at regularly that involves standing on stepladders or a chair, lower it for the duration.

The embryo's eyelids

appear and its body elongates. The internal sex organs are starting to develop into boy and girl bits, but you can't tell the sex from the outside yet. An ultrasound will be able to show the embryo's early movements. The ends of the limbs are looking a bit more like hands and feet but you still couldn't play 'This little piggy goes to market' unless you changed the words to 'This little webby bit . . . ' Birth guru Sheila Kitzinger's fruit alert says the embryo weighs as much as a grape.

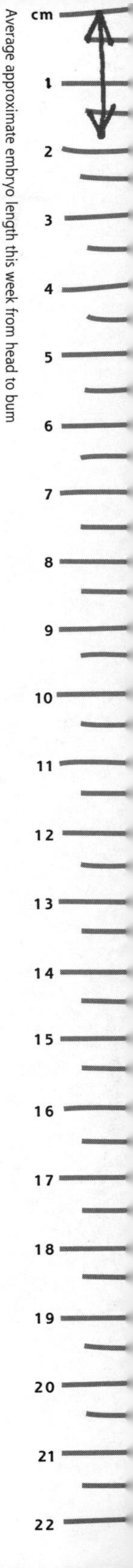

Average approximate embryo length this week from head to bum

cm
1
2
3
4
5
6
7
8
9
10
11
12
13
14
15
16
17
18
19
20
21
22

DiARY Apparently the current conservative-government policy is to pay us $820 for having a baby (means tested). What the hell is that about? As if this encouraging-family-values dumb policy works like: oh I don't think I want to have children because I'm a heathen left-wing feminist, but gee, $820, that's an incentive. 'Oy! You, yes, the bus driver! Want to have unprotected sex?'

And as for all those ratbags who complain about paying for single mothers – who, incidentally, stay on the benefit for an average of less than three years at a time – I've been paying for everyone else's children and their hospital care and their education and their roads even though I've been a childless, unlicensed, non-driving taxpayer for almost fifteen years. So you can all bugger off.

Where was I? Oh yes.

Even though it still seems miles off, I have to make plans for the actual (it's hard to say this out loud), um, you know . . . birth. I picked up a pamphlet advertising the services of independent midwives at Beck's clinic. You could tell they were very modern because the mother on the front cover, holding her minutes-old baby, had a very charming tattoo on her arm.

I have informed Beck she will have to be my private midwife and I refuse to get a tattoo. Beck has agreed to this cunning plan, and now I have to ask Dr Herb if an independent midwife can come to the delivery. It feels like being a kid and asking if a friend can stay over, like it's his decision and not mine. The doctor is already in charge. Still, best just to check. You don't want any punch-ups on the day.

Marg is going to Dr Herb as well, and because she hasn't got private health insurance she'll be having the baby in a public hospital so she'll end up paying less than we will in the private hospital fully insured. We'll both be out of pocket about $1,000 to Dr Herb for prenatal visits and the delivery, which is not totally covered by Medicare or private health insurance.

I have also booked into hospital. Luckily (or not, now we know we'll be paying more), I forgot to cancel my health insurance. It's a small private hospital only 10 minutes away that is owned by some religious people. I don't share their religion, but I'll take their private room. All this stuff arrives from the hospital, which I'm supposed to read and fill in.

There's a hospital admittance form that has on it 'Diagnosis: confinement'. Confinement?! Hello, can we just shuffle on up to the twenty-first century here for a nanosecond? It's a word out of a Jane Austen novel, or some 1950s sitcom, when pregnant bellies were hidden indoors for the last few months so nobody had to be reminded that pregnant women HAVE HAD SEX. Confined, for Christ's sake. It's a wonder the form doesn't say 'BYO handcuffs'.

The hospital has a lot of patients who believe in circumcising their boy children before they are old enough to have an anaesthetic. If I have a boy, I might have to write 'No circumcision' on his forehead until I leave. And if I can hear all the boy babies screaming, I might just check out and stay at the Sheraton. By the look of how little private health insurance pays back, the Sheraton might be a lot cheaper. Read in a magazine yesterday how Elle Macpherson checked out of hospital in a day and went to stay in a luxury New York hotel. Lucky sod. Dr Herb reminds me that the Sheraton is unlikely to check your haemorrhoids, but I guess you could always try room service.

The list of things we're instructed to bring to the hospital on Cellsie's birth day is more mystifying the longer I look at it. 'Underclothes including underpants and maternity bras.' Well, what other kinds of underclothes are there? Do people usually take flounced petticoats and lace teddies? 'One to two packets of nursing pads.' Oh dear. Not a clue what they are. Surely nurses can look after their own period needs? 'Two packets of super-adhesive sanitary pads (maternity sanitary pads such as Whisper).' I can't imagine why they don't have maternity pads called 'Ungodly Shrieking'. 'Whisper' just doesn't seem appropriate somehow.

Then there's a whole list of baby stuff they want you to bring, for which we'll need to borrow a road-train. 'Four bunny-rugs.' Four? What's going to happen to the other three? Does the baby shred them during tantrums? Do they all go on at once? How cold can the kid get? What exactly constitutes the bunniness of a rug? 'Baby hat, and bootees or socks, and mittens (optional).' Well, I'm glad it's all optional. Because to be honest it hadn't previously occurred to me that a person less than a week old should have a hat and gloves. Stockings, maybe, but let's not go overboard. The kid can develop its own sense of elegant matching accessories when it leaves home and can afford to buy its own formal wear.

Under 'What to bring for partner' there is a most unsatisfactorily short list. 'Men's night attire please if staying overnight e.g. tracksuits, pyjamas, dressing-gown.' (I asked about this, and apparently most of the nurses have seen willies before, but an elderly nurse at the hospital copped an eyeful of a bloke's leopard-skin posing pouch early one morning and took early retirement.)

As Des has none of the recommended items except tracky dacks this could be a bit of a problem. And anyway, why assume the partner is male? Why should a lesbian partner be forced into 'men's night attire'? It's downright unnatural. And the list of what a partner should bring to the hospital should include: enormous boxes of chocolates, latest magazines, new and attractive clothes, tickets to Paris (springtime) etc. Diamonds would be acceptable. And a boat with a bowling alley. What am I saying? By the time I give birth we'll have $2.50 between us.

The upshot of reading all this material from the hospital is that you get wildly ahead of yourself. You've still got months and months to go and you're wondering what to pack. Not to mention a few decisions about ambience.

For delivery, the hospital suggests 'relaxation music'. Not a good start. Relaxation music always makes me very tense. Comedian Mark Little once pointed out it sounded like dolphins playing the piano. Besides, if you gave birth to Enya music, the quietly contemplative ambience might be somewhat offset by the fact that you are screaming the place down and something huge is coming out of your vagina and at least two people you don't even know are watching. And anyway, if we can subliminally remember birth, why would you want the poor child to forever associate pain, screaming and fluorescent lights with Enya's latest hits?

Anyway. Further suggestions include 'camera'. Oh for God's sake, if I want a photo of myself red in the face, grimacing and drooling and shouting I can take a happy snap next time I'm pissed at a party. Also 'essential oils, glucose lollies, large T-shirt or old nightie, socks, toiletries, book or magazine, etc., T-shirts and shorts or swimwear for partner if desired'. I have never imagined labour as a scenario in which I am lying back reading while Des does a few laps. It is all very confusing. And at what exact point during labour would one read a book? 'The baby's head is crowning!' 'Don't bother me now, Mr Darcy's just going for a swim in the pond.'

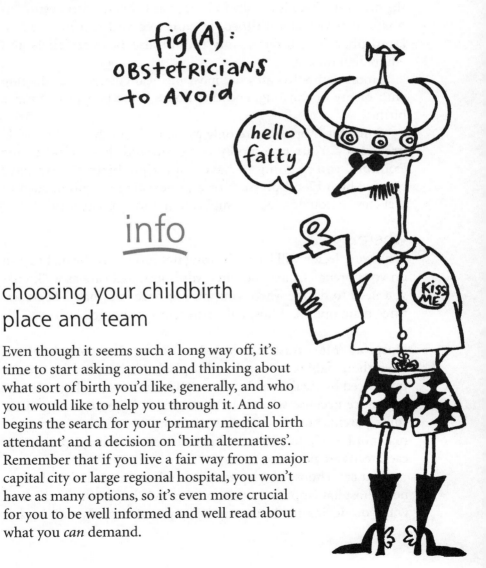

fig (A):
OBSTETRICIANS
to Avoid

hello fatty

info

choosing your childbirth place and team

Even though it seems such a long way off, it's time to start asking around and thinking about what sort of birth you'd like, generally, and who you would like to help you through it. And so begins the search for your 'primary medical birth attendant' and a decision on 'birth alternatives'. Remember that if you live a fair way from a major capital city or large regional hospital, you won't have as many options, so it's even more crucial for you to be well informed and well read about what you *can* demand.

Most people these days look for a safe balance between a comfortable environment and the best medical care available. Giving birth on the kitchen floor is a much safer proposition if there's an ambulance minutes away than if you're in the middle of the outback with only a confused sheep and a potato peeler instead of an experienced midwife.

Because birth can become a medical emergency very quickly, the medical advice is usually to have your baby in a birth centre or hospital that has a philosophy you like and can provide an atmosphere you'll feel comfy in, but also has specialists and equipment on call.

Homebirth advocates say most medical emergencies develop with plenty of warning, and that home is the best place to give birth.

Some birth options are only available if you have a 'low-risk' pregnancy. Your pregnancy is considered 'high-risk' if, for example, you're going to have a multiple birth or you have chronic high blood pressure or a pre-existing condition such as diabetes, or you develop a complication during pregnancy.

where?

What you decide will have a bearing not just on the birth, but also on your prenatal care, and often your postnatal care as well. First you need to decide where you want to have your baby. There are three main options – hospital, birth centre or home.

Hospital   Most Australian and New Zealand women choose to have their babies in a public hospital. All hospital births are influenced by legal considerations. Obstetricians pay high rates of insurance because when a baby dies or is injured during birth, some parents sue the attending doctor. This means you may or may not be able to video the birth (it's almost always policy that caesareans are no-video zones).

You can choose to hire an independent, 'freelance' midwife – not a hospital employee – who advises you before the birth, stays with you during the birth, and helps you afterwards with breastfeeding and other issues. Make sure you check whether the hospital will accept your midwife as your primary carer during the labour. For legal reasons, some hospitals will insist that procedures and the delivery itself are decided and performed by hospital staff, relegating your independent midwife to 'support person'.

PUBLIC   Usually you'll have your check-ups at the hospital's prenatal clinic or an obstetrician's rooms. Or the hospital may have a midwives clinic, which you'll attend for most of your prenatal visits. Your prenatal visits to the obstetrician or clinic and your stay in hospital are covered by Medicare but you can't choose your midwives or obstetrician. If you want an independent midwife you will have to pay privately. When the time comes, you'll go to the hospital's maternity ward. You'll be attended by hospital staff midwives, perhaps trainee midwives, and possibly obstetricians in training (called registrars), general doctors doing their hospital training (called residents) and an obstetrician (called Sparky).

Usually the hospital will run prenatal classes, and often post-natal classes on breastfeeding and other baby-care subjects. A large teaching hospital in a capital city can be the best place to be in the rare case of an emergency because there are specialists on call.

PRIVATE   If you've got private health insurance, you can choose your obstetrician and have a private room in hospital (depending on availability the day you give birth). You'll be attended by the hospital midwives, and you may bring an independent midwife. Make sure you know exactly what your private insurance will pay for: it may cover only your time in hospital – not visits to the obstetrician – and it may not cover meals or all of the obstetrician's fee. It probably won't cover your independent midwife, but it's worth trying to negotiate. Privately paid obstetricians can deliver babies in private or public hospitals or birth centres: find out where yours goes. Check also that in an unexpected emergency your private hospital can keep a baby breathing until the specialised ambulance arrives to take it to the nearest major hospital.

Birth centre

HOSPITAL AFFILIATED   Many hospitals have birth centres, which are more 'homey' places to give birth in than a surgical-looking room. They are often seen as the result of hospitals responding to public demand – a safer option than giving birth on a couch at home and a more pleasant and natural option than giving birth on a trolley under klieg lights in a room that smells like industrial-strength Dettol. But 'There's much more to a birth room than a double bed and a potted plant', according to one midwife, who warns that some hospital birth centres look inviting but have the same hospital attitudes that women are often trying to avoid. She suggests you compare rates of caesarean deliveries, and other interventions such as rupture of the membranes, inductions, monitoring and vaginal examinations during labour. And find out how crowded the birth centre usually is – mothers in labour could be 'bumped' to the hospital wards if the centre is full. Mothers can also be quickly transferred to the hospital if necessary. Public patients are fully covered by Medicare.

Birth centres may be staffed by midwives, who run prenatal classes, give prenatal care and help you through the delivery. These are usually used by public patients. Or you can have an independent midwife you bring in, if the centre allows it. If necessary, an obstetrician will be called in during the birth. If you're privately insured, you could arrange to have available an obstetrician you choose. Otherwise, it's whoever is 'on call' for the centre.

FREESTANDING   Some birth centres are not affiliated with a hospital, and are not in hospital grounds. Usually you will have to pay extra for these, and you'll need to check whether your private health insurance covers the one you choose, and how much you get refunded by Medicare.

Home   A homebirth is usually attended by one or two midwives. You can choose to have an obstetrician there as well, but your choice will be limited by the fact that very few obstetricians want to be involved in homebirths, considering them dangerous or uninsurable. You should be transferred to a hospital if it becomes necessary during the delivery. Most health funds will not cover homebirths, but you may be able to negotiate part payment for independent midwives and some other services. Check with your fund. Also check if the doctor's involvement is covered by Medicare or a private fund.

Shared care This is just what it sounds like – a team approach to your pregnancy with a combination of visits to a local doctor and a hospital; or a community health centre and a hospital; or a team of independent midwives and a hospital; or an independent midwife who visits you at home and a private or public-hospital obstetrician. Shared care is available to rural and city women – ideally, you should be able to have flexible options so you can put together the team you want.

For many women in remote areas, choices will probably be more limited. Although GPs are qualified to deliver babies and will certainly roll up their sleeves if nobody else is available, it's much better for you to have access to specialists and special equipment (including ultrasound operators) during your pregnancy and especially when giving birth. Look for a midwife and doctor who are experienced and whose philosophy is compatible with yours.

who?

The relationship with your obstetrician and a midwife who goes with you through pregnancy and beyond is intimate, and dependent on trust, mutual respect and free communication. You'll come to depend on them over a number of months. You will be entrusting them with your life and your child's life. In an ideal situation, they will be equal partners with you in the process.

It's worth spending some time researching and even seeing a couple of candidates before you decide. Recommendations often travel through word of mouth or from your local doctor. If you feel intimidated, patronised or confused by, or at odds with, an obstetrician or midwife, change to somebody else.

Obstetrician You might prefer a woman obstetrician. Maybe you want a woman obstetrician who has had at least one child herself. Or maybe you don't care if it's a bloke or a woman as long as the person is fully qualified, pleasant and easy to talk to (and not called Sparky).

You can ask around for the name of a good one and then get your local doctor to refer you, or ask your local doctor for a recommendation.

Questions you might like to ask an obstetrician on your first visit include:

◉ Will you be in the country on my due delivery date?

◉ Who covers for you when you're not on call?

◉ Under what circumstances are you happy to be contacted out of hours?

◉ What are your views on pain relief, different labour positions, electronic foetal monitoring, episiotomy and forceps delivery?

◉ Under what circumstances would you recommend inducing birth or performing a caesarean?

◉ What do you consider the roles of the midwife, doctor, mother and support person or partner to be during the birth?

◉ How do you feel about following my special wishes for the labour? (We'll get into the birth plans later . . .)

If you're not satisfied with the answers, find another obstetrician.

Tell the obstetrician what sort of birth experience you are hoping for and what sort of patient you are; say, for example, that you like to have clear explanations given to you about why things are done, or that you will be needing extra reassurance because your last pregnancy ended in a miscarriage, or that it's important that you can continue with your alternative health care as well as seeing the obstetrician, or that you are terrified of the whole idea and thinking of a general anaesthetic as well as being interstate at the time or hiding under a rock.

Remember: wherever you are, whether you are in a community health clinic, a birth centre, a doctor's office or a teaching hospital, it is your right to refuse to allow students to attend consultations or procedures.

It's important to know that few obstetricians are able to attend an entire birth. They usually pop in and out during labour and are there at the end, for the birth, unless something unusual is happening. So your other support people are very important.

Midwife There are a few options to choose from.

⊚ You can hire an independent midwife who'll consult and examine you throughout your pregnancy, attend you at the birth, however long it takes, and visit to help and advise you on care and feeding in the first weeks of your baby's life. An independent midwife is most likely to give you the best continuity of individual care. (Ask the midwife who the 'back-up' will be in case they can't make it to your birth.)

⊚ An independent midwife can be part of a 'shared care' team with your local doctor or your obstetrician, or your hospital. They can attend home or hospital births. Check with your hospital or birth centre whether your midwife will be respected as your primary caregiver and decision maker during the birth and when or if a doctor may overrule the midwife. Remember that some hospitals will not allow independent midwives to deliver the baby, and the service is not covered by Medicare or most health funds.

⊚ If you're having a hospital birth, the hospital will allocate you a midwife or midwives on duty. This could include trainee midwives in a public hospital – if you're not happy about this, kick up a fuss. Hospital midwives can go 'off shift' in the middle of your labour and be replaced by the new midwives on duty.

⊚ Some independent, birth-centre and clinic midwives work in teams. This means a few midwives in rotation might be responsible for your prenatal, delivery and postnatal care, depending on who is on call or on duty. They will refer you to an obstetrician if that is necessary.

 For contact numbers, see under Midwives in 'Help'.

Support person If you have a partner, you'll usually want to have them at the birth. But if your partner isn't keen, it's probably better to choose somebody who'll be more useful and supportive at the time. Other common support people are sisters and friends. More rarely, parents are involved, especially mothers. Don't forget that if you have a long labour, it's better for everyone if your support person gets rest breaks or even a bit of shut-eye. They won't have your endorphins, and you don't want them fainting at the wrong moment. (Whatever a right moment is.)

Many people want a record of the event in photos or on video: some even want it shown live on the Internet. It can be hard for somebody to be in charge of support, lollies and multimedia at the same time.

Some people invite a cast of thousands, only to regret it later. Don't forget the people who are actively involved need room to do their work. Some midwives and doctors believe that the more people in the room, the longer the birth. Most women don't want to be distracted by visitors or worried about how their small children are coping with what can be a pretty heavy scene for them.

your record

What kind of prenatal and birth care have you chosen? How did you find your obstetrician or midwife? Who did you choose? Who else will be on your support team and why?

ultrasound

WEEK

cm

1

2

3

4

5

6

7

8

9

10

11

12

13

14

15

16

17

18

19

20

21

22

what's going on You're hungry. Eat.

Your body is doing a lot of work and you need more fuel than usual.

The embryo officially becomes a foetus this week. Very few organs are actually working yet, but they're in the right spot. The head is still big in proportion to the rest of the foetus. The nostrils and tear ducts are finished off. (If anybody asks why you're tired, just say you've been making eyebrows all night long.) Around about now the little tail will 'disappear' as the rest of the foetus grows. The limbs get longer; the arms can bend; hands and feet can touch each-other; and toes and fingers lose their webbing and become fully separated. Sheila Kitzinger's never-ending supply of fruit comparisons says your uterus is now the size of an orange. Weight: about 8 grams.

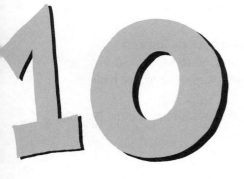

Diary   I'm not sure but I think some of my wrinkles –
sorry, I mean character lines – are less obvious.
This is because my body is making extra collagen
and all that stuff the cosmetics companies would
probably kill us pregnant women for if they knew how to get it
out of us.

Most of my daily thoughts consist only of the following
mantra: 'I have no interest in food, I cannot cook, I must lie down,
I need to watch crap on television, would you get a load of Ricki
Lake's hairdo. Help me. I can't get off the couch.' It's all just too,
too exhausting. If only I was the sort of person with four servants
and a heart-shaped box of chocolates and a four-poster bed with a
quilted-satin doona cover, it would probably all look quite
glamorous. I could have a negligee and a peignoir, and other
French words for jarmies.

I go for the nuchal fold ultrasound. This is an ultrasound that
looks for a thickening at the back of the baby's neck, which is an
indicator of Down syndrome. For some reason everyone thought I
might be eleven weeks pregnant but it's actually only about ten
according to the ultrasound operator, Dr Donaldson. Which means
it's too early to see much and I'll have to come back again.

It was kind of disappointing not to get a definitive answer
about the nuchal fold thing, but I'm happy that somebody else is
as bad at maths as me. Des comes for a look. There's Cellsie on the
screen, waving its wee bits.

'There's your baby,' says Dr Donaldson.

'It's not, it's a Christmas beetle,' I retort, looking at an insecty
shape stuck on its back and wiggling a lot of little legs in the air.

'Look, it's waving,' he says, pointing out a head, two arms and
two legs.

The head seemed to turn towards us, like something out of an
alien movie.

'Oh fuck, that's too weird,' I say and nobody answers.

It occurs to me that you're not supposed to say fuck during an
ultrasound. Repeat after me: Mummies ought not to say fuck.
Sigh. So much to learn.

The creature on the screen looks like any sort of foetus. It could grow into a lizard, or a laptop-dance club owner, or something equally hideous. And even though inside me it's actually only about 3.5 centimetres long, on the screen it looks as long as an adult hand. This is very disconcerting. Makes it seem more advanced and less human at the same time.

Suddenly the heartbeat monitor at the bottom of the screen shows an up-and-downie, mountain-shaped graph running along like something out of 'ER' – and the sound! Like a Latin techno beat! The fastest heartbeat I have ever heard. Looking closer, we can see the heart actually beating inside the lizardy thing. I begin to feel quite fond of it.

'That's not my heartbeat is it?' I ask. 'Because if it is, I think I'm having a heart attack.'

Dr Donaldson doesn't know why foetal heartbeats are so fast, but he says it's quite normal. Everything is normal. Size, normal. Shape, normal. All bits present so far. Normal. Normal, normal, normal.

Normal? I want to sneer. I've spent my whole life running away from normal. I don't DO normal. I refuse to live in the suburbs. I want to be special, I want to be interesting, I want . . . Okay, it's kind of reassuring that everything's normal. I'll admit it. You don't want to hear an ultrasound operator saying 'What the . . . ?', 'That can't BE!' or 'Holy catfish! I've never seen that before. Do you mind if I call some friends to come over and have a look?'.

(Des confesses afterwards that he checked out the electronic equipment and was watching the $5,000 monitor while I was watching the $1,000 monitor. He promises to point out the superior hardware next time we go.)

Dr Donaldson gives us a speech about how we shouldn't do any further tests unless the nuchal fold ultrasound shows a possible problem. He says once you start getting tests done they show falsely high possibilities, and then you just have more tests. He says our chances of having a baby with Down syndrome are less than the chances of losing a healthy pregnancy because one of the tests – amniocentesis (often called 'amnio') – may trigger a miscarriage. More statistics. There's a one in 500 chance of Down syndrome and a one in 200 chance of the test causing a miscarriage.

Another consultation with Dr Herb, clutching the normalnormalnormal ultrasound report in my hand. There's got to be a more civilised way of arriving at the doctor's than putting your jar of wee on the counter and then trotting off to the scales and shouting out to the doctor's assistant, 'Seventy-seven kilos, Lorraine, but 10 kilos of that must be these hiking socks I'm wearing.'

Lorraine, of course, invariably calls across the waiting room, 'HOW much do you weigh, again?' or 'IS THIS YOUR WEE, HERMOINE?'.

I imagine we're now going live through the hospital's public address system: 'Hermoine Harridan is 77 kilos, Hermoine Harridan is 77 kilos, code red.' All heads turn. 'Look, Lorraine, just write down: "Has entered bovine stage. When she walks, bass drum and tuba music plays. Was mistaken for a dugong off the beach early this morning".'

I further distinguish myself once I get into Dr Herb's room by whipping off my trousers and undies when he just wants to feel my tummy and 'measure the fundus'.

The man obviously thinks I'm some kind of crazed exhibitionist who enjoys lying on couches naked from the waist down except for boots, with her ankles somewhere near the light fittings, while her boyfriend sits in the corner reading a pamphlet.

Well, maybe I am. What's it to ya?

I wonder what a fundus is? Oh. It's the top of the uterus.

Dr Herb expands on the statistics for various risks. It leaves my brain in a whirl of confusing maths, so it seems best to just wait and see what's on the next ultrasound.

I have started to wrestle with constipation: I decide to adopt Beck's secret seed-breakfast method. Every time I get constipated I get at least one pimple, probably two. But after a day or two of crushed mixed seeds on my muesli, I'm running like a train again and zit-free.

info

chromosomes and genes

At conception the egg and sperm join to make a single cell. This one cell, combining twenty-three chromosomes supplied by the egg and twenty-three from the sperm, contains the entire genetic blueprint for your child. At that moment, your baby's genetic destiny is decided: what sex it will be, how tall it will be, how much natural musical or sporting talent it will have, what colour skin, hair and eyes, what shape it will become after puberty, and maybe what kind of illnesses it will be prone to.

Even though its genetic inheritance comes equally from both parents, a baby will not be an exact 50:50 mix of both parents' characteristics. It may end up with red hair that has 'skipped' a generation, or with a skin colour that is far more Dad than Mum, or vice versa. Your child may look not much like either parent, but more like long-lost Great-Aunty Nuala. Some families have genes that always seem to win out, such as a distinctive family nose or a particular build.

Your baby will eventually have millions of cells. The forty-six chromosomes inside the nucleus of each cell are made up of two chains of your genetic code, called DNA (deoxyribonucleic acid), which control growth and functioning of the baby. The chromosomes contain thousands of genes, which determine the physical and intellectual characteristics.

problems with chromosomes and genes

The term 'genetic disorder' refers to changes in the genetic code – like a typing error – that occurred in the formation of the genes and chromosomes in a particular baby, as well as to medical conditions or health problems, often also called genetic, which are inherited through the family.

Some inherited genetic diseases such as cystic fibrosis happen when both parents carry a recessive gene that can cause a problem. This gene doesn't affect either of the parents, but when the two potential problem genes are combined the foetus is affected. Other problems such as haemophilia (in boys) may be 'activated' only if the baby is of a certain sex. Some genetic disorders are linked to geographic regions or ethnic groups. Sickle-cell anaemia is the most common genetic disease in people of African descent, for example.

Down syndrome is a genetic condition with a high profile. The most common cause of intellectual disability, it affects about one in 800 to 1,000 pregnancies. It is also known as trisomy 21. Because of an accident during the division of cells when still an embryo, the foetus has three copies of chromosome 21 instead of the usual two. A baby (and adult) with Down syndrome will be mentally disabled, will have characteristic facial differences (especially a distinctive eyelid shape), a stocky stature and loose muscle tone, and may also suffer from medical problems, such as heart abnormalities, that need corrective surgery.

The incidence of Down syndrome increases dramatically in the foetuses of older women. According to the Victorian Clinical Genetics Services the ratios are:

21-year-old women – one in 1,520 pregnancies
35-year-old women – one in 355 pregnancies

WEEK 10 ⊚ 111

40-year-old women – one in 90 pregnancies
43-year-old women – one in 40 pregnancies

genetic counselling

Your hospital or your obstetrician can refer you to a genetic counsellor for any of the following reasons, but it is not automatic. If
you have any worries you may need to bring up the subject.

⊚ You've had a diagnostic test confirming a chromosomal
abnormality.

⊚ You've had miscarriages.

⊚ You or your partner has a family history of inherited physical
or psychiatric disease.

⊚ Blood tests have indicated a partner carries a genetic disorder.

⊚ You've already had a baby with a chromosomal or genetic
abnormality.

⊚ You've had a baby who died before or shortly after it was born.

⊚ You or your partner or a member of either family was born
with an abnormality caused by a genetic problem that was not
inherited through the family – this is known as a 'congenital
abnormality'.

⊚ You and your partner are related (cousins, for example).

⊚ You or your partner is over 35.

Genetic counsellors can accurately assess your risk of having a
baby with a hereditary disorder. If you have already had a child
with a disorder, they may be able to predict your chances of it
happening again. They can tell you if you carry genes that cause
certain disorders, and very often reassure you that the chances of
a problem are very low. The techniques used to arrive at this information can include blood tests, genetic analysis and examination
of both families' medical history. So of course it will always be a
bonus if you have access to family histories on both sides. If you
don't have access because you don't know who the father is or he is

unco-operative, you probably don't need to worry at all. Genetic problems are very rare.

more info on gene and chromosome problems

There are support and info groups for various genetic disorders. Check the phone listings for your area or go through the counsellor at the biggest hospital in your area.

Prenatal Testing: Making Choices in Pregnancy by Lachlan de Crespigny, Meg Espie and Sophia Holmes, Penguin, Ringwood, 1998.

A wonderfully informative book that explains risks, tests, results and the decision-making process during what could be your most confusing moments. Compassionate case histories add to the non-judgemental tone. Importantly, it is up to date and completely relevant to Australia.

your record

If the baby's dad is on the scene, how does he seem to be reacting? You might like to get him to write down his thoughts here, or you could put your hair in a bun and take dictation and then take all your clothes off and . . . excuse me.

Average approximate foetus length this week from head to bum

what's going on Nausea should

start to settle down from now on. Hurrah.

Outside influences, such as certain

drugs and chemicals, could have damaged the

foetus while it was still forming; the dangers are still

there after week 10, but are no longer so

acute. (This does not mean you can get on

the vodka.) The placenta is continuing to get

bigger, keeping pace with what the foetus

needs. The heart is completely formed

and pumping away. The ear and hearing

structures are nearly finished and

ready to grow. Your foetus is looking

a lot more like a tiny human with a big

head, short limbs and not much clothes sense.

(In fact, about now the head is almost half the size

of the whole foetus.) Weight: about 10 grams.

oops

WEEK 11

INADVISABLE ACROBATIC DANCING

DiARY I've been lent a lot of baby-care books for the duration. One is Aunty Peg's decrepit second-hand copy of Dr Spock from approximately the Jurassic Period, which she immediately borrowed after Mum died to work out what she and Uncle Stan should do with this small creature (me) suddenly on their doorstep.

I fancied a look at the modern pregnancy and child-care books, but I discovered most of them are absolutely shocking. For one thing, they're always banging on about husbands as if every pregnant woman had to have one. Mind you it's not just insulting to the single mother-to-be. The blokes don't come out of it well either. One book actually recommends that you teach 'your husband' to make his own breakfast before you go to hospital, say by week 32 to be sure. If a bloke doesn't know how to make his own breakfast, I say you're better off without him.

It's kind of comforting that even the experts disagree – this means you don't have to get worried if you're not at exactly the stage a book reckons you should be. On almost every major yardstick I'm not. And quite frankly I don't expect to have a multiple orgasm the first time I breastfeed.

Even some of the good books have the most absurd photographs to enliven their pages. Under the section on nutrition or appetite there is usually a photograph of a woman with a plate of food, in case you have forgotten what a plate of food looks like.

And I don't wish to be rude, but I'd like all the people who have done illustrations for pregnancy books rounded up and killed. They can't be allowed to go on. Who ARE all these women in the illustrations, pale-as-pastry, frumpy, with disgusting haircuts, wearing doona covers? And who are these husbands looking manfully into the distance with gigantic sideburns? They are the line-drawing equivalents of knitting-pattern photos from the 1970s. With captions like 'A new father can bottle-feed a baby'. Yes, and given half a chance he can tie his own shoelaces, and all.

One book has four filthy drawings of bright pink couples 'making love' during pregnancy, in different positions. In the first position they look bored. In the second position they look like they've had a lobotomy. In the third they look really smug, and in number four, I don't know how this is quite conveyed, but I'm pretty sure they were singing 'Michael Row the Boat Ashore'. (This could be dangerous. If you don't know by now that it's possible to have sex from behind, a line drawing is going to send you into shock.)

Another book, called *A Child Is Born*, has graphic photos of the foetus in the uterus. It's disgusting. Des reads it every night. He's fascinated by the pictures. They make me want to projectile vomit.

'Look, that's what Cellsie looks like now.'

I scream and hide under the sheets. 'That looks like a prawn made of snot!'

'But it's amazing. Look at this one – this is what it'll look like next week.'

Great. A portion of especially dumb plankton, with eyes like ball bearings. I cannot relate to this. It is a greater test of maternal instincts than anyone should have to undergo. Nobody could love a snot prawn. How can I bond with a crustacean?

There really is too much information in these books, and yet not enough. For example, 'Acrobatic dancing is, of course, unwise at any stage during pregnancy'. How acrobatic? Are we talking those circus girls who can put their head up their own bum? Do we refer here to the sort of wafty crap, Stevie-Nicks-type hippie dancing while waving shawls? Which is surely ultimately more offensive and therefore more dangerous than the lesser known acrobatic dancing. Perhaps it means chandelier work.

And personally I cannot take anybody seriously who uses the word 'brassiere' in a complete sentence. Especially if the sentence is 'The advantage of having a well-made and properly fitted brassiere cannot be emphasised too strongly'. Certainly not, Mrs Shelf-Bosom. Emphasise away.

Unfortunately I can't seem to stick to the bits of the books relevant to me this week. I go racing ahead to the things like, 'To take with you to the hospital for the baby: seven pilchers and three fluffies'. What the bollocky blue blazes is a pilcher? Will there be enough space in the hospital room for seven of them? A fluffy *what* exactly? 'Fluffy' is not a noun. 'Fluffy' is an adjective.

One of the books, by Miriam Stoppard, has an entire section

devoted to how to wear make-up during pregnancy (on your face, I presume). Anyway, there are handy hints such as how to cover up dark circles under the eyes; and camouflage puffiness by shading a little brown blusher subtly beneath the jawbone and on either side of the neck. Look, this might work if you are standing still, being professionally lit and photographed, but if you're walking around like a normal human being no amount of brown blusher on your neck is going to disguise the fact that you're a bit puffy.

You would be better off constantly introducing yourself to people by saying, 'Hello, I'm a bit puffy. It's because I'm up the duff and a big fat baby is going to come out of my vagina', and getting on with things. I can guarantee nobody will mention any puffiness after that. Not to your face, anyway. Here's a great pregnancy make-up hint: 'To draw attention away from your jawline, try using a blusher at the temples so that your eyes become the focus'. Or, say, wear a hat with a rotating stuffed zebra leg on it.

info

screening and diagnostic tests

There are lots of screening and diagnostic tests that will give you an idea of how your baby is developing, although not all of them are 100 per cent accurate.

A screening test is one that assesses your risk (against the average risk) of carrying a baby that has certain abnormalities. A positive screening-test result does NOT mean the baby has an abnormality. In fact, chances are very much in your favour that the baby is perfectly fine, but the result means that a further test is offered to you, a diagnostic test.

Diagnostic tests, such as amniocentesis and CVS (see below), can provide you with a definite answer about whether your baby has a specific abnormality. Ultrasound tests are also used, but they're not a failsafe way of detecting problems. For the best chance of useful results, an ultrasound test must be conducted by a specialist operator.

More than 95 per cent of women having prenatal tests will have babies with no abnormality at all.

routine ultrasound

An ultrasound examination bounces high-frequency soundwaves into your body to create an image of the foetus and your internal organs on a computer screen. You lie on your back while an ultrasound technician or obstetrician performs the test. A small object a bit like a computer mouse will be run over the top of your tummy, after some gel has been spread on it; or, if the test is done before twelve weeks of pregnancy, a 'probe' is put into your vagina. Luckily the probe is only about the size of a large pen. Ultrasounds don't hurt, and these days you don't have to have a full bladder.

An ultrasound is usually offered to you at about eighteen weeks. It's a great chance to see your foetus on screen for the first time – so bring your partner, or a friend who might get a kick out of it. If you're lucky, the foetus will give you a wave. It can be quite an emotional moment seeing your foetus for the first time; be prepared to get misty eyed.

The operator will compile a report for your obstetrician. The ultrasound can confirm an estimation of how advanced your pregnancy is (give or take a few days); catch sight of twins or other multiple births; and locate the position of your placenta (if it's low lying, another ultrasound will be done later in the pregnancy to see if placenta praevia has developed – that's when the placenta grows over or very close to the cervix). The ultrasound will show any uterine growths, such as fibroids. Most fibroids are harmless and don't get in the way of anything – you wouldn't even know you had them unless you'd had the ultrasound.

An ultrasound allows the operator to measure and observe

limbs and organs; it also shows the baby's sex (it's about 98 per cent accurate, but sometimes the position of the foetus can make identification difficult). If you don't want to know the sex of the baby you should let the operator know, otherwise they're likely to blurt out something like 'It's a girlie!' or 'Look out, there's a big willy.'

A specialist ultrasound operator can usually identify certain foetal abnormalities such as spina bifida, cleft palate and mis-shapen feet by using measurements and observation.

Digital technology has made it possible now to have a three-dimensional ultrasound. Distributors of this technology say it is better than the routine ultrasound at picking up some abnor-malities early on. It is still too expensive (about double the price of the standard machines) for routine use in Australia.

nuchal fold ultrasound

You may be offered, or you can request, an ultrasound at eleven weeks that is sometimes called the nuchal fold, or nuchal trans-lucency, test. The operator gets a good image of your foetus's neck on the screen and measures the skin layer at the back of the neck. The thicker this layer is, the greater the chance the baby will have Down syndrome. (This test picks up about 80 per cent of Down syndrome cases it surveys.) If the neck swelling is there, you will be offered a more accurate diagnostic test – amniocentesis or CVS (see below) – which can tell you whether or not your baby has Down syndrome.

blood test

If your nuchal fold test result doesn't give you the 'all clear' or you have a worrying family medical history, your doctor will probably suggest a blood test, carried out at between fifteen and eighteen weeks, to find out if you have an increased risk of Down syndrome or neural tube defects such as spina bifida. A small amount of blood is taken from your arm and sent off to a laboratory. The result comes back within a week as either 'low-risk' or 'increased risk', often expressed as a statistic (a one in 30,000 chance, one in 100, and so on). Nineteen out of twenty women tested will have a 'low-risk' result.

An 'increased risk' result does *not* automatically mean your baby has the conditions tested for, but it does mean you'll probably be offered a further diagnostic test: an ultrasound, CVS or amniocentesis. (Most 'increased risk' women will be found to be carrying a healthy baby. Unfortunately this means you often sweat on a 'one in 30' result for two weeks until you get the all clear.) The blood test works by measuring levels of substances in the blood including the hormone HCG, the oestrogen called oestriol, and a protein called alpha-foetoprotein.

amniocentesis and CVS

Some diagnostic tests are usually recommended if you're over 35, you have a family history of Down syndrome or spina bifida, you've had a foetus with a neural tube defect in a previous pregnancy, you've had an 'increased risk' blood test result, or you've had an inkling from the nuchal fold test that your foetus may be at greater risk.

The two main diagnostic tests are amniocentesis (known as 'amnio') and CVS (chorionic villus sampling, but it's almost always just called CVS). These are both invasive tests that slightly increase your existing risk of miscarriage – amnio by half of 1 per cent and CVS by 1 per cent when carried out by experienced, specialist practitioners.

It's this risk that makes the tests an option rather than a routine for every pregnancy. You will be weighing up a statistical risk – the chance of discovering a defect versus the chance of causing the miscarriage of a healthy foetus. Help in making that decision is available from your obstetrician or hospital prenatal clinic.

Operators' risk rates can vary enormously, so insist that your obstetrician refer you to a place where the procedure is performed by experienced specialists (this might mean you need to travel to your nearest capital city), and ask the obstetrician about the risk rate of the particular person who will be performing your procedure.

Amniocentesis is used to test for Down syndrome and other chromosomal disorders, neural tube defects such as spina bifida, and other genetic conditions. The test is carried out at about fifteen weeks. It involves you lying very still, while the technician uses an ultrasound to see exactly where the foetus is inside the amniotic sac. The technician will then insert a needle through your abdomen and into the uterus but not near the foetus. The needle draws in a small amount of amniotic fluid, which contains cells from the foetus. It is these cells that can give a definitive answer to questions about chromosomes.

CVS is used to test for most of the same conditions as amnio, but cannot test for spina bifida. The test is often done earlier than amnio and can be done at any time after about ten weeks. The technician operates in much the same way as for amnio, but takes a needle sample of tissue from the chorion – the name for the placenta in its early, growing phase. The needle can go in either through the abdomen or through the vagina.

Both tests are usually considered to be uncomfortable rather than painful, although it's no fun having a big needle put into you near your foetus; besides which, you may be worried about the result. It's good to have someone come with you to the procedure, who can then take you home, where you should lie down for the day, or even two, depending on the advice of your obstetrician.

Results for both tests take up to three weeks. Because CVS can give a result earlier in the pregnancy than amnio, it's often helpful if you have to decide whether to discontinue a pregnancy involving a foetus with an abnormality. It is easier emotionally and physically to terminate a pregnancy as early as possible. Most people do decide to terminate a foetus with a severe abnormality, but some would not do this whatever the circumstances.

Decisions about terminations are always difficult, even if you're sure you've made the right choice. Take as much time as possible to thoroughly work through and feel comfortable with the decision. Non-directive counselling will be available to you (help to understand and process the issues, without any urging in a particular direction); it can also be useful in resolving any differences of opinion between you and your partner.

Some elements to consider are the nature and severity of the diagnosed condition, the likely survival or quality of life of the baby after birth, any ethical and religious aspects, your willingness or ability to deal with the baby's condition, and the likely impact on members of your family such as other children.

If your obstetrician does not wish to terminate the pregnancy once you have decided you want to, see another one or go to a family planning clinic (see Family Planning Clinics in 'Help' for contact numbers). If your obstetrician strongly advises you to terminate, and you are unsure or don't want to, the same alternatives apply.

Even if for religious or ethical reasons you would not consider terminating your pregnancy, these tests can help you and your family to prepare both emotionally and in a practical sense for the birth requirements and care of a special needs baby, or for the possibility of a miscarriage.

Scientists are running clinical trials of a new method as accurate as CVS that can be done when a woman is six weeks pregnant, using only a sample of her blood. If that proves successful, it will still be some time before it's available to everyone.

more info on tests and beyond

 Which Tests for My Unborn Baby? Ultrasound and Other Prenatal Tests by Lachlan de Crespigny with Rhonda Dredge, Oxford University Press, Melbourne, 1998. Written by an obstetrician and a journalist specialising in genetics, this is a surprisingly easy to follow, up-to-date explanation of the hows and whys of ultrasound, CVS, amnio and foetal abnormalities, and also a wrap-up of less common testing procedures.

Prenatal Testing: Making Choices in Pregnancy by Lachlan de Crespigny, Meg Espie and Sophia Holmes (for details and full review see More Info on Gene and Chromosome Problems in 'Week 10').

Your nearest family planning clinic, maternity hospital or obstetrician will have staff and counsellors to help you, and pamphlets or booklets you can read on specific issues. There are support groups for parents of babies and children with special needs. Your doctor or nearest hospital should be able to help you get in touch.

Grief counsellors can help with anything from a decision to terminate or miscarriage, to dealing with a special needs baby.

See also Grief and Loss, and Babies' Health Problems in 'Help'.

your record

What tests have you decided to have?

How do you feel about waiting for results?

If you had an ultrasound, what was it like? What could you see? You can paste in any ultrasound 'photos' here.

what's going on

This is often the first time you'll visit the obstetrician. Don't forget beforehand to write down questions as they occur to you, for the obstetrician. You may be feeling very tired – after all, you're not just a fascinating, sophisticated minx any more, you're a walking host organ.

Inside, your foetus looks more like a baby but with the head still bent forward. The face has a human profile and the jaw hides twenty developing tooth buds. Muscles are growing and increasing the movement of the foetus, but you still can't feel it because it has plenty of room to slosh about in the amniotic fluid without touching the sides. As the placenta has been doing since week 5, it is routinely sending oxygen and nutrients down the vein of the umbilical cord, and taking away waste such as foetal wee, which travels back up the two arteries in the cord. Weight: about 18 grams.

DiARy

For some reason my sense of smell has become really acute. I can only wear men's aftershaves. Any even slightly girlie, florally scents make me go bleuuuergh. God help me if I get stuck in a lift at a department store.

Finally I get to have the proper nuchal fold ultrasound. This time Dr Donaldson pokes Cellsie around to get it in the right position by pushing hard on my tummy, and I really don't feel good about this. All the measurements are fine, he says, and so he would advise against me having further, invasive tests. Again we are at the whim of statistics, reminded that the test picks up 80 per cent of Down syndrome cases. For a wild maths-phobic moment I think this means we have a 20 per cent chance of having a Down syndrome baby, but of course it doesn't mean that at all.

We leave, and I surprise myself by bursting into tears. For some reason I feel great indignation at Cellsie being unceremoniously poked to get him or her into a better position. I guess the baby must be starting to feel more real. I didn't expect to feel protective of my little space prawn.

We're close to the magic, don't-have-to-be-so-scared-about-miscarriages point, and we decide to tell everybody we haven't told. Des's parents are thrilled, and send us a lovely fax from Canada, where they are on assignment investigating rare fungus up some mountain. Aunty Peg is very happy, I think, but it's hard to tell. Aunty Peg cries no matter what happens.

Uncle Stan seems very happy, but then he's cheered up immensely since the initial shock when Aunty Peg changed the locks after the Raelene the Magnificent Incident eleven years ago. Sure it took him ten years, but he's certainly coming good in the jollies department. He seems seriously avuncular about the idea of a grand-niece or -nephew.

He makes the same joke he does every two months about being glad we're not getting married so he doesn't have to pay for it. Anyway, he continues, the State should have nothing to do with religion, which is why Stan's a Pagan. He likes to write it in purple ink on his census form each four years. Actually I think he's decided to be a Pagan because at Pagan Rituals you get to meet a lot of mature-age ladies who wear shawls, listen to Fleetwood Mac and agree to have Sex with Stan.

As Aunty Peg snorts: 'Pagan, my bum. He's bloody C of E.' Even though she hasn't been to a church, except for a wedding, in thirty years, as far as Aunty Peg is concerned everyone is Church of England except 'foreigners' and Irish persons. (When I told her I was having the baby in a Jewish hospital because it was the closest, she had to lie down with a cold washer on her ankles and suck a Tarzan's jube.)

At the news of our impending bundle of joie de vivre, Stan's girlfriend Aurelia shrieks, throws herself off her stilettoes onto Des, gets coral-coloured lipstick in his eyebrows and his ears (she's thorough), and expresses the opinion that a few good thumps never hurt anyone and she hopes we won't be the type to mollycoddle the little bastard. I repress the urgent desire to reassure her that we'll start whacking the living daylights out of it as soon as we see its head coming out, but I find it harder than usual to be jocular about child abuse in my present state. Guess it's those pesky 'baby hormones' the books blame everything on.

Aurelia demands that Uncle Stan take her down to the pub to celebrate. Uncle Stan departs, saying he's very happy for us but he's never changed a nappy in his life and he doesn't intend to start now, bugger it. I think everyone has made their position clear. Five minutes later Uncle Stan comes back to get Aurelia's gold Glo-mesh cigarette case.

'Your mother would have loved this,' he whispers.

I get tears in my eyes. I've always missed her, but I think I'll feel it more when the baby comes.

Apparently the minute she got to the local, Aurelia announced my pregnancy to the public bar, the saloon bar, the ladies' lounge and the men's urinal, as well as to a guy called Scott who was rewiring a pokies machine.

Des's cousin Annie, mother of six, which is a truly appalling prospect, the one who spent years before the pregnancy asking when I was going to get pregnant and then, when told to knock it off, asked everyone else in the family every time she saw them, is continuing to be insufferable. She announces loudly and frequently,

'I *knew* you were pregnant!', and has taken to poking me in the stomach and squeezing me on the arm as if she's about to buy me as a Shetland pony for one of her children. 'Mmm,' she says each time. 'Yes, you're definitely pregnant!' 'No, I just said I was for something to do, you idiot,' I feel like saying. Or 'Yes, I had an inkling. I feel pregnant and the hormone tests say I'm pregnant and I've seen the foetus on ultrasound.'

Other immediate reactions to 'I'm pregnant' have included:

'You'll never get rid of them!' (60-year-old woman)

'That's wonderful!' (all the nice people I know)

'Your life is over!' (Miss Francine, my beauty therapiste)

Complete silence and choking sound. (my boss)

One of my clients buying the latest range wants me to commit to a fashion conference four hours away by plane, in September. Cellsie will be four weeks old. 'It will only be for a day and a half,' he says. 'You'll be dying to get out and about by then, and reclaim your identity. I mean, I know when we had kids it satisfied my creative urges for a while, but then you really need to reclaim your own space.' Lordy. What a dork.

Another visit to Dr Herb so he can check out the ultrasound results, and me. Wait in the waiting room while he delivers somebody else's baby. (Well, one can hardly complain about *that* as an excuse for being late, can one?) The woman next to me has a small child she speaks to in a Very Loud Voice. She is Extremely Annoying. The child looks at pictures in a book.

'Here's Daddy,' he says, pointing to a man.

'That's not *our* daddy,' she bellows, cheerfully.

Our daddy! 'Madam,' I feel like saying, 'he is the child's daddy. He is not your daddy.' I ponder the whole spooky idea of calling your sexual partner mummy or daddy.

Finally I get to see Dr Herb. He gives the old tummy a bit of a poke and a feel (this is called 'palpation' apparently) and seems pleased with the progress.

'It's definitely growing.'

Despite the obviousness of this banality I am absurdly pleased. He smiles.

'Everything's going as well as could be expected. Couldn't be better.' I beam. Oh hurrah. I feel like I've received a gold star and an elephant stamp on my homework.

'By the way, I had some reeeeally alcoholic punch at a party when I was already pregnant,' I 'fess up.

'How much?' asks Herb.

'About two glasses. Erm. Maybe three. Four, tops.'

'It's very unlikely to do any harm at all.'

Phew.

I have written down three questions: can Beck be the midwife? (Yes.) Is the hospital set up for any emergency, and will he perform a caesarean if it's needed? (Yes.) And what books does he recommend? (Janet Balaskas's *New Active Birth*.) I think it's interesting that, of all the books on pregnancy and child-wrangling, he has chosen one about birth, but I realise afterwards that he must have thought I MEANT just books on childbirth because I had asked about the hospital facilities. You have to be so specific. They see so many women in a day. God knows how many Peter Pan collars on tarpaulin-frocks the poor man has had to endure in his lifetime.

Aunty Peg is driving me insane. She has been depressed since 1957, but carries about her the air of a wounded martyr delivering vital messages to the front. Unfortunately now she knows I'm pregnant, she has decided the front is me and the messages must be as tragic as possible. Aunty Peg always has a horrendous story to tell, usually about some dreadful thing that has happened to a small child: left in the wilderness, flung from a train, attacked by feral guinea pigs – you name it, Aunty Peg can tell you the long version.

'I'm not congratulating Des yet, dear,' she announces on the doorstep instead of saying hello, 'in case something goes wrong.'

Tact and optimism are strangers to our Peg. After a few other pleasantries (babies who have been abused, small children murdered by their estranged parents, the children of women who drink too much in pregnancy), she bursts into tears – just as I am about to shovel her into the gutter and get to work.

'Oh, poor wee thing!' she sobs.

I am bewildered. 'Who?'

'Kimberley.'

'Kimberley?' I reply, mystified. The only Kimberley I know is a strapping second cousin of 42 years, who lives in ignorant bliss with her gormless husband and five children.

'Yes,' sobs Aunty Peg, who's related to this person by marriage. 'Her mother lifted a bluestone block when she was six months and seventeen days pregnant, and Kimberley came the next day.'

'But Kimberley is perfectly fine, apart from being a complete idiot,' I reply.

Aunty Peg looks at me accusingly. 'You're not lifting anything, are you?'

She leaves, after pressing some packets of herbs into my hands, neatly labelled with their names.

'Make yourself some tea with these, dear, they're very natural,' she confides.

Not bloody likely. After she goes I ring Beck for the herb inside story, and sure enough, one of the herbs is an abortifacient, which means it could abort or deform a developing foetus. Now I have to ring Aunty Peg and tell her to stop being an amateur herbalist around the joint before somebody comes out in hives, loses their hair or carks it. (What is it about pregnancy that brings out the amateur doctor or herbalist in people?)

'Your Aunty Peg,' says Des that night, 'is mad. It probably runs in the family.'

pregnancy hormones

Every time you mention a symptom of pregnancy – from bigger breasts, to being grumpy, to wanting an ice-cream, to feeling unspecific morbid dread, to wanting to stand on the roof and shriek – somebody will say in tones of enormously ponderous knowledge, 'It's the pregnancy hormones.' Well, what exactly are the pregnancy hormones, and which ones do what? After all it's not as if those medical professors sit around at university and in hospital meeting rooms going, 'Ooh, you know, pet, pregnancy hormones, whatever they're called.' At least I hope not. Many of the pregnancy hormones are produced by the placenta, the organ inside the uterus that sustains the developing baby through the umbilical cord. This is kind of a neat trick as the placenta comes out just after your baby does, right when you won't need those hormones any more.

❻ The 'thin blue line' hormone is called human chorionic gonadotrophin (HCG). HCG in wee triggers a 'positive' result in pregnancy tests. A high level during the first three months is one of the suspected reasons for nausea. HCG stimulates the ovaries to produce more progesterone, which in turn shuts down the monthly period department for the duration of the pregnancy.

❻ The 'Oh my God, look at these bazoombas' hormones needed for milk production are the human placental lactogen (HPL), prolactin, oestrogen and progesterone. HPL is responsible for enlarging the breasts and the secretion of colostrum, the 'pre-milk' or 'practising milk', which may leak from your nipples from about the fifth month (or not) and is produced for the first few days after the birth.

❻ Relaxin, the 'hang loose' pregnancy hormone, makes ligaments and tissues soften up and become more elastic, which provides the increased flexibility in the joints of the pelvis and back needed for labour. It may also contribute to the 'waddle' of later pregnancy. (The other contributing factor being that you've turned into a giant wombat.)

❻ Oxytocin is the squeezer hormone: it stimulates the practice (Braxton Hicks) contractions of the uterus and the contractions of childbirth. Injections of this hormone are often used to induce labour and to expel the placenta.

❻ The 'colouring-in' hormone is melanocyte-stimulating hormone (MSH). In the later months of pregnancy, high levels of MSH can make your nipples darken, and can cause dark patches on your face and a dark vertical line down the middle of your tummy called the linea nigra (Latin for 'black line').

❻ One of the big two girlie hormones, progesterone affects every aspect of pregnancy. It's produced by the ovaries when you're not pregnant, but eventually the placenta takes over the task during pregnancy. It relaxes smooth muscle: in the uterus so it's less likely to contract and cause miscarriage, and in the bladder, intestines, bowel and veins so they're more flexible as they're squashed by the growing uterus. It increases your body temperature and breathing rate, causes dilated blood vessels, which can reduce blood pressure and make you feel faint and nauseated, and helps produce breast milk. Immediately after the birth, the level drops and continues to drop for a number of days.

❻ The other major girlie hormone, oestrogen (or more correctly group of oestrogens), is also produced by the ovaries and then the placenta during pregnancy. Oestrogens help make everything in the reproductive department behave as it should throughout the pregnancy, including the breasts (enlarging nipples and developing milk glands), the uterus (strengthening) and body tissue (softening). Many believe that excess oestrogens cause nausea in the first three months. As with progesterone, the relatively high level of oestrogen drops immediately after the birth, and continues to drop in the days that follow.

❻ Endorphins, which mimic the effects of morphine and help blunt perceptions of pain and stress, are hormones produced by the brain up until and during childbirth. After the birth the levels drop sharply. This has been implicated in the temporary 'baby blues' most new mothers experience, and the more lasting feelings of depression that sometimes follow. One new mother complained, 'They've turned off my happy hormones.'

your record

What are your fears and hopes for the pregnancy?

WEEK 13

what's going on Your tummy is probably starting to stick out. Soon it will seem to 'pop' and everyone will begin noticing. Any nausea will probably stop or trail off about now.

Down in foetusland, reflexes for sucking, swallowing and breathing have begun. The amniotic sac surrounding the foetus is full of 100 millilitres of amniotic fluid, a fully appointed unit still with lots of room to bob around in. The ears are finished but can't hear yet. The lungs, liver, kidneys and digestive bits are still maturing. The head has been growing more slowly than the body since week 11. By the end of this week almost everything should be formed and ready to grow. But the foetus almost certainly wouldn't survive on its own because the organs wouldn't function well enough. Weight: about 30 grams.

Diary

I am so grumpy. All I want is an extensive personal staff to clean the house, fluff the pillows, cook my dinner and suck up to me. I have injured myself by sneezing in the middle of a yoga stretch. It felt like I tore through muscles or ligaments on each side of my tummy, down low near the hip bones. Bloody exercise: it's bad for you.

And there is far too much palaver written these days about balanced meals for the pregnant woman. A perfectly nutritious and attractive meal can be had by eating three pieces of Vegemite toast and half a packet of milk chocolate in 7 seconds flat. Although it is true that I'd probably be dead if I wasn't taking all those vitamins (but not vitamin A, which you can't if you're up the duff).

It's the weirdest thing being nauseous and getting no fun out of food, but still feeding your face relentlessly.

My gums keep bleeding. This is obviously some sort of design fault. Again, many of the books are hopeless, presuming the 'mother-to-be' has the brain of the average anteater: 'The baby hormones may be making your gums bleed. Take special care with dental hygiene.' I always lose consciousness at about the word 'hygiene'. Beck suggests more vitamin C and that seems to help. Maybe I just had scurvy.

weepiness

At times during pregnancy you can feel ecstatic, elated, like a fertile winged mythical love goddess (well, okay, maybe not), contented, confident, optimistic and relaxed. But you can also feel depressed, terrified, worried, tense, crabby, moody and like a blundering water buffalo. Tears are almost inevitable.

Sometimes it can seem that you're on a hair-trigger. Anything can suddenly set you off: sad movies or the news stories about bad things that happen to babies or mothers. The rest of the world goes on despite your pregnancy, and with a bit of bad luck yours might coincide with a relationship break-up, other personal complications, or a death in the family.

Even without extra stress, you can feel miserable, especially during the first trimester when your hormones seem to be stuck on the spin-cycle. Maybe you recognise some of the symptoms from PMS (premenstrual syndrome). About 10 per cent of women have mild to moderate depression while pregnant.

Your moodiness might be manifested by you being cranky and overcritical; or flying into rage or panic about something that isn't really so important; or crying for no specific reason. Or at the long-distance phone ads.

Thinking about pregnancy and becoming a parent can bring up unresolved issues you may have with your own mother and father, or feelings of sadness or anger about your own childhood. And it's natural to feel ambivalent about being pregnant, and worried about many aspects of pregnancy and parenting, and grief for a lifestyle lost.

Your pregnancy worries can include (but are not strictly limited to) the following.

Will my baby be born healthy and 'normal'? (Very probably.)

Do I deserve a healthy baby? (Oooh, yes.)

How will I juggle parenting and career? (You won't know until you get there, but you can talk to people who do it and see if any of their strategies might suit you.)

How will I cope with childbirth? (The best way you can.)

Sleep deprivation? (Get all the sleep you can now.)

Breastfeeding? (There's lots of help available, and in the end it isn't compulsory.)

Curtailed freedom? (There are compensations. But yes. Life ain't perfect.)

And loss of autonomy? (It will pass in about twenty years or so.)

Will I have 'maternal instincts'? (Being a good parent is about being kind, patient and ready to learn, not about 'instincts'.)

Will I bond with my baby? (Probably, and if you don't there is lots of help available.)

How will my relationship with my partner be affected? (You'll probably both be sleep-deprived and grumpy for a while. Express your fears and keep talking.)

How will my partner cope with the demands of parenting? (Don't know, but there's lots of help available.)

Will my baby suffer from me being a single parent? (Children need a stable, loving environment. You can do that.)

Will I ever recognise my body again? (Yes, and you should stop looking at photos of famous actresses and models who have had children. They also have forty-seven nannies, personal trainers and teeming hordes of hair and make-up artists.)

How will I/we cope with a reduced income and increasing expenses? (Have a strategy.)

Why wouldn't you have the occasional wave of panic when you remember any or all of the above, plus the fact that your life is about to be transformed, and there's no going back?

Maybe you just need a good cry every now and then or to share your feelings with your partner or a friend. If a particular issue is really getting you down, or if you feel depressed most of the time, it might help to get some professional counselling. It's better to sort things out now than when you have a real, live, non-theoretical baby on your hands.

Here's the bit everyone bangs on about, but only because it's true: if you're feeling shocking, don't guzzle alcohol and caffeine and stuff your face with junk food. Eat a healthy diet, and get yourself some exercise, fresh air and plenty of rest.

Partners and friends, who are always on the lookout for a way to help you, should be ordered to cheer you up. And you need to hang out with some cheerful parents.

the way people react to the news

When people react to your pregnancy, it's not about you, it's about them. If they say negative or rude things, it comes from their own experience or their own personality, their own fears or their own problems with body image, babies, their mother, whatever. Every time you hear something discouraging ('Your life is over') or ludicrous ('Childbirth doesn't hurt at all'), just say to yourself, 'It's not about me, it's about them.'

what's going on

The second trimester kicks off this week. You'll probably start to feel a bit more energetic. With a bit of luck the nausea should be gone or almost gone. You may get a dark line from your navel to your map of Tassie. This is called the linea nigra because doctors think 'black line' sounds soooo much more sophisticated in Latin. On white skin it's not a black line: it varies from a pale, shadowy pink to a browny colour. On dark skin it can look darker, or not be visible at all. You will almost certainly be 'showing' – have a bump in your tummy. According to the fruit-metaphor brigade your uterus is the size of a large grapefruit.

By now an expert ultrasound operator can see whether the foetus is a boy or a girl, by the presence or absence of a suspiciously willylike object. The bones are forming in the arms, legs, rib cage and skull. It's the start of your baby's skeleton. Weight: about 45 grams.

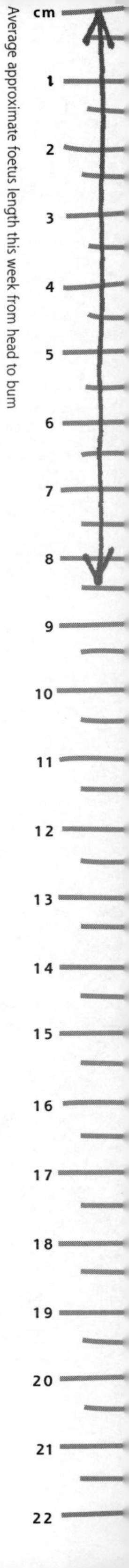

Average approximate foetus length this week from head to bum

cm
1
2
3
4
5
6
7
8
9
10
11
12
13
14
15
16
17
18
19
20
21
22

DiARY

I've stopped being grumpy and started being weepy. I'm trying to regard this as progress. I'm getting more forgetful: this might be pregnancy hormones, or just having more to think about. So much for the alleged energy surge of the second trimester that everyone goes on about . . . I feel a little better by the end of the week. At least the nausea's gone and only pays a surprise visit now and again.

I investigate my sneezing/yoga injury. There is a muscle called the psoas that extends from the lower back to the front groin and I have injured mine waving my legs in the air. My chiropractor, the second-most sensible woman in the world (strangely not called Lorraine), gives me an extremely gentle exercise to do three times a day and says a walk of 10 minutes or so at a time is plenty until it gets better. She can't feel around because the foetus is in the way, and she says since everything is changing in the pelvis, healing the muscle isn't going to be top priority for my body.

I decide that my ill-fated attempts at yoga are simply folly. If you're not already a yoga enthusiast you can end up injuring yourself. On the other hand, if you are the sort of person who ties themself up into a pretzel every Wednesday night, if you stretch every day and can climb up your own left leg, well, there's no problem. But if you start yoga cold in pregnancy, you can do more harm than good. I should have taken instruction from an exercise person who is trained in pregnancy – I suspect that a lot of people who work in gyms or conduct yoga classes say they know about pregnancy exercise, but don't really.

Beck asks whether I've had any puffiness. Nobody mentioned puffiness. There had better not be any puffiness. I'm against it. I've got enough to deal with, thank you very much.

The fact that I feel like I weigh about 56,795 kilos is beginning to depress me. Beck says I will have to exercise from week 20 on, but I shouldn't do too much exercise before then because my system would be not so much shocked as horrified.

'But what about the people who swim 5 kilometres a day and hike around Borneo when they're pregnant?' I ask.

'They are not your type,' she replies.

She's right.

I buy a swag of pregnancy magazines at the newsagent, call in sick, and take to the couch. Some of them seem pretty reliant on giveaways. I remind myself that a whizzbang product being given away is probably not in the magazine because it's necessarily the best or safest thing. It's there because its manufacturers get a free plug and a picture of their stuff in the mag.

One magazine actually gives away baby walkers even though an article in the same issue says they are not recommended for kids because they can slow real walking progress and cause spinal and neck problems.

Another one, from the US, called *Fit Pregnancy* is very focused on image, 'training' (exercise) and diet, with pages of suggested menus. All those models in the pictures seem to go through pregnancy a size 6 with a cantaloupe up their micro-mini frock. How appalling of me not to look like a whippet in a wig and cook up some Tuscan, three-course, delicious, low-fat, gourmet meal every 2 minutes.

One mag claims to have 'Amazing facts about pregnancy and birth'. And they're right. They *are* amazing. 'A child born feet first will have the power of healing later in life.' This is such amazing bollocks it makes you doubt some of the rest such as 'The heaviest baby born to a healthy mother weighed 10.2 kilograms (more than 22 pounds)'.

info

second-trimester hassles

This is often the most comfortable trimester of the pregnancy. For most women, nausea stops or decreases, energy levels are up and mood swings moderate. However, in this trimester, you may need to deal with one or more of the following.

sore, bleeding gums

Your gums may develop gingivitis, becoming sore, puffy, inflamed, and prone to bleeding, especially when you brush your teeth. This is caused by the increased progesterone and oestrogen in your blood, which makes gums softer and increases the blood pressure in the capillaries at the point where gums and teeth meet. This makes gums more susceptible to damage from food and being bumped by your toothbrush.

Try daily flossing, frequent brushing with a soft toothbrush (after each snack or meal if possible) and at least one dental visit during pregnancy for a professional cleaning job. (Make sure the dentist knows you're pregnant so you're not given an X-ray or medication. Many dentists say local anaesthetics are safe during pregnancy, but if you wait until you're not pregnant any more there will definitely be no risk.)

Proper levels of calcium, vitamin C and other nutrients will also help. As well, avoid eating toffeelike stuff or sticky date puddingy things that can get stuck in all the nooks and crannies and encourage infection.

congested nose

Something else you may share with the pregnancy sisterhood is a blocked, congested nose or one that is runnier than usual. You may also get nosebleeds. These schnoz problems are the result of the same hormonal effect that creates gum problems, which causes an increased blood supply, softening and swelling of the mucous membranes inside the nostrils, increased mucus production and easier bleeding. This means colds and upper respiratory tract infections can take longer than usual to clear up.

Bleeding can be triggered by unrestrained honking (overstrenuous nose blowing) or even by a dry atmosphere, which can harden mucus and make it more likely to cause damage to mucous membranes when you blow your nose. Try to avoid allergens. Humidifying the atmosphere and making yourself steam inhalations can help relieve the symptoms. You can also rub some emollient cream inside each nostril at bedtime.

To stop your nose bleeding apply gentle pressure on the affected side of the nose while leaning your head forward. Frequent or heavy nose bleeding should be mentioned to your doctor. Don't use any nose drops or sprays without checking first with your doctor. And . . . er . . . hate to sound like your granny, but don't pick your nose.

vaginal secretions

I realise this is hardly dinner party conversation, but you'll be pleased to know that all those extra-wet knickers are actually normal. Your vagina is producing more mucus and I think it's time we had a better term. Like lady's lotion. God. Sorry. Maybe not.

It's caused by the combined effect again of progesterone and oestrogen: the softer, more swollen mucous membranes of pregnancy produce more secretions. (Unpoetically, the medical description is 'an increase of normal mucoid discharge', which sounds like something a special-effects technician would say on the set of a critter movie.)

This normal discharge, called leucorrhoea if you want to get technical, should be clear or milky white. There can be rather a lot of it, and it's likely to increase as the pregnancy progresses.

To help with the hassle of vaginal secretions in overdrive:

⊚ avoid tight undies or trousers

⊚ wear undies and trousers made from natural fabrics such as cotton or wool – avoid nylon and polyester

⊚ wear panty-liners and change them frequently during the day

⊚ don't use tampons when you're pregnant because there is a higher risk of vaginal infection

◎ if it's easy, take a couple of changes of underpants with you in your handbag (and if you think you need a bigger handbag to leave the house now, just wait until you have a baby!).

Increased blood flow to the genitals can mean a more sensitive than usual clitoris (another reason to stay away from tight undies or trousers). (Or not.)

infections

If your vaginal discharge is yellowish or greenish or has an unhealthy smell, you have probably got an infection, which will need to be treated. An imbalance of friendly and unfriendly bacteria and high oestrogen levels in the vagina can make you more prone than usual to thrush, also known as candida, which may need to be treated by a doctor who knows you're pregnant. Symptoms include a curdlike white discharge and an itching and burning feeling.

If you are having thrush problems, remember to be careful to wipe front to back after going to the toilet. This is because thrush can hang out in the bowel and be transferred to your vagina. Thrush is linked to a high yeast diet, so try avoiding refined sugars, and eat lots of yoghurt with live *Lactobacillus acidophilus* cultures. Yoghurt can also be applied inside the vagina.

Air the nether regions when possible. You may do this by running around in the nuddy and waving your legs in the air, or by doing things like wearing no clothes or a nightie to bed instead of pyjamas. If you're lucky enough to have warm weather, wear a sarong or skirt with no undies when you can.

your record

How are you feeling now you're in the second trimester? Tick the applicable boxes.

❏ better

❏ happy as a clam

❏ get out of my way, I'm going to throw up

❏ excited about my changing body

❏ like my wardrobe just shrank to one ensemble and a queen-sized sleeping-bag

❏ full of beans

❏ completely exhausted, now that you mention it

what's going on

Your heart is doing a lot more than it used to and has a lot more blood to pump. (Contrary to old ludicrous persons' tales, your heart doesn't actually get bigger.) Nausea might come back if you let yourself get too tired or hungry. You may be looking even more divine than usual as your hair isn't falling out at the rate it normally does, so it looks thicker, your skin looks plumped out and the extra blood in your system is giving you what they call the 'glow'.

The foetal fingernails are developing, and the facial features are clearly defined. The foetus may suck its thumb. (All together now: awwwwww!) The skin formed is still very thin, so if there was a tiny camera in there transmitting pictures you could see blood vessels underneath. The foetus begins to put on weight more rapidly about this time. Starting soon the arms and legs will begin to be more co-ordinated when moving – imagine languid foetal aerobics.

Weight: about 80 grams.

DiARY Des and I go for a tour of the maternity ward at the hospital we're booked into. Our tour of Maternity is conducted by a very capable, nurse-type Lorraine. In the nursery we look at babies in plastic boxes with the tops cut off. I mean, they're posh plastic boxes on wheels, not homemade or anything.

Because they are in the middle of being renovated, the delivery suites and private rooms look like tacky country motel rooms after being trashed by a desultory heavy metal band. Awful, hideous, floral, flouncy bedspreads I couldn't possibly give birth on. Afterwards I remonstrate with my obstetrician.

'They like things to be feminine,' he says.

'Herb,' I point out, 'if you're squatting down with a baby coming out of your fanny, I reckon you'd know you're a woman.'

Some random realities: Sunday. Valentine's Day. We realise we've forgotten our anniversary nearly a month before. Start eating Frosty Fruits all the time. Drag myself around. Leg hurting. The bottom half of me is a milk-white sea of cellulite.

I'm starting to have the feeling that there's no going back. Getting to bed far too late, then not sleeping, then waking early and can't get back to sleep, then finally sleeping in and being late for work. I think I may have jet lag, without any jetting.

Nausea gone except when I allow myself to get tired and hungry. Weeing all night long. The idea of wearing my normal clothes – e.g. anything with a ZIP or WAIST – is totally laughable. And the books say, 'You won't be showing yet'. Showing? I'm not just showing! I'm showing OFF!

Searching for maternity clothes in the shops is like wading through the rejects of every other season. A few years ago it was orange and lime-green clothes for women – so now it must be orange and lime-green maternity wear. Cack!

As a clothes designer I know people try to reduce costs by cutting things thinner rather than wider, and shorter rather than longer, but in this case it seems pretty damn mingy. You don't want to be in a hobble skirt when you're already going to be waddling, surely? And why is there nothing between mini- and maxi-length? It's as if only Queen Victoria and one of Rod

Stewart's girlfriends buy maternity clothes.

I end up buying sensible items in black – two pairs of pants, one T-shirt, one jumper, a frock, two pairs of tights – and hand over the equivalent of the Mexican national debt. You'd think they had emeralds sewn into the hems. And that's in the normal maternity shop. The posh maternity shop has shiny polyester jackets that aren't meant to be shiny for $250 and various other rich-lady outfits. I look like the *Titanic* in all of them.

info

exercise

Moderate exercise during pregnancy is good for you and your off-spring. When we say moderate exercise, we do not mean flinging yourself about like a non-pregnant person with a gym obsession and a desire to go a marathon before lunch. Sensible exercise is good for circulation, relaxation and energy levels, and helps to stop constipation, cramps and backache.

If you're not fit before pregnancy, this is not the time to adopt a strenuous exercise regime. Try things like walking, gentle yoga and stretching, swimming, dancing, prenatal exercise classes, and aquarobics. Look for gyms, swimming and recreation centres or physiotherapy clinics that run exercise classes designed for pregnancy and have instructors with a special qualification in pregnancy exercise; at the very least make sure your instructor knows you're pregnant. Check with your obstetrician or prenatal clinic that the exercise you're doing or about to do is safe for you.

Many instructors are not aware of the special risks and strengths of pregnancy. The extra release of the hormone relaxin, which makes your ligaments and joints more stretchy, can make you more prone to injury. Sit-ups are generally a bad idea during pregnancy because they can cause a separation of muscles in your stomach, creating a hernialike effect.

Yoga can help you become aware of how comfortably you are standing, sitting or lying down. Its breathing and meditation practices can relax you during pregnancy and labour. Special prenatal yoga classes can help with many of the discomforts of pregnancy, as well as improving the body's suppleness and strength for labour. The mind-body-spirit approach of yoga can be a good match for the mind-body-spirit-altering experience of being pregnant.

Even if you've been super-fit before pregnancy, you'll need to apply some limitations to your regime. Consult your gym or fitness professional as soon as you know you're pregnant to get some expert advice on exercise modifications, and choose a slower pace, lighter-impact class and hand weights not exceeding half a kilo.

If you have played sport regularly before pregnancy, you can usually continue until the third trimester, unless it's a sport that can cause impact injuries, such as football (contesting for the ball), trick rollerblading (falls), baseball (sliding collisions), water polo (being kicked, accidentally or otherwise) and tennis (rabid opponents prone to attacking you with a racket).

Other activities not recommended during pregnancy include horse riding, any kind of skiing, backpacking, and lifting heavy weights and other heavy manual work. Jogging, running and other athletics can be too stressful on joints, breasts and baby, so check your exercise program with your doctor.

You shouldn't exercise while pregnant if you have a history of medical conditions such as recurrent miscarriages, placenta praevia, 'incompetent cervix', pre-eclampsia or heart disease. Other conditions, including diabetes, thyroid disease and anaemia, may sometimes mean exercise is not recommended.

when exercising

⑥ Wear supportive footwear and a sports bra.

⑥ Drink plenty of water before, during and after, and make sure you have some healthy snacks handy.

⑥ Remember your centre of gravity is changing, which will affect your balance and co-ordination, so take it easy.

⑥ Listen to and trust your body – stop if any activity makes you feel uncomfortable, overtired, hot, dizzy, faint or crampy.

⑥ Don't worry if your resting heart rate is higher during pregnancy even when you're not exercising. It doesn't mean you are losing fitness; it simply reflects your increased rate of circulation.

⑥ Don't get overheated for prolonged periods – this can be damaging to the foetus, particularly during the first trimester.

⑥ Exercise intensity should be measured during work-outs; a foetal heart rate stays normal when exercise intensity is moderate and your heart rate doesn't exceed 140 beats per minute (bpm), whereas if your heart rate reaches 180 bpm this can cause foetal distress and a lowered foetal heart rate. You can wear one of those pulse monitor thingies (that's the technical term) to check your heart rate.

⑥ You can walk until you are slightly puffing or reach 140 bpm, then keep this up for 15–20 minutes. Puffing work-outs should be only every second day and depend on your fitness level.

⑥ Go gently with abdominal exercises, and support your tummy with your interlinked hands while doing them; about 30 per cent of women have a separation of the abdominal muscles. If this happens, you need to stop any exercising that affects the area.

⑥ Strictly limit exercises that involve lying flat on your back to a maximum of 2–3 minutes, especially from the beginning of the second trimester, and omit them altogether after you reach twenty weeks. The weight of the uterus can compress the inferior cava vena, the vein that carries blood back to your heart from your lower parts, ultimately resulting in a reduced blood flow to your head and to the baby. So if you feel dizzy or faint while on your back, turn onto your left side and rest.

⊚ Don't forget to exercise your pelvic-floor muscles (Kegel exercises, as they are called in the US) – these muscles are like a hammock or sling that sits underneath all your inside organs and has holes in it corresponding to the various openings to the outside. Tighten your pelvic-floor muscles, as though you are trying to stop a wee, three or four times a day. Do as many of these as you can before getting tired. Every prenatal exercise class will tell you how important these are. Doing the exercises will mean faster pelvic-floor recovery after delivery, and will help prevent accidental weeing (also known as stress incontinence) when you sneeze, cough or laugh after childbirth.

⊚ You probably need to do some light abdominal exercises or the spine will be pulled forward by the weight of the baby and throw your posture out. Check with a specialised instructor.

 See also Exercise in 'Help'.

your record

What exercise did you do before pregnancy?

What exercise are you doing now?

what's going on It is possible you might feel the movements of the foetus as 'butterflies' in your stomach from now on, especially if you know what to pay attention to, but you also mightn't feel it for weeks.

You now have about 180 millilitres of amniotic fluid. Your uterus is kind of like a balloon full of yellowish water. All the joints of the foetus are working and the fingers and toes are all there and waving about. Toenails are just starting to form. The head still looks kind of oversized but the rest of the body is catching up. The downy foetal hair called lanugo has started to grow on the body. (Lanugo means fine wool in some ancient language.) There are various opinions about what the lanugo might be for: it might help keep the foetus warm, or it might be an underfelt for the gooey stuff that eventually covers the baby. Or maybe the foetus is just trying to develop a fashion instinct. Weight: about 110 grams.

DiARY

No idea what happened this week.
Blinked and missed it.
Oprah's hair's looking tremendous though,
I must say.

Reading for Dads·to·Be

info

'fess up to being pregnant

You're slower, you're more tired, you're more scatty, especially in
the first three months, and apparently we've got it to look forward
to again in the last three months. (That leaves these middle three
months in which everyone tells us we're looking divine, just
glowin' up a storm.) Tell people you're tired. Let them help. And
let them make allowances. Forgot to pay the phone bill? It's
because you're pregnant. Have to sit down on the floor during a

meeting and put your feet on a chair and show everyone your undies? Because you're pregnant. Had to buy a new pair of red shoes? Pregnant. See? It's easy.

the pursed-lip brigade

Not married? Married but wearing tight clothes? Planning to go back to work before the baby turns seventeen? Somewhere, somehow, someone will disapprove of you. Get used to it. If you stay home with the baby, some idiots will start asking, 'What do you DO all day?', as if you're just sitting at home watching Oprah and eating Mars Bars (ahem). If you're at work, people will ask, 'You haven't put your baby in child care/hired a nanny, have you?', as if it were the same as asking, 'You haven't tied it up and popped it in a tree for the day, have you?'. Apply the same logic as you do for unsolicited advice: it's not about you, it's about them.

stuff you didn't know before

1   Breast milk comes out of the nipple like water comes out of a sprinkler – there are heaps of little holes, not just one. And one breast may produce heaps more milk than the other.

2   What the inside of your navel looks like.

3   You *can* want to throw up and eat at the same time.

4   You *can* go and wee all the time and still retain fluid.

5   Sleep deprivation starts well before the birth.

stuff that people don't know

It makes people be nicer to you when they know:

⑥   you are carrying a quarter again the amount of blood you usually do

⑥   in the second half of the pregnancy the baby whacks you in the internal organs all the time, and it's not always a cute little whack – sometimes it's really uncomfortable, sometimes it actually hurts

❍ your feet swell to twice their usual size (well, that's what it feels like)

❍ you can't get the required amount of deep sleep because you have to wee all night – it's the equivalent of someone waking you up every couple of hours.

stuff for blokes

Warning: We're assuming your partner is a bloke for the next few paragraphs.

If your partner won't read or learn anything about childbirth, at least tell him:

a) there's going to be a lot of blood

b) there's not much he can do about the pain, and that's not his job

c) the obstetrician or midwife may well feel the medical necessity to put their hand all the way inside you – this is not a cue for your partner to say, 'Steady on!'

d) if he thinks he is going to faint, he should put his head between his knees or stand on tippytoes, or go outside and have a rest. (I say let's see 'im try all three at once.)

BOOKS FOR BLOKES

 Most of the books available for blokes aren't much chop as 'how to' manuals for dads who are at home, being the 'primary caregiver', but blokes can read the usual books and stuff that's aimed at mums (see Baby-care Books in 'Week 43'). After all, it's the same problems and the same advice.

So You're Going to Be a Dad by Peter Downey, Simon and Schuster, Sydney, 1998.

Hilarious book from the engagingly honest Mr Downey: one to make fathers-to-be laugh out loud. There are quite a few practical hints for dads, mostly working ones rather than stay-at-home ones, and lots of stories that see the funny side of stuff like . . . well, poo.

Babyhood by Paul Reiser, Bantam, Sydney, 1997.

Comedian and star of 'Mad About You' Paul Reiser gives a stand-up-style account of becoming a dad.

Father Time: Making Time for Your Children by Daniel Petre, Macmillan, Sydney, 1998.

A company big-wig type guy, Petre writes about how to make more time to be with your kid(s), and what makes a good father. Includes a section for dads separated from mum.

Men and Pregnancy, a pamphlet available from the Canberra headquarters of the Australian Medical Association.

The pamphlet gives a point-form run-down of what to expect. Includes the classic line: 'If you see something that needs doing (e.g. the washing up), why not surprise her by doing it'. Yes, and why not make it a habit so she doesn't get such a nasty shock?

WEEK 17

what's going on

You may be sweating, spitting and running like a tap at the nose as well as having those pesky vaginal secretions. Basically you're a leaking bag of various fluids. I'm sorry, but there it is. Find room in your handbag among the lipsticks, spanners and panty-liners for tissues, spare deodorant, spare undies, a couple of Wettexes, maybe a beach towel. (It's really not that bad.)

By now the baby's sex organs are completely formed. The foetal kidneys produce lots of urine: the foetus wees about every 40–45 minutes (at least you don't have to change nappies yet). Icky though it may sound, the foetus takes in some of this wee when it swallows mouthfuls of amniotic fluid. But most of the foetal waste products go through the placental membrane and into your circulation, where it's dealt with by your body's usual functions.

Weight: about 150 grams.

STARTLING BOSOMS

Average approximate foetus length this week from head to bum

cm
1
2
3
4
5
6
7
8
9
10
11
12
13
14
15
16
17
18
19
20
21
22

Diary   My bosoms are getting bigger, and none of my bras are comfy, even the bigger ones I bought. My bosoms used to stick out straight from my body, practically in opposite directions from each other. They were known as East and West. Now they're kind of bigger and lower slung, meaning there's a bit underneath where it gets sweaty. And all these little skin tags have grown there as well. Thank God I finally found a book that said this was perfectly normal.

Sports crop-tops seemed the best, but now they feel like elastic-bandage boob-tubes three sizes too small. If I'm sitting around at home I don't wear a bra at all. No doubt this means I'll end up having bosoms shaped like tube socks that I can tie in a knot behind my neck when they get in the way. Don't care. Those areas around my nipples I can never pronounce have started to go brown and are getting bumps on them.

Farewell, my strawberries-and-cream nipples, my horizontal, pointy bosoms! Will you now both be called South forever? Why don't I have a photo of you?! Was my youth so misspent that I never even posed for nude photographs? What was I thinking!

I'm feeling very annoyed with myself for not being a supple, lithe, yoga-frenzied woman.

The bath in the new house is of such a ludicrous design by some kind of deranged handyman that before I can get in it I have to crawl over about half a metre of tiles or take a huge, dangerous step on one leg. (Well, obviously, otherwise it would be a jump, not a step. I'm losing my mind.) And given that there isn't enough room in the bathroom to swing a cat – actually there isn't even enough room to *shout* at a cat – it won't do. The whole thing is a disaster waiting to happen for a woman whose centre of gravity is changing every day.

I call Wayne the plumber to come and fix it. (All sensible handymen types are called Wayne, just as all sensible women are called Lorraine.) Wayne, of course, finds that the bathroom floor is practically rotted through as well and that there's some other piping-style disaster, which means the job turns out to be five times bigger.

One of the reasons I feel like I'm going mad is sleep deprivation. It never occurred to me this would happen BEFORE the little tacker arrived. One of the books says this is because I'm sleeping like a baby – not much deep sleep but plenty of REM sleep. That stands for Rapidly Enraged Mother-to-be.

Call me dense, but it's only just hit me I'm not one person who's pregnant – I mean, I am – but I'm also two people. No. I'm not two people but there are two people – a big one and a little one – sharing the same body. Well. That's a bit spooky.

Apparently many people at this stage of pregnancy find that they can have a few sips of wine or beer occasionally without a violent reaction. Des poured me an enormous thimbleful of what he described as 'a very smooth cab sav' but it tasted like metho to me.

He's reading bits of a book for wannabe fathers, which argues that men shouldn't be expected to be at the birth because they can't fix the pain, and if they prefer, they can plant a tree or invent a new dance instead, to celebrate the birth. I'm afraid Des is the sort of bloke who thinks this is a load of old cobblers, and the way that book is being hurled about it won't last the evening. I don't think he's the making-up-a-dance type.

info

breasts

Ah, bosoms. On the one hand there are the people who go 'Phwoaaarrr' and, on the other, people who worship them as sacred life-giving vessels of compulsorily acquired nourishment. Blimey. Get a grip. They're just bosoms.

Probably one of the first pregnancy changes you noticed were your breasts getting larger and more tender. They'll keep growing, but extreme sensitivity usually settles down after the first trimester. From here on, the hormones oestrogen, progesterone and prolactin stimulate more growth and the production of some pre-milk stuff called colostrum.

Each breast contains about twenty segments or lobes; each of these is made up of grapelike bunches of glands called alveoli; and each of these is lined with milk-producing cells. During pregnancy your bosoms get bigger because not only do your dormant milk-producing cells and ducts enlarge, your body also grows new ones to help out. (Your original breast size bears no relation to milk production.)

the changes

Breast changes are usually more extreme in a first pregnancy. Your breasts may feel tender, tingling, warm, full, heavy, painfully sensitive or lumpy. You may even have some stabbing pain.

You'll be able to see more veins, often blue, close to the skin's surface, carrying the extra blood supply to the area. They're especially noticeable if you have fair skin.

The nipples and areolae (the areas around each nipple) become larger and darker, particularly if your natural skin tone is dark. Most nipples and areolae go a shade of brown, even if they have been pink before. This can happen gradually to the entire area, or in patches.

Each areola is dotted with sebaceous (oil-producing) glands called Montgomery's tubercles (those little bumps), which secrete a fluid that keeps the nipples supple. The glands become more prominent during pregnancy, so you get a bumpier effect.

You may have a small amount of colostrum – a thin, yellowish liquid – leaking from your nipples towards the end of pregnancy, and even earlier on, but not everyone does. This can cause wet patches, but can be soaked up and hidden by breast pads, otherwise known as nursing pads; you can buy these in the baby section of the chemist or supermarket. Actual milk production won't start until after the baby arrives.

bras

Wearing a well-fitted supporting bra during pregnancy is recommended. You often need to increase your bra measurement and cup size by at least one size. The increase might even be more, depending on the overall weight gain and whatever your breasts feel like doing. (For example, you  might go from 12B to 14C.) You can buy bras to fit your changing size, even though it might mean buying a new size a couple of times during the pregnancy. You don't need a maternity bra (with front fasteners that make for easy bosom access) or new size while your present bra fits well, is comfortable and gives you enough support.

Good features of a maternity bra include wide straps, a wide band of fabric under the breast and a high cotton content. Anything that digs into the skin is even more intolerable than usual, so make sure you get a comfy fit.

Maternity bras often fasten at the front between the cups; or where the straps meet the cups at the front; or they don't fasten at all, but rather stretch so you can just pop a bosom out the bottom to breastfeed. Whatever suits you best. If you started with big bosoms, you'll probably need more support than the stretchy crop-top style.

afterwards

Don't be sucked in by cosmetic surgery hype that breasts are 'deformed' by breastfeeding and need to be 'enlarged' with sacs of plastic and saline. Sharky cosmetic surgeons don't really care about your bosoms, they just want your money. And there are many possible hideous side effects, including rupture, pain, scarring, lost nipple sensation and inability to breastfeed again.

Likewise beware the faffy marketing techniques of the cosmetics companies trying to sell you 'bust firming' and 'breast cream' and 'body treatment' moisturisers. (Often the names are in French or pseudo-French.) They will not prevent your breasts from changing shape or sagging. These creams don't affect the tissues inside the breast, and many are a shockingly expensive waste of time. A cheap moisturiser that smells nice is just as good at keeping the surface of your skin moist, and just as likely to keep your breasts firm – that is, not at all.

Often these creams and oils have ingredients that feel tingly or make the skin seem tighter – the same tightening feeling can be achieved by putting eggwhite on your breasts and waiting for it to dry. Don't be fooled – there's no lasting effect on your bosomry and certainly these creams are no match for Mrs Gravity once she's decided to make her presence felt.

your record

Do a little drawing of what your bosoms used to be like, and what they look like now. Oh, what the hell, draw your whole body or paste in a photo.

what's going on

You'll find many pregnancy books tell you that this is the week you'll start to feel a first baby MOVE around. Don't hold your breath: you might not feel it move for weeks yet, and that doesn't mean there's anything wrong. Babies mostly move when you're resting at night: basically after 8 p.m. and before 8 a.m. When you move around during the day, you rock the baby to sleep. Use pillows to support your growing tummy while you sleep.

According to some pregnancy experts, this week the foetus can make facial expressions. Oh yeah? Like what? Astonishment? 'Euwww yuk, that amniotic fluid tastes bad'? Anyway, the foetus is definitely able to move around a lot, swing on the umbilical cord (well, that's what it looks like) and can bite its own fingers or do the hokey-pokey if it feels like it. There is lanugo hair all over the body, and blood cells start to form in the bone marrow. Tastebuds are forming. Weight: about 200 grams.

DiARY

I 'pop along' to a group physio lesson at the maternity hospital. It is mostly couples, except me, and exactly the sort of thing I hate – name tags and a white board and splitting into two groups to workshop questions such as 'What does fitness mean to you?' and 'Will exercise help?'. (Duh, I think. 'Course it will.)

I am very annoyed to discover that mad exercising in the last few weeks of pregnancy will not actually guarantee a short labour. This seems to be another major design fault of this whole caper, along with painful childbirth.

A woman called Anthea, wearing a black velvet Alice band on her long blonde hair and shoes that cost more than all the rest of the clothes in the room added together, tells the class smugly that she is still going to gym every day and doing a special program of exercises and weights. She looks bloody shocking – has a grey pallor and is scarily thin for someone who is up the duff. Lorraine the physio asks her if her gym instructor is qualified by the State government health department gym person's fully trained accreditation pregnancy type arrangement. No, Anthea says, rather patronisingly, explaining that it's a very superior sort of gym and they do know she's pregnant and IT'S FRIGHTFULLY EXPENSIVE.

Later in the class when Lorraine explains an abdominal muscle injury that causes bits of your organs to poke through in a line under the skin of your tummy in a characteristic shape, Anthea squeals in recognition, 'Oh my GOD, I've got that!', and goes a bit quiet for the rest of the class. One imagines the very superior gym is about to receive a call from her frightfully expensive lawyer.

We practise (a) sitting on giant inflatable balls to strengthen our squatting muscles and straighten our backs, (b) sprawling in beanbags, and (c) a relaxation technique that I fail at miserably. Not for me relaxing in a hospital room full of strangers lying on nylon carpet with the fluoro lights temporarily off, thank you. We are informed about the importance of pelvic-floor exercises and I just know I'm not going to do them. I've tried. I did six in a row one Saturday and got bored. We all pass around a plastic pelvis and stare at it as if it might suddenly have something to tell us.

Here's what I learn in group physio.

✳ The average female pelvis is ludicrously small for what's expected of it.

✳ Pelvic-floor exercises exercise the pelvic floor (hello). (The pelvic floor is the trampoliney bit that is stretched under all the pelvic organs.) The main jobs of the pelvic floor are to stop all your organs from falling out of your fanny (well, they wouldn't really, but it would all get a bit saggy in there); contracting around the holes to prevent unscheduled leaking, especially during coughing or sneezing (that is, it's a continence accessory); and allowing your vagina to contract rhythmically if you are in any way interested in sex, which is hard to imagine.

✳ How to exercise the pelvic-floor muscles without anybody noticing. My favourite instruction was 'Your buttocks should not be moving'. I often think that.

✳ They now say to work your pelvic-floor muscles to fatigue three to four times a day, rather than five times thirty times a day or thirty times five times a day, which was the old-fashioned advice.

✳ It is difficult to have a mid-class snack while the physio is explaining to a young woman how to poo properly. (Tragically I walked away, so I'll never know.)

✳ Nap when you can, even for 15 minutes.

✳ Bend and rotate your arms backwards like you're doing a chicken dance, when you can. Also put your feet up when you can and, if you can't, flex them back and forth. Both of these will keep your muscles flexible and help your circulation.

✳ Don't hunch over your stomach. Sit backwards on a chair, with a pillow between you and the back and your legs to each side, or sit on a giant inflatable ball, which you can buy from midwives and physio supplies shops.

✳ If you have to pick something up, use the lunge position (bend at the knee, one leg in front, keeping your back straight). If you vacuum, hold the cord behind your back with one hand, which automatically keeps your back straight. When you're at the sink, stand on one leg and put the other foot on the shelf under the sink, as long as the shelf is low enough for you to feel comfortable. Anthea says what are we thinking of, we should all hire a housekeeper. (I suggest we could dress her in a long, black frock and call her Mrs Danvers.)

✳ A diagram of a uterus looks like a bagpipe with a tent rope on it.

✳ Being fit may not ensure an easy labour, but it will mean a better labour and recovery than you would have had if you were unfit.

✳ Don't go into spas and saunas. Their temperature can be raised to dangerous levels for the foetus without you realising.

✳ Don't get really hot and then jump in a cold pool, or otherwise shock your system with sudden temperature changes.

✳ Because the relaxin hormone goes into overdrive during pregnancy and slackens all the ligaments, joints and muscles, don't overstretch or bounce on stretches.

Jill, who'll probably be a godmother without the God bit, and Des come to this week's ultrasound. I'm a bit nervy. In my heart I feel that everything is fine but my head is saying, well, things do go wrong. My left ankle just doesn't know what to think. Actually it probably has nothing to do with my head – instead it's got a microprocessor implanted by Aunty Peg to flash signals at me regularly throughout life: 'TERRIBLE things can happen'.

It all turns out all right. Going by the pictures on the screen the foetus is seventeen weeks four days, but ultrasounds are only 'guesstimates'. Jill is pretty gobsmacked. I think she was expecting it to be a fairly static side view. Instead the camera goes in from all angles – top of head, soles of feet – and measures the length of the thighbone and the arm bone, and thankfully everything's all right and connected to the other right bits.

The foetus face still looks pretty spooky, sort of like a skeleton face with black shapes where the eyes should be. The shot of the spine makes our little darling look like the remains of a flounder on a dinner plate. It's hard not to think it's really waving or having a chat or playing peekaboo when really all it's doing is instinctively having a rowdy time, practising grabbing, sucking and Morris dancing. Dr Donaldson takes quite some time and is very thorough, checking the four valves of the heart, measuring a whole lot of circumferences and lengths and widths. He speaks very quietly to his assistant, who types it all into a computer.

Des and I turn up afterwards at Dr Herb's and I take one look at the waiting room, which looks like an upper-middle-class refugee camp or an Alice-band convention, before rolling my eyes at Lorraine and saying, 'I just had a clear ultrasound and I'm going home.' She agrees, and accepts a small bottle of my wee as a token of her gratitude.

'Shall I weigh myself or just get out?'

'Just get out,' she says. Good old Lorraine.

This carrying around of the wee is getting on my nerves – what if I get arrested and searched? And why do they give you the empty jar once they've tested the wee? Carrying an empty wee jar is even weirder. Look, I'm all in favour of recycling but there is a limit. Remember that ad 'You can tell a lot about a woman by what's in her handbag'? It had pictures of celebrity girlies with all sorts of glam stuff in their bag. Not a wee jar between them.

Suddenly sleeping a lot better and floating through the days. If I didn't know better I'd say I was on drugs.

Another thing I have started noticing: people who warn you against unsolicited advice already have their own. 'Don't listen to any busybodies,' they say. 'What you'll need to do is . . . '

info

repelling unwanted advice and comments

When people give you that firm advice – 'You *must* have a nanny', 'You *must* always look after the baby yourself', '*Men* can't look after babies', 'You *must* use disposable nappies' – remember it's about them, not you. They're usually just telling you what THEY did and insisting that you do the same, maybe partly because that's all they know and partly because if you do it the same way it will make them feel better. Don't forget: your experience will be different from everybody else's. Listen, but don't automatically follow their advice.

It starts as soon as you tell people you're pregnant, and continues throughout parenting life. Having babies is such a universal experience that everyone has opinions and advice to share, whether you want to hear them or not.

You'll hear things about whether you can tell if you're having a girl or boy based on how sick you are, how much your baby moves or what shape your tummy is; why you should only see an obstetrician/midwife; why you should/shouldn't use pain relief drugs during childbirth; how to avoid an episiotomy/caesarean/cracked nipples; why you must/mustn't breastfeed; why you should always use/never bother with cloth nappies; how you make your baby sleep through the night (pick it up/ignore it/give it a stiff gin); how to avoid nappy rash; why you must go straight back/never go back to work; what sort of child care is best; what sort of schooling is best; what to do when your child is arrested in its mid-thirties. The list seems infinite.

Some advice will be useful and compatible with your own ideas, and some won't. Read books you like the philosophical feel of, and choose a couple of friends to listen to. In the end you'll find that having to deal with your own, real baby will provide the best information.

Another mind-boggling thing is that people want to touch your tummy, and sometimes they don't even ask if it's okay. This is easier to cope with than the advice. You can say, 'I'd rather you didn't', or grab hands that are heading towards your belly.

at work or parties
Sometimes people, even in a meeting at work, will bang on about anything to do with pregnancy, including cervical mucus, in front of anyone at all. (Make sure this isn't you.) You can learn to get out of these mortifying situations by saying pleasantly and firmly, 'Let's stick to the agenda, shall we?'. Even if it's a lie, you can always try, 'Oh, I've got a rule – no pregnancy talk at work/parties/whatever', then gently disengage and move away. You can go to the loo and come back if you think someone will have changed the subject in the meantime.

strangers
Advice can be worse in your first pregnancy because people assume you want their opinion, and you have no ammunition to defend yourself against it. You can give strangers a distant smile and no verbal response. A lot of pregnancy/baby chitchat when you're out and about is from people who are just looking to pass the time of day or strike up a conversation. These ones are easily dealt with: 'Gosh, is that the time? Must fly.'

friends

Advice from friends is usually offered with good intentions, and they can give you some invaluable insights and shortcuts. Store away anything that seems useful and ignore anything you don't like the sound of. Alternatively, you can always tell friends you'll come to them if you have any questions, or that you're sick of everybody giving you advice and could they please shut right up before you slap them.

the older generation

Take with a grain of salt any of the pregnancy and baby-care advice from parents or parents-in-law, which is likely to have a long-expired use-by date. It's worth having a tactful chat early on about how you see their role in relation to the baby. Without putting too fine a point on it, they need to understand that as far as the baby goes, you're the boss.

Unfortunately, some members of the older generation, including grandparents, may have fixed ideas about how things should be done (the way they did them). Here are some of the outdated notions you may have to firmly explain are not acceptable.

BEFORE THE BABY ARRIVES

'Eat lots of lamb's fry and liver.' (No, too much vitamin A can damage the foetus.)

'"Morning sickness" is a myth.' (It isn't.)

'You should try to hide your "bump".' (Oh for God's sake!)

AFTER THE BABY ARRIVES

'Breastfeeding/bottle-feeding is bad for your baby.' (It's your choice.)

'There's no need to use a baby restraint in the car for every trip, particularly short ones.' (This is potentially lethal, and can lead to horrific injuries.)

'Put the baby to sleep on its tummy.' (This is a sudden infant death syndrome – SIDS – risk, according to statistics.)

'Throwing the baby into the air is perfectly okay.' (No, this can be as damaging to the brain and eyes as shaking a baby.)

'Put honey on a dummy.' (It rots teeth and can create a 'sweet' dependency.)

'Hitting, smacking and threats of violence are good disciplinary measures.' (These teach the child to hit other children and creatures smaller than they are.)

'That child is being "bad".' (This targets the child, not the behaviour.)

'Of course dropping around without ringing to check if it's convenient is all right.' (Aaaargghhhh!)

'Give small children lollies and sugared soft drinks as a treat or a reward. And milk or juice in their night-time bottles is fine.' (All these are a major cause of children having to have all their first teeth removed under anaesthetic.)

'Always leave a baby to cry/never leave a baby to cry even for 30 seconds.' (Both of these are extreme.)

'Insist on a sleep routine/refuse to follow a sleep routine.' (Whatever works for you is fine.)

Grandparents might say, 'But we did this with you and you turned out fine.' Rather than replying, 'Well, that was bloody lucky then, wasn't it?', try saying, in the case of safety issues, 'You did the right thing then, but they've done all this new research and the right thing to do now is . . .' When all else fails, just say, 'I really need it to be done this way.' In the case of safety issues, if a friend or relative is likely to ignore your wishes, it's safer for you to be there whenever they have access to the baby or your children.

solicited advice

Advice from experts and pregnancy books is often conflicting, which can be confusing. You only need to experience the nursing-shift changeovers at a hospital when you're learning how to breastfeed to find out just how varied professional opinion can be. It can be tricky to filter it, and – as always – you need to assess the individual you're dealing with, whether it be a physiotherapist conducting a prenatal class or a breastfeeding consultant or a paediatrician after the baby's born.

Find women who you relate to who are pregnant, or who have had children, especially recently. Ask them anything you need to know, and they'll tell you their experiences. But bear in mind you're just researching – your experiences will not be exactly the same, though you may get pointed in a few directions. New mums will have a few hints about settling babies or the best nappies, that kind of useful stuff. Mums whose kids are older may have forgotten the details.

your record

Write down all the unsolicited and solicited advice you get.

Useful	Not useful

cm

Average approximate foetus length this week from head to bum

1
2
3
4
5
6
7

13
14
15
16
17
18
19
20
21
22

WOMB SWEET WOMB

PLENTY OF ROOM

WE

what's going on

Your waistline is missing, presumed obliterated. You may have backache, skin pigment changes, and a tendency to vague . . . somethingerother. The foetus still has plenty of room to hoon around in the amniotic sac, but it's a tighter fit than, say, a pear in a bucket of water – that's why, if you haven't already, you will feel movements any time from now on.

Its muscles have developed enough for the foetus to be doing loop-the-loops, and it can get itself tangled and untangled in the umbilical cord. The foetus is putting on brown-coloured fat deposits, which produce heat to keep it warm. Weight: about 260 grams.

EK 19

DiARY I have been reading Sheila Kitzinger. She abandons comparing the foetus to fruit for a moment to solemnly declare, 'You may notice that you are putting on weight on your buttocks'. Actually I've been noticing that for the last nineteen weeks, sunshine. If they're going to get any bigger, people will start to think I'm shoplifting a futon.

The finance experts in magazines and on the radio all suggest that when you stop using contraception you should start saving for all the stuff you're going to need, especially because one person is probably going to drop an income for a while. Accordingly, we are spending money like it's the last day on earth we can.

I have $105 left in the bank. We've got security screens, we've got built-in wardrobes coming, we've got trees going into the garden. We've got new maternity clothes. For some reason I'm in a manchester frenzy and keep wanting to buy towels even though we've got enough. Must be some innate memory of all those films where the baby's come early and some gnarled old trusty shouts, 'Boil some towels and splice the mainsail!' Or perhaps I'm thinking of pirate movies. 'I've boiled the water and trained the parrot, dear. Everything's going to be fine.'

Back, legs and neck all painful. Get hysterical. Ring the chiropractor at home. Make an appointment for the next afternoon, so of course by the next morning after a reasonable sleep (only four or five wees during the night!) most of the symptoms are gone.

Rush from the chiropractor to Dr Herb's because I skipped seeing him last week after the ultrasound. I can't wait to listen to the heartbeat again. I am beginning to get quite worried because I can't feel the baby move like all the books say I should by now. Maybe Cellsie's gone out.

Thankfully there are no infuriating mothers in the waiting room. Lorraine asks for my wee.

'I gave you some of my wee last week, Lorraine. Now you're just getting greedy.'

I sit in the waiting room remembering my weekend of feeling weepy, hideous, fat, disgusting, spotty and vilely repellent in every degree, and getting really freaked out about the sea of cellulite. So far I've been Sneezy, Sleepy, Dopey and Grumpy. I'm hoping for the full complement of the Seven Dwarfs before the confinement. There wasn't a Weepy, sadly. Or a Crappy. Or a Dippy. Spotty never got a look in. Or, indeed, a Fatty. Can't think why.

Try this out on Dr Herb, who says I could be Happy. I feel like saying you can be Doc, Doc. When it comes to the crunch I suspect I'm going to be Shrieky, or at least the Evil Queen. Then he tells me somebody has already made the Seven Dwarfs joke in a book he can't remember the name of. Great. So now I'm Plagiary as well.

'Listen, Herb,' I say, 'all the books say by week 20 you should have felt the baby move, and it's week 19 and mine's gone out for coffee or is playing possum.'

Herb's opinion on the matter, basically, is bugger the books (except that Dr Herb probably never says bugger), I'll feel it soon enough.

I realise that I don't know whether you keep feeling the baby once you've felt it for the first time or if you have to wait another week. Herb says once you feel it you feel it every day. He puts the little instrument on my stomach and it amplifies the baby's heartbeat. It makes me grin.

'It sounds groovy,' I say. 'Kind of swishy.'

'I always think it sounds like Rolf Harris,' he says. 'That wobble board thingo. Anything else worrying you?'

'Yes. I am 78 kilos.'

'That's okay.'

'Am I putting on too much weight?'

'No, and you can't diet.'

'Yes, I know. I was just wondering whether I should hire a wheelbarrow to get around in.'

Quite often in the street I suddenly find myself rubbing my stomach in the unselfconscious way men scratch their scrotum or stick their hand up between their buttocks to arrest some jockettes making a bold upward bid for freedom. And I don't care who sees me. My stomach sticks way out in front and people ask, 'When are you due?', and I say, 'August', and they look at me as if I've got a bullock up my frock. Their next question is usually 'Is it twins?'

If it wasn't for the phone, I'd never talk to anyone. All my childless friends are flat out at work (so am I) and the ones with kids are worse. I never go out at night any more, and when I do I leave parties at about 10 p.m. stone-cold sober, wishing people wouldn't smoke. Miss Francine was right. My life is over . . .

info

maternity clothes hints

⊚ Length does matter. If you weren't the type to wear a miniskirt before you were pregnant, why would you wear one during pregnancy? Because except for a few ankle-skimmers that's all they make – obviously saving money on materials. In magazines you can even see pregnant models in minidresses wearing long socks, leaving their thighs as the only exposed skin. There are probably only three women in the world who would want to wear this outfit when they're heavily pregnant. If you want a plain dress that ends in the vicinity of your knee, rather than your gusset or your big toe, astonishingly enough, you may have to get someone to make it for you or sew it yourself if you're that way inclined.

⊚ Always remember: this is a TEMPORARY wardrobe. Don't spend a fortune unless you're a diamond heiress, in which case stop reading this book and go and invade Corsica or something.

⊚ Borrow everything you can from a previously pregnant friend, but only things you know you'll wear. Don't clutter up your

drawers with stuff that doesn't fit or you wouldn't wear. Write down who has lent you what – with the label and description recorded – so you can give it all back. (Some friends will just say you can pass it on down the line in the great pregnant-women swap-meet of life.)

⑤ Don't borrow anything really flash if the person you're borrowing from wants it back. You never know what could happen to it, and it might be a financial hardship to replace it, even if you could still buy that style, which is unlikely.

⑤ Check out the racks in the following sections: sports, dance wear, men's, and full-figured women's clothes. Bear in mind that in the last month or two of pregnancy just 'big' may not do it. You'll probably need at least a couple of items that have the properly designed stomach bits you only get in maternity clothes.

⑤ Don't worry if your maternity wardrobe is all black, or all navy, or all incredibly boring in some way or other. At least everything will match. You'll be so sick of the sight of everything by the time you give birth, anyway, that it doesn't matter.

⑤ Be wary of the pregnancy 'kit', which is usually a box containing stretch pants, stretch skirt, a long T-shirt and a frock. The first company to make the kits was very generous with fabric, but some of the 'knock-offs' and department store copies, while cheaper, are often really mingy with fabric, so everything is tighter and shorter than the original.

⑤ The maternity fashion police will tell you not to wear overalls or stirrup pants because they are unflattering. May I just say that from about the thirty-second week of the pregnancy, you might as well be wearing an armoured tank: *nothing* is flattering.

⑤ To cut down on searching every morning, look through your wardrobe ONCE, now. Put all the possible maternity clothes up one end of the wardrobe and clear a drawer for the non-hanging possible clothes and maternity undies and bras. As each item of normal clothing outlives its usefulness, put it in the normal-person part of the wardrobe or chest of drawers.

⑥ Work out what the weather will be like in the last four months or so of the pregnancy and plan accordingly.

winter

See if any of your friends have a swing-coat (also known as an A-line or knee-length overcoat) that you can borrow to get you through. If you're going to need to wear huge socks, you're probably going to have to buy a pair of gigantic shoes for the duration. A basic winter maternity wardrobe could include:

1 frock for best
1 skirt
2 pairs black trousers
4 pairs opaque black stockings
gigantic jumper
maternity jeans
2 maternity-sized bras – maybe one pale and
one black
gigantic cotton underpants

summer or the tropics

Please, just forget that polyester was ever invented. Go for cotton, or microfibre or a rayon if it's the cool, floaty kind. Corner a big bloke and confiscate all his T-shirts and shirts. A basic summer or tropics maternity wardrobe could include:

1 frock for best
1–2 everyday gigantic frocks
large T-shirts
large 'men's' shirts
2 maternity-sized bras – maybe one pale and
one black
loose maternity trousers
gigantic cotton underpants
shawl, wrap or giant jumper for cold evenings:
use a horse blanket if necessary

undies

⊚ The most important word on undies is cotton.

⊚ Undies can either be worn under the belly, if you like a bikini style; or if you find up-to-the-waist styles more comfortable, you can probably just buy bigger sizes of your favourite brand – if or when these become tragically inadequate, you may need to invest in maternity knickers.

⊚ Women who have bad backs, are overweight or are carrying twins may be told by their doctor to wear a maternity girdle to give some extra support late in the pregnancy. Maternity girdles should not be designed to make your stomach look smaller.

⊚ Real tights usually just don't fit at all as you progress in size. But why doesn't anyone make matt-black opaque maternity tights that don't fall down so you don't get that sagging gusset thing happening? Until they do, you could take a tip from Superman and wear your underpants OVER your tights to keep them up.

shoes

Yes, your feet are getting bigger – firstly, they're probably puffed up with extra fluid (and if you go on a plane they puff up like stonefish), and secondly, they're probably broader because of all that extra weight you're carrying. The ligaments in your feet are softer and stretchier than usual, so your feet will 'spread' and well-fitting, comfortable shoes are essential.

⊚ Your feet may end up one size bigger permanently. You may want to wait and see before buying lots of hideously expensive new shoes.

⊚ If you wear socks, buy thin ones or stocking socks.

⊚ Buy a new, larger, all-purpose, flat-heeled pair of shoes to 'live in' for the duration – many very pregnant women wear sports shoes. Or pop a couple of rowboats on your feet.

Average approximate foetus length this week from head to bum

cm 1 2 3 4 5 6 7 8 9 10 11 12 13

what's going on

Probably by now you will have felt the baby move, but maybe not. It's usual to laugh or cry. Doing both at once is perfectly fine. It might still be too early for anyone else to be able to feel the movements from the outside. For a while, it's your little secret bond.

The foetus puts on more muscle and tests it out by moving around. One book says your baby is as heavy as 'a medium-sized Spanish onion' (do let me know if you find a Spanish onion weighing 320 grams). The skin's sebaceous glands (needed, of course, to make pimples later) become active and make the oily stuff called vernix caseosa that covers the skin. It's the foetus's do-it-yourself wetsuit made, disgustingly enough, of fatty material and dead skin cells. (If that doesn't make you feel sick, how's this: doctors say the coating looks like cheese.) Vernix caseosa waterproofs the skin against the amniotic fluid, and protects the foetus from scrapes when it bangs into the wall of the uterus. Weight: about 320 grams.

16 17 18 19 20 21 22 23 24 25 26 27 28 29

DiARY

I'm not depressed any more but I still haven't bloody well felt the baby move and I'm sick of all these books saying I should have. It makes me really anxious. I feel very cheated about it not kicking and really cross with the books for making me feel like a freak because I haven't felt 'the quickening'.

Beck says, 'You have felt the baby move, but you just don't know you have. You probably thought you were going to fart or something.' How romantic.

We go out to dinner and I have two glasses of French champagne and am so shickered I sleep for 11 hours and only go to the toilet four or five times. Remarkable.

Feeling suddenly bigger and paradoxically less fat. Probably because it all seems like it's out the front there, now. I really feel like I'm carrying weight, though – when I try to run, this galumphing, hilarious big tummy precedes me like a big beer belly. Des says soothing, private things like, 'You are *not* a fat old moll. You are the Tummy Princess.'

Suddenly feel connected to other mothers a bit – certainly more than I ever have before. Not all mothers. Well, obviously. Not Pamela Anderson Lee or the Queen or anything.

I saw Peter X in the street today. Nothing like the wildly startled look of an old boyfriend who's about to say, 'Hi, you look well', and then has to restrain himself from fainting as he realises you're pregnant and he doesn't know what to say. His eyes rolled around in his head like the eyeballs of a mad blue heeler – lots of white. Poor thing. I suspect that just for a split second he thought it might have had something to do with him – until he came to his senses and realised that six years' gestation is probably pushing it.

Yesterday I paid for all my literal slackness in not doing my pelvic-floor exercises. I sneezed and wet myself. Not a huge gush, but enough to make a tiny splash on the floor. Luckily I was standing on the wooden floor at home.

When I sneezed Des said, 'You look absolutely mortified.'

'Well, I just wee-ed,' I explained helpfully.

I am also having a recurring dream that I'm having an affair with a freelance sausage maker. I wonder if freelance sausage makers mind if you wet yourself.

My old friend Luke and his wife, Fatimah, call to offer a pram. Excellent. Uncle Stan insists on buying the cot even though he will no doubt complain for six weeks about how much it cost and express the view that the baby should be sleeping in a hammock in the open air dressed in a robe knitted from chamomile or something.

Marg's getting on in her pregnancy now. She just rang to say she was in the shoe shop and a woman told her she had good posture. Marg, completely vague and stuffed full of pregnancy info, meant to tell the shop assistant that's because when she walks she 'leads with her sternum', the breastbone. Unfortunately what she actually said was she 'leads with her perineum', which is the area between the vagina and the anus. No wonder the shop assistant looked startled.

Marg's not putting on enough weight and I've got plenty extra. We're considering a transference.

info

weight gain

Weight gain is an important part of a healthy pregnancy. You'll find pregnancy 'experts' are all over the shop when it comes to saying how much weight you should gain. The right weight gain for you is different from the right one for somebody else (you know, depending on your height, weight and body frame when you became pregnant, and whether you give a stuff about it). The ranges nominated for a one-baby pregnancy vary from 12 kilograms to 16 kilograms. Many slender women put on 20–30 kilos during pregnancy and then lose it again afterwards.

About a third of the weight gain is baby, placenta and amniotic fluid; the rest is new bits of you – increased blood volume, breast growth, fluid and fat. The body needs to build up stores of fat during pregnancy, which is then used in breastfeeding. The weight you gain will probably go something like this:

baby, placenta, amniotic fluid: 4.5 kilograms
increased size of uterus: 1 kilo
increased breast size: 0.5–1 kilo
increased blood: 1 kilo
retained fluid: 3 kilos
increased fat and protein stores: 3 kilos.

Most of the weight gain is in the fourth to the seventh month of the pregnancy.

At the birth you can lose up to 12 kilos at once, and in the days following, the excess fluid will also be lost through sweat and urine.

You will probably weigh yourself every time you visit the obstetrician or midwife, and they may give you advice on diet if they think you are gaining too much. If you're not gaining enough weight and they are concerned about foetal growth, you will be offered an ultrasound to check this and may be put on a weight-gain diet.

Your obstetrician or midwife will be on the alert for any rapid increase in weight during the last ten weeks of pregnancy, which can be a sign of pre-eclampsia (see the info in 'Week 31'). Some other conditions associated with too much weight gain in pregnancy are gestational diabetes, high blood pressure, varicose veins, haemorrhoids and uncontrollable Magnum addictions.

more info on weight gain

What to Eat When You're Expecting by Arlene Eisenberg, Heidi E. Murkoff and Sandee E. Hathaway (for details and full review see More Info on Eating and Supplements in 'Week 2').

See also Eating and Supplements in 'Week 2' and Exercise in 'Week 15'.

your record

Time capsule for your child:
What's in the news this week?

What are the most popular songs? (By whom?)

What are the most popular films? (Starring whom?)

What outfit is the height of fashion right now?

WEEK 21

what's going on

You could start to get heartburn and indigestion. Get used to people judging your size – 'You're not very big for dates' and 'My giddy aunt, that's enormous!' – sometimes on the same day. This could be a good time to spend a day with a friend or friend-of-a-friend who has a baby under 9 weeks old, just to get a feel for the future. The foetal eyelids are still fused closed (until week 27), but the foetus can hear sounds from within and outside your body. The brain has been developing very quickly, but its surface is still very smooth, not like the textbook pictures of adult brains we're used to. Weight: about 390 grams.

You could catch stingrays in my UNDERPANTS

DiARY

I have new moles and skin tags everywhere. It's like my skin is hyperactive and throwing out extra bits wherever it can. Basically, I'm getting extra tags and moles in every area I already have them, plus a whole new bunch of tags under each breast.

My hair also appears to be attempting an Afro at every available opportunity. It seems to be growing faster and getting thicker, but perhaps this is an optical illusion.

My tummy's sticking out about where the rest of the world used to be, so when I squeeze through to get out of the lift at work and automatically calculate I've got a 10-centimetre clearance I actually rub myself against someone, who starts to look very frightened at the idea of being groped by a pregnant woman.

Young men look me up and down in the street, and when they realise I'm pregnant there's this look of panic that crosses their face and they quickly swerve out of my way. It makes me want to rush over and get them in a vicelike grip and scream: 'The baby's coming! You'll have to do something!' I reckon most of them would faint dead away or just run.

I was standing in the street the other day waiting for the lights to change, and just as they did a beaten-up Kingswood stopped and a bloke with dreadlocks and a cowboy hat stuck most of his body out the window and started shouting, and then the driver was honking his horn and wolf-whistling, so I started rubbing my big tummy up and down, pulling up my frock and vamping across the road – because of course it was some blokes from Des's work falling about laughing. You should have seen the looks on the faces of the other drivers banked up at the lights: like, this used to be a bad area but now it's just *disgusting*.

Shopping with Aunty Peg. Thank God no horror stories, although she does tell me encouragingly at some length that ALL first babies cry CONSTANTLY and wriggle all the time and drive their parents mad, and the parents *never* get any sleep, and this is the inevitable fault of the parents, who are necessarily inexperienced and tense so make the baby tense. Quite serene, this shopping caper.

See a small child in a clothes shop and say 'Hellooo' in exactly the same tone Aunty Peg uses. Reel back in horror and hope I won't automatically start trying to feed small children grey mince on rice and boiled chops four nights a week. A few minutes later say 'Peekaboo' to another strange child just as if I am channelling Aunty Peg, who is at that moment looking at a pink floral suit and saying, 'This is lovely, dear, unless it's a boy.' (She is very worried about cross-dressing babies.) The child seems to take it rather well and in the jaunty manner it was intended.

Shopping for baby clothes is actually just like being size 14 in a shop for grown-up women where all the sizes are 6 and 8. Everything's teeny tiny. Except there are slightly more snap fasteners at crotch level than usual. When shopping for myself I can still go into a shop and say, 'Yes, I'll have one of those in size ginormous, thank you.' If they have them. At this stage you could catch stingrays in my underpants.

Anyway, back to baby gear. Some kids' clothes are $50 a throw, even $100 a throw, for something that they must grow out of in a nanosecond. I'm thinking I might just coat my child in Vaseline to keep it warm. There are T-shirts and rompy suit things you can buy with 'Baby' written on the front – you know, in case you think you've given birth to a ferret, or you get confused and start dressing your bedside lamp. 'No, that's right, tea-cosy on the teapot, T-shirt on the BABY.'

And there are these hair bands with flowers on that go around a baby's head, and basically they're used on a baldy baby to indicate that it's a girl. Oh, say it loud and say it proud: 'The kid's bald.'

People keep asking me if it's going to be a boy or a girl and I say, 'Yes, I believe so. So I've been led to understand. But we're not fussy. We're just hoping for a life form of some description.' They say, 'Well, you should find out so you know what kind of clothes to buy for the baby.' I'm like: is it going to matter? Is somebody going to accuse a 4-month-old child of cross-dressing? 'You perverted infant, you're dressing like Julian Clary – get a hold of yourself!!'

And sometimes people ask, 'What are you hoping for?' 'A giraffe. They're up running around the paddock an hour or so after birth and starting to feed themselves.'

If you don't know much about babies, the sizes are very confusing. They start at 'premmie', followed by 000, but when I say that looks too small the sales assistant shows me a doll that's size 00 and fair dinkum it could play full-back for Essendon. There's no way something that big is going to come out of me without some kind of major rearrangement of the laws of physics. So triple zero for newborns it is – about the size of one of those gowns starlets wear to the Oscars, in fact.

I'm feeling much better, but still sleeping up to 10 hours a night easily. The whole food thing is weird. I still eat when I'm hungry but nearly hurl at the sight or smell of any slight sliminess, like green leafy things more than a few minutes out of the ground. I can't go to the market with Des any more because I go whey-faced the minute I smell the delicatessen section and have to go outside.

I watched a TV documentary on Spike Milligan and was astonished to hear that after they divorced he refused to let his wife ever see their children: that's what the law allowed then because she had left him, even though he was a manic-depressive alcoholic. He now says he was an unfit father. His kids talked about how they used to write letters to fairies and leave them in the garden, and Spike would write back tiny, enchanting letters and they really believed there were fairies, well into their teens. It sounds lovely, a man trying to make his children's world so beautiful. But then his son sadly describes how completely ill-equipped this made him for the real world. Oh, who'd be a parent?

We're off to Des's work function. Des is given a nurseryman's achievement award (a very nice shovel), and his colleague Brenda makes a speech in front of the entire workforce of the nursery chain stores about how his extra work is really appreciated, especially as his 'wife' (apparently that's me) wouldn't appreciate him working on weekends with women in skimpy shorts (no, I really think lady gardeners should wear crinolines) but I had mounted the best strategy and got him pregnant.

I spend a good half an hour restraining myself from wrestling her to the floor and strangling her with a tablecloth.

About sixteen people handle my stomach without asking. Only one, Trina, asks whether she can. Her baby is a year old and she tries to flog me her cousin's pram. Crushed to hear we are already prammed up on a promise, she changes tack by looking at me critically.

'How are you going with your weight?' she asks, swaying in the wind on her go-go boots.

'Oh, stacking it on, thanks,' I say cheerfully.

'Don't do what I did. I got up to 80 kilos.'

I break it to her gently. 'I'm already 80 kilos.'

'OH MY GOD! I've finally lost it all.'

'Breastfeeding?' I ask.

'No, it's harder than that,' says Trina. 'As soon as I stopped breastfeeding, I started starving myself and eating junk food. But I'll have to start eating properly again to set the baby a good example.' Fat chance.

At Lucretia's party that meat-faced old drunk Michael F comes up and tells me loudly I'm the last person he expected would ever get pregnant. I suggest he take a long look at Boris Yeltsin.

'Babies love me,' he says. 'I don't know why, but when they get a bit older they reject me.'

'Maybe it's because you smell like a bottle of mixed sherry and urine,' I don't say. More bloody advice about how to get them to sleep from a man with four children by five different women, who thinks a hearty breakfast is a bottle of stout and a packet of Styvos.

Today's newspaper says a new study shows that 'unborn babies' can hear at twenty weeks. I hope Cellsie didn't get a load of Brenda's speech. Mind you, I'm really not sure about the research methods in some of these surveys that provide quotable statistics. Ten pregnant women listened to one music tape in the twentieth week of pregnancy. Two to three weeks after birth, the babies kicked less when those songs from the tape were played.

Well, this is just not enough information. Were the babies forced to listen to Garth Brooks, Celine Dion or Mating Calls of the Lesser Yak? Couldn't the lack of kicks have been incredulity?

info

at work

In a healthy pregnancy and a healthy workplace there is no reason why you shouldn't keep working for as long as you want to and your doctor and health and safety officer agree, especially because the money will come in handy. How close to your due date you work will depend on how you feel.

Most women value some time alone before they begin the horror! the horror! Oops. The extremely rewarding and divinely bondworthy, magnificent experience of childbirth and caring for a newborn baby. It's common to take maternity leave for at least the last four to six weeks of the pregnancy, and longer if you can afford it. You'll probably feel really tired and uncomfortable in the last few weeks. Resting well, exercising gently, eating right and thinking serene thoughts during the last weeks of the pregnancy certainly won't hurt.

From week 32 your heart, lungs and other vital organs are working really hard and getting more and more squished up by the growing uterus. The strain on your back, joints and muscles

is increasingly intense, and you might be vaguing out a lot. Not to mention that by week 36 that baby head bouncing on your cervix can make you swear and jump around as if you've suddenly developed Tourette's syndrome: not a good look during a meeting.

If your job requires a lot of standing up, working in the last few weeks can get really difficult. Even a desk job can become hard. You might just want to lie on the couch and read magazines or watch videos.

Some doctors recommend that if your job has you on your feet more than 4 hours a day, you should stop work by week 24, and that if you need to stand half an hour of each working hour you ought to stop work by week 32.

Other work conditions that should be discussed with your doctor are exposure to possible teratogens – substances or environmental factors that could harm your baby (see the info in Looking After Your Foetus in 'Week 4') – work that involves lots of lifting, carrying or bending, or shift work, which can upset sleep and eating patterns.

Being pregnant at work should probably be dealt with like any other personal issue: don't blab everything to everybody, especially gossipy people and ones who couldn't care less and drop off for a nap at the first sign of the word 'trimester'. This will also allow you to feel more professional for the time you are there and when you come back.

Regardless of what the law requires of them, managers can vary dramatically in how they view the whole deal of pregnancy and maternity leave. Bosses in some large companies have done cost-benefit research and realised it's cheaper and smarter to give valued employees leave, then welcome them back with flexible working hours, than drive them out and start training new people (who may also get pregnant). Other bosses try to sack you as soon as they find out: this is illegal.

While you're busy being your same old reliable, efficient self, you might really be feeling very different, hiding how you feel and worrying that you might overlook something important. Here are some suggestions that might help.

❂ Keep a stash of healthy snacks at work, which are useful for keeping your blood sugar up and nausea at bay during the first trimester, and for general nutrition the rest of the time.

❂ Make yourself comfortable. Put your feet up when you can. Sit rather than stand. Practise squatting for labour during private moments. Have regular walks and stretches if you're bent over a desk for much of the day. Drink plenty of water. If you feel really tired, use your lunch hour to sleep in a spare office, organising to have someone wake you up at the end of the break. If you do this, don't forget to make time to eat.

❂ Take it as easy as you can. Bring work home, or go home for a snooze if you can.

❂ If work is stressful, try yoga or meditation classes and learn some good relaxation techniques.

❂ Keep the best work diary you could imagine and religiously consult it every morning. Make lists. Invest in Post-it notes for reminders. Get colour-coded folders. Get other staff pals or an assistant to remind you of things, including 'Go and have lunch'.

If you think you're being discriminated against, check your rights with your union, lawyer or government departments dealing with employment.

your record

Is being pregnant affecting your work? If so, how?

Describe your job or what you do all day. (Your child
will be interested to know eventually.)

what's going on

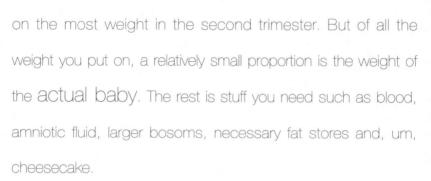

You may have back pain, cramps, varicose veins, vivid dreams, and feel strangely calm. You also put on the most weight in the second trimester. But of all the weight you put on, a relatively small proportion is the weight of the actual baby. The rest is stuff you need such as blood, amniotic fluid, larger bosoms, necessary fat stores and, um, cheesecake.

Downstairs there may well be some exhibition somersaulting going on. The inner ear has reached adult size. There are now eyebrows and head hair (unless you've got a baldy baby). The lungs are starting to produce stuff called surfactant, a detergentlike substance that will help them to function properly by keeping them expanded after a breath. Weight: about 460 grams.

Average approximate foetus length this week from head to bum

cm 1 2 3 4 5 6 7 8 9 10 11 12 13

DiARY My horoscope this week says: 'Dating is invested with potential. Those who are pair-bonded ought to beware sudden attractions to deeply inappropriate types'. In my case, I presume, this would mean . . . anybody else in the entire universe.

Des talks to all the men at work about weird things their wives do when pregnant. I don't have enough people to talk to about this stuff. Most of my friends who aren't childless have forgotten what it's like to be pregnant. Even a lot of my lesbian friends (or as my niece Seychelle calls them, ladies who love ladies) who want to have kids haven't got around to working out how yet. We are about to leave the baby-free zone.

I've been organising a nappy wash service for Marg for when she gets out of hospital with the new baby. I've been sending out a form letter to all our friends.

Dear Friends

As you may have noticed, Marg Anderson is about to have a baby any minute now. Possibly at this very moment. What you may not know is that newborn babies need their nappies changed up to sixty times a week.

Yes.

Horrible, isn't it?

To help deal with this rather confronting fact, we have organised Marg a gift account at Snappy Nappy – which will deliver clean nappies (and take away the other kind) each week, as soon as she gets home from hospital. (She has expressed a firm wish to receive a gift of nappies rather than flowers, which will only make her sneeze.)

You might like to contribute a week's worth of nappies ($28.50) yourself or as part of a cartel. Please fill in the enclosed coupon, add a cheque and send it straight to Snappy Nappy. Marg's account number is 62240. Don't forget to add your name to the coupon so Marg will receive a card with your name on it.

Love, Hermoine.

I am prostrate with exhaustion and self-admiration after such efficiency. Then I realise I forgot to put stamps on the letters.

This not-feeling-the-baby-move business is getting embarrassing. Beck, with absolutely no tact in sight, tells me I'm a 'bit remedial'. She assures me again that I have felt the baby move but haven't realised it, and tells the story of a fat woman who came into casualty when Beck was a nurse.

The woman was complaining of terrible, sudden, intermittent abdominal pains. (You know what's coming, don't you? Well, she didn't.) The ambos told the nursing staff the pains were coming at regular intervals and were probably labour contractions, although the woman kept saying she wasn't pregnant. Beck said to her, 'But haven't you felt the baby move?' 'It's just wind,' the woman said, shortly before being joined by her offspring, whom she regarded with some astonishment.

I've popped into Beck's clinic, after another visit to the chiropractor, to see if I'm in early labour or just constipated. What a glamorous job she has.

'I'm not giving you a laxative without feeling what's going on,' she says. 'Otherwise you might be having a baby instead of a poo.'

Charming.

Speaking of wind, am nearly crippled by it in the babies' wear department of a gigantic department store this afternoon, and have to walk around bent in half and rubbing my stomach. People look rather concerned but I can hardly announce: 'It's all right, move along, I think I just need to do an enormous FART.'

Once again some of the baby clothes have Paris couturier prices, and although I am careful I end up spending $150 on small hats, singlets, cotton jumpsuity things and oh, all right, a couple of expensive cute things like a red denim jacket and matching leggings. Bought a few light blue items. Not because I think I'm having a boy but because that pale pink makes me feel queasy.

I think it's better if I stay out of babies' and children's wear departments. It will be cheaper, and I don't want to end up with a child resembling anything remotely like those demented-looking blond children with bowl haircuts you see in glossy kids' wear brochures, dressed in velvet frou-frou knickerbockers with matching bow ties, looking like their parents would have conniptions if they got dirty. I'm thinking of dressing Cellsie in a plastic mac from dawn till dusk and just hosing him or her down before bedtime.

info

skin

A whole lot of stuff happens to your skin when you're pregnant. Everything is working overtime, generally resulting in more oil, sweat and pigment (colouring) being produced. More blood is flowing closer to your skin, making it warmer; and increased oil gland secretions, giving skin a shinier appearance, add to the pregnancy 'glow'. Retained fluid can give the skin a fuller, smoother appearance than usual. Necessary fat stores mean more cellulite on buttocks and thighs for the duration.

It depends on the individual: although many women find their skin looks better than ever during pregnancy, some may be prone to pimples or acne, while others may find themselves with dry, scaly skin. Oestrogen slows down oil production, but progesterone promotes it – and they are both very active during pregnancy. Most skin changes, including some skin tags, are temporary, but some are permanent: you may end up with darker

nipples forever; a few more moles and stretch marks will stay, but fade to be hardly noticeable unless you run around in the nuddy under fluorescent lights.

pigmentation changes

Pigmentation changes, also known as melanin or colour changes, are caused by increased production of melanocyte-stimulating hormone (MSH), which acts on the cells that affect the colour of your skin. These changes are usually more obvious on dark skin. The theory is that darker nipples make it easier for breastfeeding babies to find them. If you have fair skin and red hair the changes will probably be slight.

linea nigra

The dark line called the linea nigra, which divides your tummy into halves along the site of the stretching rectus muscle (from your navel down to the map of Tassie), often appears by week 14, though sometimes not until weeks later. (The line is actually there before pregnancy – imaginatively and inaccurately called the linea alba, the Latin for 'white line' – though it's not particularly noticeable on any skin colour.)

The area around and inside your navel can also become darker. So can existing freckles and moles; and the skin under the eyes and arms, between the thighs and of the genitals may also be noticeably darker during pregnancy. Some pregnancy experts say the vagina turns purple. But who's game to look? It doesn't matter what colour it is. (Tell a lie. Lime green would be a worry.) Oh, let's just take their word for it.

irregular patches

Irregular patches of slightly different-coloured skin might turn up on your face; these are called chloasma, or by doctors who used to watch 'Zorro', the 'mask of pregnancy'. The patches are dark in women with light skin and light in women with dark skin.

Folic acid deficiency is linked to too much colour change in the skin. Exposure to the sun will intensify changes such as the face patches. A hat and a 15+ sunscreen cream will protect you.

stretch marks

Stretch marks that look like thin pink, red or purplish lines on pale skin, and paler brown lines on dark skin, are the result of collagen fibres in the skin tearing and breaking. They can happen on breasts, tummy, thighs and bottom. (The same hormone that makes ligaments relax during pregnancy, relaxin, also decreases the amount of collagen in the skin fibres, making them more fragile.) After pregnancy, stretch marks gradually fade to silvery lines in the skin, usually barely noticeable.

You can't stop or heal stretch marks, but as they are caused by the skin being forced to stretch a lot and quite quickly they are generally worse in cases of rapid, excessive weight gain. How many you get and how quickly they fade will largely be determined by the skin and body type you inherited. Some skins have more elastin and collagen than others.

Gradual weight gain may help to minimise stretch marks, and a good diet that includes plenty of protein and vitamin C will help keep skin in a generally healthy condition. Many people swear by vitamin E cream, but there's no scientific research that proves it helps, and many women who use vitamin E cream still get stretch marks.

skin tags

Skin tags are little extra bits of skin that often develop in places where there is some friction, such as the bra line under your breasts, or under your arms. They are caused by small areas of skin getting overactive. Sometimes they disappear a few months after birth, sometimes you've got them forever (but dermatologists can remove them). Guess you'll just have to wait and see what happens to yours.

visible veins

Some people develop spider veins: threadlike, wiggly red lines, usually on the cheeks. They are small broken blood vessels caused by rapid dilation and constriction of the blood vessels when circulation increases during pregnancy. Blue lines under the skin, on the breasts and on the tummy just show some of the extra blood you're carrying. They will go away after the baby arrives. Bulging varicose veins in the legs can be painful. Your doctor can tell you how to avoid them (usually: put your feet up when you can and wear special 'support' tights). They may eventually disappear or in severe cases have to be surgically removed.

rashes and spots

Heat rashes can be caused by the combination of increased circulation, body temperature, sweating and skin friction in pregnancy. Rashes might cause itchiness. It may help to dress in cotton clothes that allow good ventilation and to wash using a non-soap alternative or special oil (ask your pharmacist).

Red spots sometimes appear on the face, arms, torso, palms and soles of the feet. These too are caused by increased blood flow through dilated vessels, and go away after pregnancy.

Some medications for acne and psoriasis can be very dangerous to the developing foetus. Discuss alternative treatments with your doctor. Conditions such as eczema and psoriasis often improve during pregnancy.

what's going on
Your bladder is getting squished up even more, so you may need to wee more often. You might feel practice labour contractions from now on, called Braxton Hicks (or they may not start for weeks, or you might not ever experience them).

WEEK

Average approximate foetus length this week from head to bum

| cm | 1 | 2 | 3 | 4 | 5 | 6 | 7 | 8 | 9 | 10 | 11 | 12 | 13 |

The foetus is growing like gangbusters, and the brain is maturing. Some researchers believe the foetus has started to think. Others, to be safer, say we can't really tell when this happens, and it may be much later. (And anyway, it's probably just stuff like 'Gee, I like to suck things' and 'La, la, la, whatever' or 'It's a bit wet in here, innit?'.) The skin is growing very quickly, but there's not much fat yet developed for plumping up underneath it, so the skin looks a bit pruney. Weight: about 540 grams.

| 16 | 17 | 18 | 19 | 20 | 21 | 22 | 23 | 24 | 25 | 26 | 27 | 28 | 29 |

Diary

Just ate entire block of chocolate. Feel sick. This won't stop me from having lunch, mind you. By this stage I find I am in need of some even more simply enormous underpants. They are the kind of thing you could wave if you were surrendering. Later I might recycle a pair as a doona cover. I find it is infinitely more soothing not to think about the size of my bum. I also picked up a bargain – a free pair of socks with every pair of maternity tights! Some bargain – the whole package was $20 and the tights laddered when I looked at them sternly.

The only time I can get a sense of weightlessness is in the bath. I'd rather be swimming, even if I did resemble the opening sequence of *Free Willy*. But the public pools are infested with some hideous staphylococcus, germy thing that's front-page news. The reports include a hideous diagram of minute quantities of 'faecal matter' floating around public pools and spreading the bug. Not for me, thanks. And the sea is too cold to swim in at this time of year unless you're one of those 80-year-old fanatics with elaborate floral bathing caps.

Marg's baby has arrived. She's a very beautiful girl with gigantic feet and no name, but never mind that: Marg did the whole labour as Warrior Woman without pain-killers!

She had a trainee midwife who made her push too early – apparently the midwife thought the distension of the vaginal wall caused by the pushing was the baby's head! Marg's fanny, by this stage, was looking like it had been thoroughly bashed up. Poor Marg was very happy to see Dr Herb, who marched in, terribly calm, put a suction cup on the baby's head and pulled it outta there. He had to give her an episiotomy, so she has heaps of stitches. She said she was in shock afterwards and thought she'd rather die than ever do that again, but a few days later she'd kind of forgotten.

Marg has stories of over-bustly nurses coming in at all hours and patting the baby around as if she were a football, which unsettles her. So she's told them all to bugger off and will only let in the nicer nurses. She had the 'baby blues' day on day 4 when the real breast milk came into her breasts, but she reckons it wasn't

too bad – she just let herself cry all day without feeling weird
about it. She looks terribly glamorous and serene in her silky
nightie, and the baby seems to be an old hand at the breast.

Marg's hospital ensemble reminds me I don't have anything
like it. I go straight to a department store to get myself a nightie
and dressing-gown because a T-shirt, explorer socks and an old
overcoat obviously will not do. I also try to buy a back-supporting
maternity-girdle-type thing. But when I mention the girdle, the
saleslady asks sternly through cat's-bum lips, 'Has your doctor told
you to get one? They're not recommended these days. Have you
told your doctor?'

'I don't want one to hide my stomach, I want it to support my
back.'

'I see,' she snapped. 'We haven't got any.'

What a ninny.

Boy, do I have this Nesting Thing really bad. All afternoon
I daydream about moving the furniture. Why can't I live in a
minimalist house like the ones in *Vogue Apartments* magazine?
Pout for a while. I collect more boxes to put things in and cut out
magazine articles that introduce a new verb, 'de-cluttering'.

Thank God I am removed from the house by the necessity to
travel interstate and do a bit of promotion for the new fashion
range. Realistic sizes are flavour of the month, but you watch – by
summer every other fashion house will be back to toddler-sized
persons jigging about in grown-ups' clothes. I have to do an
interview at ABC Classic FM, where it's so posh that as I'm eating
a muffin out of a paper bag while I'm waiting to go in, somebody
comes and gives me a plate so I won't 'have to be a savage'.

I'm supposed to say in the interview why I've chosen these bits
of classical music – and I don't even know what they are. I got
them all off this relaxing CD that my beautician plays while I'm
having a facial. So the interviewer's going, 'And why is this passage
by Debussy a favourite of yours?', and I just take a punt and say,
'Look, it's got a lot of piano, and if you're in the bath you can go
underwater to wash off the shampoo, come back up and not feel
like you've missed anything.'

And then the interviewer says: 'And you're pregnant. We had

another pregnant lady in a while ago – or maybe she was breastfeeding, I can't remember.'

I say, 'Well, did you see her bare bosoms? If you saw her bare bosoms, she probably had passed the pregnancy stage.'

Being in a huge city is really no fun in this condition. The queue for a taxi at the airport is 200 long and full of business people who look at you as if you're an alien pregnant person and never offer to help with your luggage.

And seven times out of ten when you *do* get in a taxi you're totally at the driver's mercy. Either they will not speak to you at all. You say, 'I'd like to go to Kings Cross, please.' Silence. 'Do you know where it is?' Silence. 'Do you have a pulse?' Silence. So you just sit back and relax, wondering if your family will ever hear from you again.

OR you get the ones where you say 'Kings Cross, please', and they say, 'How was your day? I'm just listening to John Laws. I'll turn it up in the back. I'll tell you what's wrong with this country today. The Immigrant Devil makes work for Andy Pandy and yea through the valley of the Beelzebub the spawn of life will be transcended. John Howard is a communist and will burn dripping in hell for all eternity for his permissive Y-frontery. You know that, don't you?' And that's when you say: 'Couldn't agree more! Just let me out at the next corner, thanks!'

Meanwhile, the State premier has refused to pass a law that enshrines the right of mothers to breastfeed in public because it is sometimes 'just exhibitionism'. Hear, hear. I am sick of these mothers pushing their prams around the streets in string bikinis, removing their nipple tassels and just flaunting themselves generally. I mean, it's too much. There are many people who don't know what a breast looks like, and when confronted with one in the street, for a split second before a bub wraps its gob round the pointy bit, people could lose their reason!

And everybody knows that when a woman is breastfeeding, it is impossible not to be reminded of such classic films as *Debbie Does Dubbo*, *Swedish Knockers Akimbo* and of course any Carry On film starring Barbara Windsor. In fact, breastfeeding is such a salacious and provocative act, I'm surprised it isn't banned altogether.

Obviously a lot of nursing mothers will pretend that they just want to feed their child to stop it from shrieking – but I think we all really know that it's just an excuse to behave like a strumpet and give all the blokes in the vicinity a bit of a saucy come-on. Apparently when you're getting 20 minutes of sleep a day and you spend your life cleaning up somebody else's poo and you haven't had time to wash your hair for three weeks, all you really want to do is have sex with strange men in public places. Can't help yourself.

All the newspapers have gone wild with letters, including one from a member of the Breast Police who has managed to insult *everyone* by saying she finds mothers who *bottle-feed* their baby in public to be offensive because everyone must breastfeed. She's alienated all those mums who would love to breastfeed but can't. I hope her nipples rotate at night like propellers and keep her awake.

Today, I officially let myself go. I spend the entire day dressed in a wheat bag and moccasins, and I haven't washed my hair since Wednesday. I know the Oprah theme music by heart.

And I've been reading the preggo mags again. One suggests that you could hint to your partner that you were pregnant by serving him a dinner comprised of veal, baby carrots, baby peas and baby's lettuce. And decorate the table with the white flowers called baby's breath. Des, at least, being a professional, could tell baby's breath from a bunch of cauliflower, but even he's unlikely to make the connection.

The magazines are full of aerobicised chicks in high heels. I haven't done any side-lying crunches and I don't walk the length of the Nullarbor every day. I have lifted no weights, cross-country skiing is a mystery to me, and I don't even know what an isometric abdominal is. I haven't done any pelvic-floor exercises. This means by Christmas I'll be incontinent, broke and 487 kilos. What I want to see is a few of these pregnancy magazines with women who were more than size 10 to start with and who've just had two nights of insomnia and half a black forest cake; and instead of male models, I want to see proper blokes looking unshaven, and shell-shocked after seeing their first ballistic baby poo.

I've 'popped' again: another growth surge in the tummy region. I popped at four, five and now six months. It makes me go around singing the blues song by Howlin' Wolf, 'Three Hundred Pounds of (Heavenly) Joy'.

info

travelling

The best time for holiday travel is the middle trimester – you're probably not queasy, there's not much chance of labour starting, your energy levels are up, you're not too huge to get comfortable and you're less likely to be mistaken for a large wildebeest in the dark.

Think twice about going somewhere hot, humid and otherwise a frenzied-mosquito festival. Pregnancy has already raised your body temperature. As well, high altitude destinations (over 2,000 metres) are not recommended because of the lack of oxygen for you and your baby.

Plan a holiday that allows for good diet, rest and relaxation, and always check in with your midwife or obstetrician before making any bookings. This is no time to press on with that adventure trek across the Mongolian plains on the back of a goat just because you planned it two years ago.

And if you are lucky enough to live in a developed country, this is probably not the time to visit a developing one. You might

not be able to have the vaccinations you'll need, and you'll be exposing yourself and the baby to disease and the sort of medical care they make scary films about. If you insist on heading for regions where gastro bugs are common, pack diarrhoea medication recommended by your doctor or obstetrician for use during pregnancy, and don't let yourself dehydrate.

If you travel anywhere overseas, get high-level travel insurance that includes medical costs. The most 'developed' country in the world, the USA, has an appalling health system. Ask your obstetrician about how to find a doctor at your destination who literally speaks your language. Carry a brief medical history, including your blood group and allergies, and your own obstetrician's phone numbers. If you have a problem, call your obstetrician at home in Australia, even if you're in Burkina Faso. Worry about the phone bill when you get home.

by car
You can drive all through pregnancy as long as you don't rule yourself out for severe vagueness.

◎ Take snacks, drinks and a back support cushion if driving for long distances (and likewise on train trips). The only snacks you can buy in most places have the nutritional content of a battered Mars Bar and three times the kilojoules.

◎ Stop, stretch and have rest breaks, and don't hold back if you need to wee: make sure you stop regularly and go to the toilet.

◎ Put the seatbelt's lap strap underneath your belly and the sash between belly and breast.

◎ You can sit on a folded towel for the last couple of weeks of pregnancy in case your waters break when you're driving, so the amniotic fluid doesn't ruin the upholstery.

by plane
Most airlines refuse bookings from pregnant passengers during the last four to five weeks of the pregnancy in case you give birth prematurely on the flight. Restrictions and medical certificate

requirements vary from airline to airline. Don't think you can fox them by just turning up, either – they may make an arbitrary decision not to let you fly if you can't 'prove' your due date.

It's not safe to fly in an unpressurised aircraft when pregnant because of the lack of oxygen. Large planes all have pressurised cabins but smaller planes may not, and you need to find out about this from your travel agent. Oxygen levels can fluctuate even in pressurised aeroplane cabins, so if you are feeling light-headed ask the flight attendant for some oxygen.

⑥ If taking a short holiday or trip, try to limit yourself to hand luggage to save having to wait on arrival.

⑥ When booking flights, say you are pregnant and ask for an aisle seat (for access to the toilets and leg stretching) near the front of the plane (you can get on last, get off first and have better air quality).

⑥ Ask about food options, such as vegetarian or low-fat meals, that might be yummier and better for you.

⑥ Check with your doctor to assess your risk of deep vein thrombosis (DVT) developing during air travel.

⑥ On long flights avoid dehydration by drinking plenty of fluid – water, diluted fruit juice or milk – but not alcohol, tea or coffee. Bring your own healthy snacks.

⑥ Take plenty of walk and stretch breaks. Elevate, flex and rotate your feet while you are sitting, to help your circulation.

⑥ Wear comfortable shoes and thin socks because your feet will swell even more than they do on a long flight when you're not pregnant, and put on support pantyhose if you have varicose veins. Puffiness may last for a day or so afterwards (see the info on swelling and fluid retention in 'Week 28').

⑥ To help get rid of fluid, take a plunger, dandelion-leaf tea and peppermint tea – in your hand luggage so they can't be sent to Botswana if you're going to Fangataufa. (DON'T get dandelion-root tea or 'coffee'.) The tea looks like a bag of shredded leaves from the cannabis plant and may amuse Customs if it's not labelled properly. Throw 2 or more dessertspoons of the tea and 1 teaspoon of the peppermint tea in the plunger and fill it with water; leave the tea unplunged overnight, then plunge and drink the lot at breakfast.

staying away

⑥ Take your own pillow in a black or patterned pillowcase (so it's harder to forget and leave it behind) – this will leave other pillows for propping under your tummy or between your legs.

⑥ In your handbag carry a few essentials such as tissues (you never know when your nose will run or stuff up or you'll need toilet paper), ear plugs and an eye mask.

⑥ Don't even think about high heels.

⑥ Lighten your load as much as possible. Some marketing geniuses now make small cosmetic travelling kits for this very purpose. Cute but expensive – you can make up your own. Put all cosmetics, shampoos and so on in tiny plastic bottles (you can buy them at pharmacies and department stores) or get sample-sized sachets, and take just enough for what you'll need while you're away.

⑥ Pack light, versatile clothes: a perfectly fine three- or four-day business trip can be accomplished with one black microfibre frock (microfibre doesn't need ironing and black won't get grubby so quickly), two pairs of tights, one pair of microfibre or cotton black pants, two T-shirts or shirts with short or long sleeves, two pairs of socks, four pairs of undies, two bras and . . . um . . . a jacket. Unless somebody else will be available to carry your luggage *at all times*, plan to be able to have everything in a carry-on-the-plane-sized bag. Or have a small bag on wheels and ask someone to get it off the carousel for you.

You are very obviously pregnant by now so if you'd like to avoid people asking you lots of questions on your train, bus or plane trip, read some erotic fiction with lurid book covers. You'd be surprised how much people leave you alone.

WEEK

Average approximate foetus length this week from head to bum

what's going on You may be feeling constipated. Changes in blood flow can mean your blood pressure drops and you may feel faint. This can happen when you lie flat on your back because the weight of the uterus can compress the big fat vein (the inferior vena cava) that carries blood from your lower parts back to your heart. If you do feel weird, stop lying on your back and you'll feel better again.

Many babies born at this stage have survived with the help of hospital intensive care, but this is by no means guaranteed. The biggest problem is that the lungs aren't really finished, so if the foetus came out early it would need help to breathe. The foetus still looks thin compared to the roly-poly Anne Geddes postcard-style baby, but is starting to get plumper. Weight: about 630 grams.

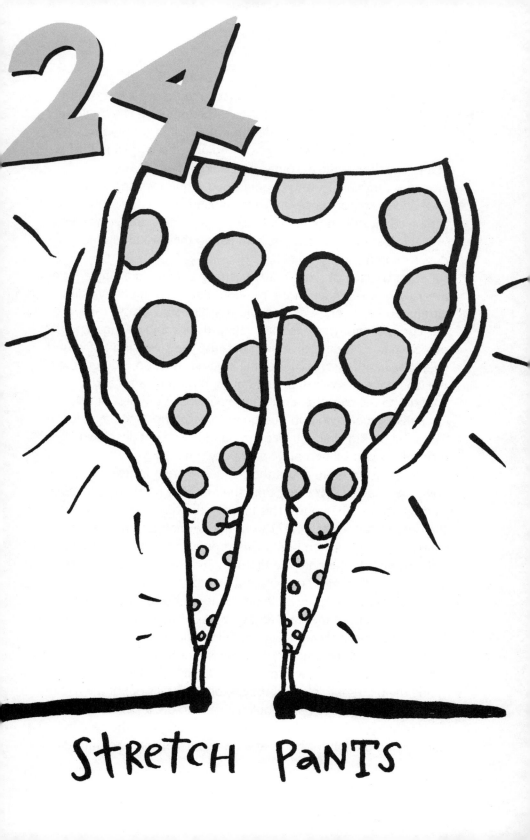

24

STRETCH PANTS

DiARY

Katie rings from interstate to say she's just been to the agricultural show, where there was a 'maternity ward' – a bustling pavilion full of twenty ewes, any one of which was 'lambing' (that is, giving birth) at any one time while a woman on a microphone made an incessant commentary and people stood around waving show bags and, depending on who they were, looking stunned (young men), completely horrified (young women), sympathetic (older women), stoical (older men), and antsy from eating their weight in fairy floss (children).

So of course last night I dreamt that it is me and a whole lot of other pregnant women in the pavilion. I am wearing baby-doll jarmies and everyone else is in Laura-Ashley-style dressing-gowns. The commentator is sitting on a velour throne and saying, 'Look at that woman. She can't give birth because she's wearing the wrong pyjamas.' I am mortified about the pyjama situation, but just then the woman in the next stall gives birth to a small lamb and confides to me over the fence that she'll 'make the best of it'.

I wish my hair wouldn't be quite so eccentric. One day it looks like a full-on Big Hair extravaganza, and the next it lies down like a couple of bad billiard players in a city pub.

I'm thinking more about the baby. The great festival of nesting continues. Rachel says every time she rings me up there is another tradesperson in the house. This time it's the carpenter, Crazy Axel (he doesn't call himself Crazy Axel, but he should). Crazy Axel makes my long-awaited built-in wardrobes in large pieces that he unloads off a trailer onto the footpath and then realises none of them will fit through the door, and he has to saw them in half.

Installation brings a whole new sense of horror, with great big bits gouged out of the wall, and Crazy Axel's frank admission that he hasn't thought about how to install the heavy top pieces. At one point I offer a crane, but luckily some Swedish circus performers who are staying next door come in and climb up the wall and help guide the pieces into place. If the bottom ever falls out of the flying-trapeze market, these gals should be able to get a job at Ikea.

Crazy Axel distinguishes himself by running into the gate in his car, leaving the job for hours at a time and walking back into the house without knocking. Finally, he says he can't finish the job because it's all too upsetting, and drives away. Leaving his mobile phone in the wardrobe. Which rings in the middle of the night.

I'm still really sensitive to smells. I try to go to the market again, but one foot into the deli section and I nearly faint and throw up at the same time. Luckily I don't try Fish – my head might have rotated.

Why do I bother to make those few social calls to remind myself I still have friends? I distinguish myself by leaving parties when most other people are arriving. It's impossible to keep up my previous, non-pregnant pace – but hard to slow down to a real pregnant pace. This leaves just the uncomfortable feeling of being boring and guilty at the same time.

My brain is suet and I can't remember anything. I have stuck Post-it notes around my computer screen so many times it looks like a clown's ruff.

I'm sitting on the couch watching the Teletubbies (practice) when I feel a sort of a feeling that could be some lunch rearranging itself, only it's too low down, and might be a fart but isn't, and come to think of it, I've felt it before. Eh-oh!

It's Cellsie! I feel intensely pleased with the world, and can't help patting my tummy in reply.

People are still trying to get us to find out if it's a girl or boy. An article in the local paper asks, 'Does discovering your unborn baby's sex spoil the surprise or does it allow for sensible planning?'. It says three-quarters of English women want to know the sex – but I'm sure it has to do with thinking of the baby more as a person, so you'll take any info you can get. If the doctor could tell whether or not the kid was going to have a natural talent at footy, you'd probably want to know that too – partly because there are so many unknowns and undercurrent worries that any hard and fast information can seem comforting.

Only a small minority of Australian women want to know the sex of their first baby. People are more likely to find out the sex of babies when they have already had a child or children. I suppose that's the one thing they are not pre-warned about.

I squeeze into some old stretch pants and wear them down the street. And I do mean stretch pants. They are so thin that the tight grey pantery shows my bum crack (a fact helpfully imparted by Des when we are two blocks from home) and threatens to simply twang off my body at any moment. A rather narrow squeak for me, if I can use the words 'me' and 'narrow' in the same sentence.

info

childbirth education classes

where?

Ask your midwife or obstetrician for their recommendation regarding childbirth education classes. Book a prenatal class as early as possible in your pregnancy to make sure you get a timeslot that suits you. Classes are held at hospitals, through prenatal clinics or birth centres, and also offered by private childbirth educators, who are usually midwives or physiotherapists.

← man watching birth video

why?

The aim is to prepare you and your partner or labour support person psychologically and practically for labour and delivery. Well, as prepared as you can be if you've never done it before. And these classes are full of first-time parents. (Already-parents are probably at home having a lie-down.) The classes often have a couple of weeks dedicated to stuff that happens after the child is born – breastfeeding, baby care and safety for L-plate parents.

what?

Also known as prenatal classes, antenatal classes and the horror video club, they're usually five to eight weekly sessions in the third trimester of pregnancy. Ask about the style of the class before you book in. Some are run as a series of lectures; others may have an open structure, allowing for discussion. Some offer hands-on sessions for practising breathing and massage techniques; others may encourage the sharing of feelings about pregnancy and childbirth, or involve lying around on lumpy, brown corduroy beanbags discussing your innermost feelings with total strangers. Some prenatal classes focus specifically on fitness or yoga during pregnancy and after delivery and may be found through hospital prenatal clinics, local sports or recreation centres, the Australian Physiotherapy Association, your local baby health centre, or a nearby yoga centre.

Ideally the person running the class will impartially present the pros and cons on issues such as pain relief, without saying things like, 'Anyone who has an epidural is a big girlie wussbag', or 'Anyone who doesn't have an epidural is a mad feral hippie.'

If the teacher seems to be going in a direction you don't like, try another teacher. Good classes should ensure you develop realistic expectations about what labour will be like, providing a balance between childbirth as a joyful, amazing event and the things that might go wrong or go against your picture of the ideal birth. Ask lots of questions: classes are there to give you the information *you* want.

Typical classes will provide information on how to recognise the onset of labour: when to come to the hospital or birth centre, or call in the homebirth troops; pain relief; and body positions that might help during labour. They almost always show videos of childbirth; provide a tour of a birth centre or labour ward; and include advice on prenatal and postnatal exercise, caesarean section, induced labour, the partner's or labour support person's role, breastfeeding, unsettled babies, how to reduce the risk of sudden infant death syndrome, and how to recognise postnatal depression.

who?

You'll find that the pregnancy and childbirth books often talk about the various schools of childbirth theory, such as Sheila Kitzinger's psychosexual approach to childbirth (a progression from earlier theorists such as Dick-Read and Lamaze), or Janet Balaskas's active-birth model. In practice, prenatal classes tend to provide a combo of the most helpful elements from various schools of thought as they relate to the experience and philosophy of the birth centre or hospital maternity department.

You can go to birth classes on your own, but it makes far more sense to go with your birth support person. This makes it less likely that they'll be asking questions during the real thing such as 'What happens now?' and 'Can I have some of those drugs?'.

your record

Spend a day with a parent and small baby.
When you've had a good lie down, record your
overwhelming impressions.

Which room or corner will be converted to a nursery?
How do you plan to decorate it?

what's going on

The foetus is about due to start putting pressure on your ribs and also on your digestive system. You could get pains down the sides of your tummy from now on as the uterus stretches.

The foetus looks pretty much like a baby at birth. It will definitely have developed its own sleeping patterns: usually awake when you're asleep and vice versa as your movements soothe it to sleep. (This is why babies can be rocked to sleep once they come out.) The foetus may be startled by loud music and start bashing you up when it hears a certain tune. Or maybe that's just dancing. This is a good time to play it music, talk to it and see if you get a reaction.

Weight: about 720 grams.

WEEK 25

lunge
lunge

TRYING to
CATCH
POSSetS

DiARy I keep forgetting where I am in the middle of
sentences: it reminds me of all those times
recovering from endometriosis operations, when
the general anaesthetic seemed to temporarily
wipe out most of my vocabulary. I have covered the house with a
confetti of Post-it notes, and I keep paper and pencil AND a tape
recorder next to the bed at night. So far I have written down really
helpful stuff like 'Remember the thing', and mumbled thoroughly
unintelligible words into the tape recorder, then dropped it and
stood on it on the way to the loo for the nine-hundredth time.

Des inquires whether, now that I'm pregnant, I intend to eat
his head. Turns out he has been watching a wonders-of-nature
program on the telly about black widow spiders. I point out loftily
that the preying mantis eats the head – the black widow eats the
whole lot. Strangely, he doesn't look soothed by the knowledge
that I have this detailed information.

A weirdy man on the bus tries to look up my skirt. I feel like
saying, 'Careful. You might meet someone coming the other way!'
I've heard about men who are affected in an unseemly way by
pregnancy, and here is the proof.

It takes some effort to think about what will happen after the
baby arrives as I can't seem to stretch my mind past the concept of
childbirth, but it must be done. Oh my God. It's not just that I'm
pregnant; there's actually going to be another person along any
minute, and they haven't even got their own room.

Actually I don't really mind if the baby spends the first few
weeks sleeping in a cardboard box, but it would probably upset
Aunty Peg. We have completely run out of money, but these are
some of the things the books seem to think we should be
purchasing:

✳ a gigantic industrial-strength washing machine

✳ a fridge with a freezer big enough to store frozen casseroles for
the weeks after the birth. The fridge we have is a legacy of the old
shared-house days. That freezer is a lot more used to ever-emptying
bottles of vodka and tubs of ice-cream with a spoon frozen into
them. Right now the fridge freezer has only enough room for four

sausages, a chicken Maryland and eight Frosty Fruits. Unless it has over-frosted again, and the door has frozen shut. We just *can't* have a baby, we haven't got the right fridge

✳ a crib. I just refuse to buy something called a crib, though I might call some friends in the Northern Territory and get them to send me a woven pandanus basket made by a nice Yolngu lady in Arnhem Land. I quite like the idea of having a baby in a basket

✳ 'muslin squares for catching possets'. Oh for God's sake. I don't intend to go hunting. If possets are required, I'll just buy them at the market. (Later it turns out that this means a 'piece of cloth to put over your shoulder that the baby can vomit onto'. Why don't they just say so?)

✳ 56,000 nappies

✳ a 'nursery', a word which previously had connotations only of seedlings – will need to strip boyfriend of personal space, manhood and shedlike environment by taking over his private room to achieve this

✳ a 'bonnet'. I presume they mean hat. Or is it compulsory to get something with bobbles on it?

✳ a nursery floor covering, as in 'The floor covering of the nursery should be linoleum or cork tiles'. Ours is carpet. Maybe we could just throw a tarpaulin down for the first couple of years

✳ a dimmer switch, 'installed for night feeds'. Have a dimmer switch installed?! How much money do these books assume you have? What, now I have to sleep with an electrician? Give me a break. Might as well say, 'Install a surround sound system with wall-sized video screen to simulate the sound and light show of the womb'. We'll make do with an old lamp, thank you. Or I could park the cot near a window that lets in street light. Or gaffer tape a bicycle lamp to my head

✳ a small sink with running water – some pregnancy books actually suggest you install one in the corner of the room. Oh and perhaps a turret might be nice.

info

baby clothes

The exact quantity of clothing you'll need will depend on things such as whether you have a very vomity baby, how often you will be washing, and whether you use cloth or disposable nappies (cloth nappies tend to create more clothes washing because their 'containment' is not as efficient as that of disposables).

It's not a bad idea to get your baby's clothes before you get too big to go charging around shops and bargain outlets. Here's what you'll need.

nappies

A newborn baby needs about sixty nappy changes a week on average. Later you use fewer nappies, but more goes into them. (That was delicately put, wasn't it?)

Cloth Depending on your washing plans, you need about thirty-six nappies. Cotton cloth nappies are usually used for tiny babies, and (more absorbent) towelling ones after a few weeks or months. When the baby first arrives, you protect each nappy with a plastic snib, which is just a shaped plastic sheet with ties. You can get these from chemists or baby shops in packs of eight or ten. You

can just throw the dirty ones in the nappy bucket or washing machine, rinse, and shake off the water afterwards. Later you'll need six to eight pairs of pilchers, the over-the-nappy-pants. The best sort come with Velcro fasteners, which are much easier to change than pull-ons or ones needing nappy pins or snappy fasteners. Get ones with extra protection at the side against leaking.

Nappy wash services will deliver clean nappies and take away dirty ones, however many you need. Order the delivery to arrive the day before you are due home from hospital, to ensure there is no chance of being caught without nappies if the company doesn't do your suburb on the day you get home, or your area is scheduled for afternoon delivery.

Disposables If you can, buy a more expensive, big-name brand in newborn-baby size, which despite the cost will be good value for money because they are much more efficient. Even if you plan to use only disposables, buy ten to twelve cloth nappies: perfect for over-the-shoulder protection after feeds and for general mopping up. You'll also be confronted with an occasional bottom so comprehensively pooey that cotton wool balls will get you nowhere. When this happens, dip a clean cloth nappy in warm water, squeeze out the excess and go in valiantly. Always use a cloth nappy to cover the change mat, which is otherwise a bit too plasticky and cold to put a baby on.

The worst nappy choice is cheap disposables, which are hopeless.

basic newborn-baby wardrobe

◉ 6 singlets

◉ 6 cotton-jersey envelope-neck nighties

◉ 6–8 front-opening grow-suits

◉ 2–3 pairs of cotton socks, or stretchy, pull-on, machine-washable bootees – forget ribbons, forget handknits except for show, and you won't need socks at all if the weather is very hot, or if you plan to use full-length grow-suits (which have 'feet' in them) all the time

⑥ 8 bunny-rugs (aka cuddlies), which are easily washed flannelette squares that are used for wrapping a baby up – they can also be tucked around the baby in a cot or pram, and laid on a floor or table as a nappy change surface

⑥ bibs – you don't need these straight away, and the number will depend on whether your baby vomits a lot, possets (does small vomits) or dribbles a lot. To be honest, all babies dribble a lot. Get big towelling bibs, not plastic-backed, which are stiff and no good for wiping faces. Velcro-fastened bibs are much better than ribbon-tied ones or ones you have to pull over a baby's head. You'll need about eight bibs once the baby starts eating solid foods (and maybe a shovel and nine bath towels). For breast-feeding, people usually just have a cloth nappy or a muslin square handy to mop up possets.

summer or tropical baby

The baby may need grow-suits with short sleeves and legs, or may be more comfy with short-sleeved cotton nighties during the day, or even a singlet and nappy as long as the insects are kept away.

A summer or tropical baby won't need as many bunny-rugs as listed, but a couple won't go astray for cool nights. Substitute a few soft, absorbent muslin or gauze squares (you can make these yourself or try proper surgical quality ones from baby shops, which are quite expensive).

winter baby

The baby will need three to four outer items: cardigans or jackets are easiest to change. If you use jumpers or windcheaters, make sure they have two buttons at the neck or are very stretchy. Fabrics such as velour, thick cotton jersey, or thermal materials are more practical than woollen knits, which are harder to wash and dry and can be itchy.

hints from mothers

⊚ Buy natural fabrics.

⊚ All clothes you get should be able to be soaked, machine washed and tumble dried, if you use a dryer.

⊚ Get long singlets, even if they seem too long – the shorter ones end up looking like crop-tops. Good singlets have really generous neck and arm holes so that you can get them on your baby quickly and easily.

⊚ Grow-suits (also called all-in-ones or jumpsuits) are so much easier to change if they have press-studs that run from the neck to the crotch and right down the inside of both legs of the suit. DO NOT BUY A SINGLE THING THAT BUTTONS DOWN THE BACK OR LACKS CROTCH FASTENERS. Remember, you need to go up a size in grow-suits as soon as they fit snugly, or they will start to hurt your baby's feet and stop legs stretching out properly.

⊚ If you buy those headbands with a bow on them for a girl baby your child will look like a demented Easter egg in a nappy.

⊚ A small baby doesn't need shoes except for show. Warm, snug socks are fine – it's not going hiking any time soon.

⊚ A surprising number of bonnets have long cords on them. Don't buy them – they're too dangerous. In fact, don't buy anything with cords or flappy tassels or long strips of loose material – they are all strangulation risks.

⊚ A tiny baby hates being dressed and undressed. Choose soft, stretchy cotton or cotton-blend clothes. To help make changes quicker and less traumatic, get envelope-neck nighties, not grow-suits, for a newborn baby: easy to get over the head, and handy access to the nappy at the other end.

⊚ Go to bargain places, but ring first to see which brands they have, and why they are seconds. Small marks that will wash out are fine, but clothes likely to spontaneously combust are not.

⊚ Borrow as much as you can. If it has to be returned, keep a list! Don't ask people to lend you baby clothes – they will offer if they want to. Sometimes they are keeping their baby clothes in case they decide to have another one, and it's all too psychologically confronting to give away their supplies.

⊚ Buy or borrow the minimum number of tiny-sized clothes: they don't get worn for very long and some big babies can skip size 000 and go straight into 00s, the size for 3–6-month-olds.

⊚ Babies grow out of things so quickly, you could well match up with someone with a slightly bigger baby and someone with a slightly smaller baby to become part of a clothes chain.

⊚ If you don't have friends with spare baby clothes available to borrow, and you're on a budget, go for recycled clothes (see the Yellow Pages). Launder everything well, particularly if it has been stored in mothballs (napthaline) or camphor, both of which are poisonous, or in drycleaning bags, which retain fumes.

⊚ Cheaper chain stores can have very good babies' and children's wear departments: sometimes the best clothes are the cheapest because they're not fiddly and made for show. At this early stage they won't need to last unless you're passing them down the line to other children. Don't overbuy, even though the clothes are so cute; your baby will grow quickly.

⊚ Op shops are good sources of knits. If need be, take someone with you who knows the difference between real wool and acrylic and buy the real wool, which is less allergy-causing and less flammable.

your record

What clothes have you bought your baby?

What music have you played the baby, and which
songs prompted a kicking reaction?

WE

YOUR BABY is SHOWING SIGNS of iNTELLigENCE

what's going on Get lots of rest and

exercise. (You should also get gifts consisting of large gems,

but this is unlikely.) If you haven't worked it out already, stop

wearing shoes with heels, and don't do any climbing or

hurling yourself about: remember your centre of gravity has

changed and you need to protect your tummy. You will be

steadily gaining weight.

Average approximate foetus length this week from head to bum

| cm | 1 | 2 | 3 | 4 | 5 | 6 | 7 | 8 | 9 | 10 | 11 | 12 | 13 |

EK 26

This coming month the foetus will really spend time putting on more fat and muscle. Each week its chances of survival outside the uterus increase as it makes more surfactant for the lungs. According to one pregnancy expert, this week in the uterus your baby 'is showing signs of sensitivity, awareness and intelligence'. So if you put a little calculator in there your foetus could probably estimate the Gross National Product of Botswana. It can detect light even through its still-closed eyelids, smell (sadly for the foetus the only thing on offer is the amniotic fluid, which smells like a swamp), as well as hear, and possibly play the slide guitar. The baby will recognise other voices from now on: friends, Daddy, aunties and Dusty Springfield singing 'Son of a Preacher Man'. Weight: about 820 grams.

| 16 | 17 | 18 | 19 | 20 | 21 | 22 | 23 | 24 | 25 | 26 | 27 | 28 | 29 |

Diary

Are the leg cramps causing insomnia, or can I feel the leg cramps because I'm awake in the middle of the night? What a fascinating philosophical question. Beck says there are two things that might be causing sore calves: blood pooling in the veins, or lack of calcium or magnesium – in my case probably magnesium as I am taking enough calcium to turn into a tusk. For the itchy, runny nose and sneezing, she suggests a special garlic-and-horseradish dose.

'What about this gigantic tummy?'

'That will settle down in a few weeks.'

My tummy is now not just a big ball out the front, but a bulge all around the sides, the supporting tissue wrapping quite tightly, like wide bandages under the skin. Not quite like love handles – too curvy to really get a grip on.

Did I mention shocking heartburn and indigestion?

Pregnancy is just an absurd strain on the body, and we don't expect that any more. We expect there to be a pill or an exercise or a mantra or a caring discussion that will alleviate 'discomfort' – and 'pain'. Nup. It's just a pure and simple pain in the arse (and the rest) for a few months. I'm sorry, but I'm not finding this a sublimely spiritual experience. It's a deeply PHYSICAL experience.

The feeling of a baby moving must be different for everybody. Some books say it feels like wind, or feathers, or gentle patting. Sometimes I think it feels like someone's twanging a ligament as they might test out a harp string; sometimes it's like a bit of inside bongo work – all these feelings still all very low down in my tummy. Although the bump seems to start under the bozoom, the top of the uterus is actually just at navel level. All the stuff above is displaced bits making way for the uterus.

This morning's paper reports that a computer-driven baby doll is being used to help teenagers realise how much work a baby is. The baby doll is taken home from school over a weekend, and is programmed to cry constantly or several times, day and night. A special sound indicates how often the nappy must be changed, and the student must decide how often the baby needs to be fed. One student who had the baby doll for the weekend said, 'It really put me off having kids.' You should try pregnancy, love.

What an incredibly raunchy life it is: so far this week I've had half a glass of red wine, nine Frosty Fruits and a Magnum, some calcium tablets, and I'm about to get my daffodils in. AND WHAT'S MORE I am becoming a stately pregnant lady and am now so considerably fattened up that that THING has happened. That THING where your thighs rub together up the top. If I wore corduroy trousers while I was walking, I'd sound like a sword fight.

So it seems a good time to check out Lisa Curry Kenny's pregnancy work-out video, which starts with some dreary footage of Lisa going off to the Commonwealth Games in New Zealand years ago; for which, of course, as she was going to be pitted against the best the Welsh had to offer, a special song was written.

What being a champion swimmer has to do with motherhood is beyond me. And the concept of 'Supermum' is a bit of a crock, isn't it? Do people get Uncle Toby's sponsorship for going without an epidural injection during childbirth? Since when do they hand out bronze medals for cervix dilation?

Next we are subjected to a gang of pregnant Queensland women, including the Supermum, dressed in very unattractive leotard arrangements doing a variety of exercises, including walking on the spot and ranging up to some rather suggestive hula-hoop-type movements. I have no idea what these exercises feel like because I am exercising my right to lie on the couch and eat another three Frosty Fruits.

So I move on to Shirley MacLaine's video, which sounds more spiritual than physical: the one in which Shirley uses a naked shop dummy with no arms and legs to explain where your chakras are. There is a lot of talk about innate spiritual reality and body fluids as they relate to creativity and the orange chakra resonating to the note D.

Shirley sits or stands around in a pink tracksuit and pink socks, and for a spiritual person she is really quite bossy and snippy. There is a lot of tinkly-dangly keyboard music. After some great kaleidoscopy patterns Shirley says: 'Question your spiritual nature. Who are you? And focus on what you very much want to happen.'

Shirl, I'd very much like you to explode. Shut up and have a Frosty Fruit.

There must be an easier way to relieve stress, so I stay on the couch for another day and check out *Nexus* magazine, which, sadly, turns out to be the organ of choice for people who see conspiracies in everything and an alien in every letterbox. This issue, for example, contains stories explaining how pet food is itself made from dogs and cats, and how the Cold War was a cruel hoax because the US had given Russia the bomb plans; and book reviews of *NASA, Nazis and JFK* and – hello, I think we've stumbled onto a mysterious connection here – *The Great Book of Hemp*. There are, however, some very impressive ads, including one for a fabulously scientific device called a Zapper, which 'frees your body from viruses, bacteria and parasites in seven minutes'! Zappers are apparently inspired by suggestions made in a book called *The Cure for All Diseases*, which as you can imagine is a bit of a medical breakthrough. I'm surprised we haven't heard more about author Hulda Regher Clark PhD ND.

That is not all, however. *Nexus* magazine also advertises exclusive products, including Kirlian photography cameras, which represent the energy levels of the body in a visual form, and aura cameras. The only further info is that the process is named after Semyon Kirlyon and his wife Valentina, who live in a small town in the Ukraine. Which is enough to make anybody send money.

The same company will deliver to your door some White Gold Powder: 'This is a unique white powder said to come directly from gold – something which alchemists have attempted to produce for centuries. Take just one-eighth of a teaspoon under the tongue twice daily.' BUT IT DOESN'T SAY WHY.

Other lovely gift and hobby ideas include building an underground library, getting a second passport, how to channel your higher self (I've never liked my higher self – she's a stuck-up cow), crapping on about guardian angels and/or interdimensional human beings, the wonders of urine treatment (I might just go for the Disprin actually), dream control – many of these, by the way, available from a post office box in Bermagui – fermented living food, herbal teaology (I looked in vain for Have-a-Good-Lie-Downology), and reversing the ageing process. Possibly by dying. That's enough exploring of my spiritual side during pregnancy, thank you. I'd rather have leg cramps.

info

baby equipment

You're about to enter the world of safety warnings – try to keep in mind that most babies are robust little critters, but they still need to be protected. All the baby-wrangling gear listed below needs to be safe and the best reference is the Australian Consumers' Association's *Choice Guide to Baby Products*. Note that many shop assistants and even some manufacturers claim certain products are 'approved by SIDS and Kids'. This is hardly ever true as that organisation rarely recommends for or against products. Always check.

If you're going to do a lot of this shopping on foot, do it now while you still feel energetic. The major items can be bought or hired from specialist baby shops. Smaller stuff can be bought at supermarkets or chemists. You can get second-hand baby equipment through trading papers, recycle shops, friends, and notices on baby health centre pin-boards. Replace any worn straps and any Velcro: there's an unofficial motto in the baby world, 'One baby, one lot of Velcro'.

baby restraint for the car

Baby restraints are compulsory for transporting a baby in a car. A 'baby restraint' is a specially designed seat, or more old-fashioned 'capsule', attached by straps to an anchor point (which must be fitted to an older car – new ones have them) and further secured by a seatbelt. You're legally required to buy a restraint that complies with the Australian Standard. *Choice* rates some as better than others. It also provides information about which restraints are suitable for which car types. Get installation of a restraint checked for safety by a local authorised fitting station. (You can find these through your local council or baby health centre.)

Don't buy a second-hand one unless it's in very good condition and you know its age and history. Ask your local council about hiring one if you don't want to buy or can't afford to buy a new one. (Replace any Velcro.)

Station wagons will need an extension strap to reach the anchor point, and a cargo barrier to stop flying shopping or dogs injuring the baby if you have to slam on the brakes. A relatively recent warning: don't leave a baby sleeping unattended in a baby restraint you may have brought in from the car. Their little head can slump forward and their airway can get blocked. Most babies will rouse themselves; a few won't be able to.

baby's bed

Whether you choose a bassinet, cradle, basket or cot for your baby's first weeks, it should meet the Australian Standard. This is no time to skimp or save money: peace of mind means a safe baby and a better sleep for you. Whatever you choose will need a firm, well-fitting mattress, two mattress protectors made of waterproof-backed fabric, and at least three sheets. You can buy fitted baby sheets of towelling or flannelette (it's not necessary to buy the sheets made of fine linen with ittle wuvvly la la duckies embroidered on them, which cost a bomb and would be covered in green liquid poo as soon as look at them); or you can cut up adult bed sheets. Bunny-rugs or pillowcases can also be used for cradle sheets. Two or three cotton cellular blankets that can be firmly tucked in are safer and easier to wash than a doona, which can cut off the air supply and smother a baby. Pillows and cot bumpers are also dangerous.

Bassinets, cradles and baskets are only for young babies, so you need to ask yourself if you really need one, since your baby will be going into a cot within a few months anyway. Before you choose a baby basket (also known as a Moses basket), you need to consider whether you will want to leave your baby safely unattended in one. It's not easy to find a basket with a firm, tight-fitting mattress. And if you have it on the floor a lot, will you do your back lifting it and the baby?

An alternative bed for a newborn baby is the sprung hammock

on a frame that hospitals use for premature babies or soothing crying ones. You can hire them for the first few months from baby-gear places – if your baby wakes up and fusses around, the movement will cause the hammock to rock, soothing the baby automatically. The frame is light enough to be carried from room to room (without the baby in it).

Cradles too are soothing; but the soothing motion can be replicated by gently patting your baby in a cot, or rolling the baby in a pram back and forth over an arm's length. (Don't leave the baby unattended in a pram.)

Bassinets, baskets and cradles are cosier for the first few months than a cot, even though they're not strictly necessary. A well-swaddled newborn baby can be comfortable in a cot, and a slightly older baby can be 'dressed' in a quilted-cotton sleeping-bag with arms (from babies' wear outlets), especially if you want to avoid the danger of sheets, blankets or a doona smothering the baby. Cots can be made up at the bottom end, so there is no danger of the baby wriggling under the blankets (new babies tend to wriggle in the direction away from their feet).

Many cot designs on the market are potentially dangerous. Babies can be trapped, or injured on sharp protrusions or get stuck down between the mattress and the side of the cot. A mattress should be firm and fit snugly, with no more than a 2.5-centimetre gap between it and the cot on all sides. Other important factors include the spacing of bars, the security of a drop side, the efficiency of wheel brakes, what the cot is made of and painted with, and the position of the mattress relative to the height of the sides. Make sure you get the latest information on the Australian Standard for cot safety before you buy.

pram or pramette

Technically a pram is the huge, old-fashioned type, with gigantic wheels, that a Mary-Poppins-style English nanny would push around with the sixty-seventh Earl of Whatever inside. Pramettes are the newer, lighter designs that can be converted into a stroller, but no one except shop assistants ever calls them a pramette.

They're all prams to us. Again, lots of prams on the market are not considered safe. As well as safety, you'll need to consider cost, durability and adaptability.

Do you need all-terrain wheels? If you live in a cold climate, make sure there are no open parts on the side through which the wind can blow, and that the pram has a cover. If you don't go jogging or hiking you probably don't need the flash-looking three-wheeler. Is the pram light and easy to fold if you are going to put it in the car or on a bus a lot? (Don't take the manufacturer's or sales assistant's word for it – fold it up and down yourself a few times in the shop.) Do you want it to convert to a stroller or will you buy one later, or do you have one lined up from a friend?

Is the pram comfortable for you and your partner to push? Is the handle height right, or adjustable? Can you walk freely or do your feet bump into the undercarriage? Make sure it has a five-point harness for the baby, good brakes and a shelf or basket underneath large enough to hold your baby bag or shopping.

It's not safe to leave a baby sleeping in a pram or a toddler sleeping slumped in a stroller unsupervised for even a few minutes.

light for night-time feeding

Either a dimmer setting for the main light in the baby's room or a small, low-wattage lamp, which provides just enough light for you to change and feed by, is useful. (Here's one theory about why nipples and areolae go darker after a pregnancy: small babies see contrasts rather than colours, and can more easily spot the feeding station in a bad light.) A dim light helps to say to a baby, 'It's still night-time. Have a quiet feed, no chatting, do the business and back to sleep.'

Recent US research indicates there may be an association between shortsightedness and a light left on in a baby's room all night in the first two years of life. If you need a night light, keep it very dim and indirect.

change table

You will be changing gerzillions of nappies, so it makes sense to do it as comfortably as possible. If you can't afford a change table, improvise by buying a plastic-covered, hard foam change mat with built-up sides and putting it on a hip- or waist-height table or dresser. Even if you have a change table, one of these is useful to throw in the car when you're travelling or out. If you can afford a flash change table, go for a solid timber one with lockable wheels – don't buy the flimsy wire ones. Timber ones usually have a few shelves underneath, which are very handy for nappies, a change of baby clothes and bunny-rugs. Everything you need to change a nappy must be placed within arm's length of the change table beforehand because you can't take your hand off a baby on a change table.

bath venue

Early on it is so much easier to wash a baby in a clean laundry trough, kitchen sink or bathroom basin (being careful of fixed spouts) than lugging a heavy, full plastic bath around. But if you do need a separate bath, consider buying a plastic laundry bowl or storage tub, which can be re-used.

You'll also need two or three soft bath towels. These are great for wrapping a baby in after a bath, but for drying sensitive newborn-baby creases and crannies you can also use a muslin square, clean flannel nappy or bunny-rug. You can buy towels with a hood to keep baby's head warm.

For toiletries, buy a baby bath liquid or soap alternative, or an unscented bath oil; blunt-ended nail scissors; a nappy change lotion; cotton balls, nappy wipes or wash cloths and a water container; and a barrier cream such as zinc and castor oil cream or other nappy rash cream. Ask around to find out what products people recommend, then buy small sizes to test on your baby.

feeding gear

You'll need nursing bras and nursing bra pads for when you breastfeed. The pads, which soak up any leaking milk before it hits your clothes, can be bought as paper-based disposables or fabric washables. Have some disposables at least in your handbag for emergencies.

A breast pump is handy for expressing milk if you're ready for a night off; your breasts are painfully full; or you need to go to work. Electric ones are better than hand pumps for expressing often; say, for going to work. You can buy or hire from pharmacies and lactation consultants. If you're planning to leave the occasional expressed breast milk feed, you'll also need one or two bottles and teats, a sterilising unit (or you can just boil things) and bottle- and teat-cleaning brushes. You can freeze portions of breast milk in special plastic bags available in pharmacies.

For bottle-feeding, you'll need six to eight bottles and teats, bottle- and teat-cleaning brushes, formula, perhaps a measuring jug (although most bottles have measurements on them these days), a sterilising unit and an insulated bottle-carrier. Bottles are supposed to be always kept very cold and then warmed just before use.

bottom re-upholstering accoutrements

Two nappy buckets with a lid are essential if you're washing your own nappies. But everyone needs one because any clothes and bedding that come into contact with poo will need to go in a bucket of water and sterilising soaking powder before machine washing. Sterilising agents have a use-by date, so check this if you are using leftover product from the last baby or have been given a friend's leftovers.

even more stuff

You'll probably find the following items useful:

◉ a baby bag – any big bag that has a shoulder-strap handle will do, but some are specially designed to fold out like a portable change table. (For details of what goes in it, check out the info in 'Week 43')

◉ a baby-monitor – like a one-way walkie-talkie set, this is helpful if the nursery is out of earshot

◉ a sheepskin (also called lambswool) or two – some people like to have these under the cot sheet, or thrown on the floor or placed in the pram for the baby to lie on. They need to be washed regularly, otherwise they can harbour gerzillions of dust mites, but can be machine washed and tumble dried

☻ one or two quilted or flannelette baby sleeping-bags – these washable, zip-up bags are very cosy in a big cot or a pram in cold weather, but make sure you remove any dangly lace, ribbon or drawstrings

☻ a pouch or sling – great for comforting a fretty or crying baby while getting on with whatever else you need to do. Wearing a pouch or sling is a good way to have walks or go shopping when the baby is little, though it can be hard on the back when the baby starts to stack on weight. A baby should only spend 1 or 2 hours in it at a time. Try it on before you buy it: look for well-padded shoulder straps, sturdy fabric, detachable dribble bibs, a head support and secure and easy-to-use clasps. Babies outgrow slings by 5 or 6 months.

☻ a safe heater – you can dry clothes in front of it if you live somewhere wet and cold. Compare the safety features of heaters on the market before you buy.

A few months further down the track you will need a high-chair, and may also want to buy a mobile, a playpen, a fold-up pusher, a baby jumper, a backpack, a portable cot, and a large aircraft carrier to put them all in.

more info on safe baby equipment

Choice Guide to Baby Products by the Australian Consumers' Association, 1999.
You can order this excellent, regularly revised and updated guide to safe baby equipment from the association itself or look for it in your local bookshop.

See also Safety in 'Help'.

THE GREAT DUMMY DEBATE

You'll find most of the baby books sternly frown on using a dummy, especially after the baby is 3 months old, but mother and baby sleep clinics often use them. Dummies aren't supposed to be used automatically as soon as a baby cries. But if a baby is fed, clean and burped and yet has got itself into a hideous, sobbing, can't-remember-why-I'm-crying-but-I'm-hysterical-now-and-can't-stop-yelling state, a dummy is heavenly. Take no notice of what the books say; the authors aren't there to hold the baby when you're going nuts. Wait and see if your baby is like this before buying a dummy.

If you do decide to use one, here's the huge drawback nobody tells you about. The baby may become 'addicted' to it, and if so there'll be a period when the dummy will actually make the baby cry more because when a dummy falls out the only way a young baby can get it back in is to cry for you to come and put it in – several times a night. These weeks can be just not worth it, and a good time to wean the baby off the dummy. Eventually, some time between 5 and 10 months, a baby is able to replace a dummy on its own, and so the 'addiction' will continue.

Make sure you get the right-sized one that meets the Australian Standard. Replace it every few weeks, and throw it out if it looks the worse for wear with wobbly or torn bits. You'll need at least two or three to rotate them through the sterilising process once your baby works out how to spit the dummy – and then to cry for it after it's hit the floor.

your record

What baby equipment have you bought?

What have you borrowed, and from whom?

List any heirlooms or toys being passed down for your baby.

What are you buying for your child to pass down to their child?

what's going on

Hurrah, you're in the third trimester. Hire a brass band: bah de bah, bah de bah. If people don't stand up for you on public transport, say 'Excuse me, I'm pregnant. Could I sit down?'. About twelve people will rise from their seats as if given 140 volts up the fundament. Your moles may be getting bigger and you may have small skin tags, especially under the arms and breasts. You need a lot more fluids from now until the birth. You can forget about moving gracefully. People will not be saying, 'Aren't you Audrey Hepburn?' You need to put your feet up when you can: at work, if possible on another chair – better still, make the boss massage your feet .

The foetus has grown so much it is running out of room, and it takes a little longer to manoeuvre about and turn upside down and sideways. Babies born now have a very good chance of surviving (they're called 'viable' in doctorspeak). The foetus has been practising breathing here and there, but from now on its breathing will become more rhythmic and constant. Folds and grooves appear on the surface of the brain, which is developing very quickly. (Of course

if the foetus is born early, all this developing will continue outside

the uterus, usually in a humidicrib with respirators and other

monitors attached.) Weight: about 920 grams.

Lordy

WEEK 27

THE MAJESTIC PROPORTIONS

DiARY

It's true, you can spend an entire week in a dressing-gown, although I accessorise it differently at work. I find when teamed with battery-operated earrings and a beehive people tend not to notice the dressing-gown. I have developed approximately sixteen billion skin tags and my moles are all getting bigger. I am looking like a currant bun, so instead of calling Cellsie Cellsie we have started to call it the Pikelet (a relative of the currant bun, how intensely hilarious).

Maybe I'm practising not getting much sleep because I wake up for an hour or so every night and lie there with vaguely aching legs, listening to the blood swishing in my ears or my heartbeat in the silence. It is very disconcerting. My blood sounds like languid wobble-board music and I don't really want to be reminded of Rolf Harris in the wee hours.

I have purchased a giant inflatable ball to sit on, which is supposed to be good for strengthening the back muscles. Des immediately lies on top of it and rolls head-first into a bookcase.

Jo rings to say she spent the first three weeks after her baby was born looking at him and feeling nothing, but now she adores him, and do I want some jumpsuits? Liz emails to say she looked at her baby for the first time and said, 'Now I have to put this weird screaming creature on my breast? What would I want to do that for?'. I'm grateful people are being so honest.

Des just found out he can get a year's unpaid paternity leave. I'm very relieved but kind of pissed off he didn't find out before. It would have saved me a lot of 'what if?' thinking time. I'm getting scared about how much has to be done before the baby is born. After 2 hours' sleepless panic in the middle of the night about coping with it all, I decide to drop another day at work: if I'm not fooling myself, I'm not going to fool anybody else. (Maybe I can get that on a letterhead.) Besides which, at the end of every day my feet smell like the world is ending – because they have swelled up to eggplant proportions all I can wear is my pair of Hush Puppies, with the elasticky bit cut.

Outrageously, Dr Herb has gone to Paris with his wife in some sort of ludicrous attempt at a private life. I spend bloody ages in the waiting room looking at pictures of thin people in magazines, then have to put up with another obstetrician, who while clearly competent and replete with all his marbles doesn't have the bedside manner of Herb, and indeed doesn't even help me to sit up after examining me. He tells me with a disapproving look that I have put on 14 kilos since the start of my pregnancy.

'Most people,' he says, 'have put on 8 to 10 by this stage.' Why he didn't just call me Mrs Blimpy I don't know.

I have a blood test after drinking a revolting sugar drink, which checks for glucose levels, anaemia and antibodies.

Afterwards I go to visit Beck to say, 'Help me, I'm Mrs Blimpy.'

She says, 'Bollocks!' (I do love a medical adviser who says 'bollocks'.) 'Some people put on 20 kilos when they're pregnant.'

However, we agree that if I can nourish the baby and not get fatter myself, this will be a lot easier to carry around. So I must take the special pregnancy multi-vitamin-calcium supplements. I must stop eating Magnums, and stop toasted muesli for breakfast. I must have porridge with some apple or half a banana in it.

'Can I have sultanas in it?' I whine piteously.

'You can have four,' she says.

I strike her.

Then I go out to dinner and have lemon tart with ice-cream. Oh well, fuck it.

info

safety

The only way to childproof a house is to never let a kid in it. But you can try to make it safer.

The older the baby gets, the more danger-ous the house gets. Baby books will tell you what tricks your baby is likely to be up to next. Remember that there's a wide age range for milestones: your baby could be an early roller; your toddler could be an early climber.

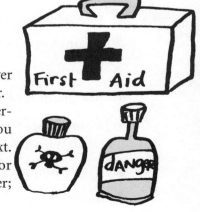

As said in last week's info, every baby-relevant item needs to be safe: cots, prams, car restraints, baby chairs, toys, change tables, clothes, dummies – the lot. Remember when you are preparing the house for small persons that the most common causes of death and injury in little kids include car and pedestrian accidents – often in their own driveway – drowning, suffocation, falling, burns, poisoning and electrical accidents.

You will need to organise:

⊚ a tamper-proof cabinet for any garden poisons and chemicals, and a first-aid kit placed higher than a child on a chair or the bench could reach

⊚ cupboards in which the following have been moved to a higher position – household poisons such as cleaning agents and detergents; medicines; alcohol; batteries; pesticides; mothballs and camphor; soaps and shampoos; cigarettes; matches and lighters; cosmetics and perfumes; essential oils; foods that could cause choking, such as peanuts and marshmallows; plastic bags (and go through wardrobes to get rid of drycleaning bags); glasses and other breakables; objects with sharp bits – babies and toddlers can be gymnastic and inquisitive. You can also get slide locks to 'lock' cupboards

⊚ an extinguisher for the kitchen and smoke alarms

⊚ electrical circuit breakers and power-point covers

⊚ no keys left in house cupboards or doors

⊚ a bathroom heater fitted high up on a wall

⊚ hairdryers kept away from water

⊚ fire guards for heaters and open fires

⊚ a hot-water service set to 50° Celsius (takes longer to burn the skin than the usual, hotter setting)

⊚ a stove hotplates guard

⊚ an out-of-reach kettle and iron

◎ electrical cords that are placed off the floor and out of reach – curled cords on kettles and irons are good

◎ topple-proof TV sets and screens

◎ stair and doorway barriers

◎ a nursery with a high shelf and a toy box with a lid

◎ a Standards Australia pool fence with a self-latching, self-locking gate at your place and the places of neighbours (if a neighbour won't co-operate report them to the council – pool fences are compulsory), relatives and friends – anyone who has a pool or pond. Your baby might walk before 12 months and crawl way before that. Always empty toddlers' wading pools and baths after use, and keep a lid on nappy buckets at all times. Babies can drown in a tiny amount of water.

other people

Never hesitate to ask people to smoke outside the house, stop drinking hot tea or coffee while nursing your baby, support the baby's head properly when holding, and not bounce the baby up and down after a feed. They'll probably be glad of the instruction: many non-baby-wrangling friends want some guidance.

Grandparents or older friends and relations may need a firmer hand. Practices from their own parenting days, such as ignoring a baby safety restraint in a car, are unsafe. Their homes will also need to be checked.

prevention

◎ Read the info on baby clothes in 'Week 25' and on baby equipment in 'Week 26' for safety hints.

◎ A nursery door lockable from the outside with a bolt (not a key, which could get lost) can prevent a toddler helpfully throwing toys or food in with the baby when the baby's asleep, or tossing the baby out of a cot like a toy.

◎ Always remove bibs before putting a baby to bed.

⊚ Never leave a small baby unattended with another small child or a dog. Never put a child, a dog and food together.

⊚ Sterilise anything that goes into your baby's mouth until at least 6 months old – okay, you don't have to boil your nipples.

⊚ Put cots, prams and baby chairs out of reach of any dangly curtain ties or blind cords and stoves, heaters, fires and power points.

⊚ Turn all saucepan handles towards the back of the stove.

⊚ When you are travelling or at someone else's place, you might need to bring safety stuff with you and be a bit more vigilant, particularly where there are other young children and dogs.

⊚ Don't leave a baby to feed unsupervised from a propped-up bottle.

⊚ Don't attach a dummy to a baby's clothes with a ribbon or string.

⊚ Don't leave a baby, even for a second, unsupervised on a change table.

⊚ Never leave a baby or young child in a bath, no matter how briefly.

emergencies

Keep a contact list near the phone or add emergency numbers to your direct-dial system. The numbers should cover the ambulance, local doctor and Poisons Information Centre. Babysitters should be told about it. You can do an infant and child mouth-to-mouth and CPR (cardiopulmonary resuscitation) course with the Red Cross or the St John Ambulance Service, or get an instructor to come to your playgroup.

Add a thermometer and baby Panadol to the family medicine cupboard and/or the baby bag. Ask your GP when you can use the Panadol.

more info on safety

Baby Love by Robin Barker (for details and full review see 'Week 43').

Gives a good room-by-room guide to looking at house safety.

The Australian Baby and Child Care Handbook by Carol Fallows (for details and full review see 'Week 43').

Has useful information on childproofing rooms and buying safe equipment.

The one-stop shop to find out what baby gear is safe is the **Choice Guide to Baby Products**, published by the Australian Consumers' Association. Failing that, make sure everything you buy complies with the current Australian Standard.

Children's hospitals are good resources when it comes to safety issues: some also sell safety products. Melbourne's Royal Children's Hospital **Safety and First Aid Book** includes, among other useful information, detailed checklists for safety in the house, outdoors and on the street, and safety hints for each age group. Or your nearest children's hospital may have their own list.

See the list of contacts under Safety in 'Help'.

what's going on For you, just more of the same, really.

Your baby may be hiccuping. It will usually decide to party while you are resting or asleep. Its eyes are partially opened – quite sensibly as who would want to open their eyes wide in a fetid old swamp of amniotic fluid? The baby is now covered all over with vernix, so it looks a bit like one of those long-distance swimmers smothered in gunk. Except babies have got more brains than to try to swim from Cuba to Florida. They just hang out in the uterus growing their bodies so their heads don't look too big. Weight: about 1 kilo.

WEEK 28

DiARY

My feet hurt to walk, and my tummy's really starting to pull forward, so of course it's time to go travelling again. I'm at Fashion Week in Sydney.

The usual lot get all the publicity, and if anyone mentions Collette Dinnigan to me again I shall have to have them killed. There's nothing wrong with a lacy wisp of froth and a scrinch of lace webbing between your headlights, but it's not like you can actually DO anything in it other than accept your best-supporting-actress-in-a-drama Logie award. As one does.

Planes always make my feet swell up, but now it seems to work on the whole body. My fluid retention after I get off the plane at midday is clearly visible to the naked eye. Have gone quite bullfroggy around the face, and the indent marks on the ankles where the socks finish are like trenches. Luckily Beck had suggested I pack some dandelion-leaf tea, which I make at my hotel in a coffee plunger I buy in the lobby shop. The tea tastes as well as looks like lawn clippings. I get so desperate, I make it up and plunge mid-afternoon instead of waiting until morning, and am weeing all night. It works, though.

People now have their routine down pat: 'When are you due?', followed by 'Do you know if it's a boy or a girl?', followed by 'Is it your first?'. I go to a very Fashion Weeky cocktail party (vodka icypoles instead of devils-on-horseback – but not for me) and meet the lead singer of Flummery, who asks 'Is it exciting?'. I think this a much better question and earbash him until his eyes glaze over and he staggers to the refreshment tent, supported by an elfin keyboards player from a visiting Canadian band called Prince Phillip's Undies.

It's becoming harder and harder to manoeuvre the body around, and I am sad to say that grunting while changing position is by no means unknown. I do it on the plane home and gross out the chemical weapons salesman sitting next to me. I find it very difficult to believe that Des would want to have sex with me, and he admits that he doesn't want to ask because (a) I seem so tired, and (b) my body seems rather preoccupied, but he does want to have sex with me because he loves me. This is the sort of answer people should win a lounge suite for on quiz shows.

We try having sex but it is really quite an absurd proposition. It is impossible to avoid the conclusion that there are three of us involved. Well, there are. I wish I could unstrap the Pikelet for a couple of hours.

I can now see cellulite on my thighs without having to pinch the skin together. Des says 'It's for a reason', and 'It's temporary', and 'It doesn't matter' (give the man another lounge suite, please), but if THIS is what size I am at six months pregnant, I am terrified to think of me at nine months. Especially the little matter of getting it OUT.

Sometimes the Pikelet kicks really hard and I get a shock. 'Sit down in front!' yells Des. And quite often I am forced to move because the baby is clearly going to make the position untenable by stretching against me somewhere uncomfortable. It's fascinating that so many women say they love to feel their baby move, but they never tell you that sometimes it's really horribly uncomfortable and sometimes it even hurts. Last night in the bath things got really freaky when my rounded tummy momentarily went up into a tentlike shape with a point. At any moment I thought Sigourney Weaver might appear in a singlet.

To add to the glamour of my relationship, apparently I am snoring like a demented tractor every night.

I have a marvellously glamorous moment in a restaurant debriefing the boss about Fashion Week. As I squeeze between tables on the way to the toilet, I attempt to keep my bump off a nearby table and instead sweep my arse along the table behind me in a majestic arc, taking the two menus and a good bit of the tablecloth with me. Talk about dignity.

info

third-trimester hassles

These three complaints can start earlier, but usually bug pregnant women the most in the last three months.

heartburn

What is it? Heartburn is that burning sensation you feel behind the breastbone, sometimes accompanied by the taste of small amounts of regurgitated food and stomach acid. It doesn't affect the baby.

Why does it happen? Because of the high levels of progesterone during pregnancy, which relaxes muscles, the muscular valve between the stomach and the oesophagus (the tube connecting stomach and mouth) relaxes, and so stomach acid flows up into the oesophagus and sometimes the mouth. It doesn't help that later in the pregnancy your uterus is encroaching on your tummy and squeezing it upwards.

What can you do?

⊚ Eat several small meals slowly, rather than wolfing three main ones.

⊚ Avoid spicy, highly seasoned, fried or fatty foods, chocolate, coffee, alcohol, carbonated drinks, spearmint and peppermint, and anything with lots of chemical additives.

⊚ Wear loose clothing around your tummy.

⊚ Don't fold yourself up on the couch because that squashes your tummy, and bend from the knees, not the waist, to pick things up.

⊚ If the heartburn is worse when you lie flat, try elevating your head by at least 15 centimetres with pillows, which will help to stop the yukky stuff flowing up into your mouth.

⊚ Try not to put on too much extra weight.

⊚ Don't smoke.

⊚ Try foods such as milk or yoghurt that help to neutralise the stomach acid.

⊚ If none of this helps, ask your doctor to recommend an antacid that is suitable for use during pregnancy. (Avoid preparations containing sodium or sodium bicarbonate.)

backache

Why does it happen? Progesterone and relaxin relax the ligaments and joints of the spine and around the pelvis. This jollies everything along for childbirth, but makes it hard to have good posture, especially when the weight of the baby puts pressure on your lower back and weakened tummy muscles, and pulls the spine forward.

Lower back and leg pain can be caused by the pressure of the enlarging uterus on the sciatic nerve. The pain may pass as the baby's position changes. If it is very severe, you may have to go to bed for an extended period (not as much fun as it sounds).

What can you do?

⊚ Avoid standing and sitting for long periods of time. When you are standing, tilt your pelvis forward so that your bum tucks under, and keep your shoulders back; when sitting, get yourself well back into the seat, and put your legs up on another chair if possible.

◉ Do some gentle stretching exercises recommended by your hospital maternity physiotherapist or yoga teacher experienced in pregnancy.

◉ The flatter your shoes, with good support, the better. This is no time for sparkly, aqua-go-green, platform thigh boots. Sadly.

◉ Avoid twisting movements.

◉ Bend from the knees when lifting things.

◉ Avoid gaining too much weight – hate that one.

For backache itself

◉ Have a massage.

◉ Relax in a warm bath or aim the shower spray at the painful area.

◉ Apply a warm (not hot) hot-water bottle or heat pack.

◉ If the pain is severe, ask your doctor to prescribe an analgesic safe for use during pregnancy.

◉ If the pain is particularly bad, ask your doctor to refer you to a fully qualified, experienced physiotherapist, osteopath or chiropractor specialising in backache during pregnancy.

swelling and fluid retention

What is it? Swelling, most noticeably of the fingers, legs, ankles and feet, also called oedema, occurs because the body retains more fluid during pregnancy. (Your face can also swell, due to the effects of natural oestrogen and cortisol, a steroid hormone, changing the distribution of fat in the body.)

Some fluid retention and swelling is perfectly normal and should cause no more than mild discomfort. However, if you feel that you are excessively puffy or if the oedema persists for more than 24 hours at a time, you should see your obstetrician. This can be normal, but it may be an early sign of pre-eclampsia (pregnancy-induced high blood pressure; see info in 'Week 31').

Why does it happen? Hormonal changes can prompt the kidneys to hang onto salt, leading to fluid retention. There is much more fluid in your body to maintain the level of amniotic fluid, and increase the water level in your blood to help the kidneys to get rid of waste.

Hot weather, standing or sitting for long periods of time and high blood pressure are the most common causes of mild oedema. It also occurs more commonly later in the day, as fluid pools in the ankles and feet – that's gravity for you. In the mornings you might see more puffiness in your eyelids and jawline. It is more likely if you're carrying a multiple pregnancy or excess weight.

What can you do?

⊚ Sit down and elevate your legs higher than 90 degrees; or, preferably, lie down – on your left side, or on your back supported by a cushion so that your back is tilted 10 degrees or more.

⊚ Wear comfortable shoes.

⊚ Avoid socks or stockings with elasticised tops.

⊚ If the oedema really bothers you, check out the range of support pantyhose (available in pregnancy fittings with extra tummy room) and knee-high socks – and remember to put these on in the morning, when the swelling is less.

⊚ Don't add salt to any food.

⊚ Drink plenty of water to flush the body of waste products. Drinking extra water won't increase fluid retention – it may even reduce it.

⊚ If your fingers swell, remember to take off any rings before they become uncomfortably tight.

more possible tests

gestational diabetes
A temporary form of diabetes: the body does not produce enough insulin to keep pace with the increased blood sugar caused by pregnancy. (Some pregnancy hormones act against insulin.) It's routinely screened, usually by a blood test, at most prenatal check-ups.

group B streptococcus (GBS)
You may be offered a test for this bacteria. Babies become really sick if they travel to the outside world down a vagina with GBS in it. A vaginal swab is usually routine in the third trimester, and if GBS is found you'll be prescribed antibiotics to clear it up.

anaemia
Your blood sample might also be checked for haemoglobin levels (indicating anaemia – insufficient iron).

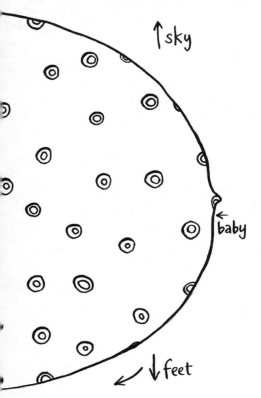

your record

Have you had: Heartburn?	What have you done to treat it?
Backache?	
Fluid retention?	

WEEK

Nesting

Average approximate baby length this week from head to bum

cm 1 2 3 4 5 6 7 8 9 10 11 12 13

29

what's going on You may be hard-pressed to find a comfy sleeping position. If you feel uncomfortable lying on your back, especially into late pregnancy, that's because the baby is pressing down on the main vein that pumps blood back to your heart. If it doesn't make you uncomfortable, sleeping on your back is fine. Most women who experience discomfort or faintness will automatically move position, even when they're asleep. (You shouldn't be examined by a dentist, or massaged, while flat on your back. Make sure there's a cushion under your right hip so you're slightly tilted to the left. Nothing makes a dentist flappier than a fainting pregnant woman.)

The baby is looking very babyesque at this point – plumper and rounder. The newborn-baby breathing rhythm is developing steadily; it's more regular, with fewer stops and starts. Weight: about 1.15 kilos.

16   17   18   19   20   21   22   23   24   25   26   27   28   29

DiARY

I think I've got interior design nesting rather than cleaning nesting. (Typical. Even when I'm nesting I don't want to do the dishes, I'd rather arrange some vases fairly artfully in the hallway. Tremendously useful skill around the house.) I am putting things in boxes and hiring large young men to come to the house while Des is at work to move furniture from room to room.

Maybe it's not just about making a nest, but about chucking out stuff from the past, stuff you don't need, and working out what you do want. That sounds a bit deep. Luckily I'm so scatterbrained my mind, having thought, immediately moves on . . . to . . . Not. Thinking. Or . . . what?

Random thoughts

Must find out whether the religious hospital I'm going into will have full facilities on their day of worship if I happen to have a day of screaming. The idea of less than full catering and no obstetrician does not appeal. Have been reading Gregory Fox's book about labour, *Your Baby and the Birth Experience*, which gives a great picture of what can happen.

Glamour check: I have discovered that pregnancy makes you sweat more – it's Mrs Fluid has come to visit. If you're not retaining it, you're leaking it – or sometimes both at once. Not to mention all that extra blood in there. I tried a strong antiperspirant, but it only blocked my pores and I felt like I was carrying a marble around in my armpit for a couple of days. I had to go without any and then went back to deodorant. I can remember at sixteen weeks when I skipped ahead in the books and thought, 'God, look at twenty-eight weeks.' It seemed so far away. But now I'm here, in a flash. Better take some photos while I'm looking pregnant.

Weeing a zillion times a night. Trying to remember to do pelvic-floor exercises. Too boring for words.

My walking shoes smell disgusting. I have sprayed them with a French perfume called Fracas.

Childbirth classes start this week. I don't want to go. For some reason it feels like having to go to Sunday School. I can't stand those things where a Lorraine at the front of the classroom asks us all to share our feelings. I've already done the physio classes, dammit. If I wanted to share my feelings with strangers I'd hire a billboard. I don't want to bond with the group. They're not going to be there when I have the child, or when it grows up. I don't care what they think or what they do, really. Perhaps I should just wear a name tag saying, 'Hi! I'm a Churlish Bitch'.

Our first childbirth class goes like this: a young, blonde Lorraine in a cuddly blue cashmere cardie and black leggings gives us all a sticky-label name tag as we walk in the door. We have to interview another couple (everyone is in a couple! – what's the world coming to?), and then introduce them to the class. 'Garry and Dianne are drug dealers. They conceived accidentally during a police raid and their obstetrician is Dr Feldman. Dianne intends to take at least a year off.' Unfortunately not quite that interesting.

We are divided into men's and women's groups. I put my middle name on the name tag out of perversity so Des has to keep squinting at my chest and saying things like, 'Um . . . Mildred here is going out to work and I'm staying home.' I feel it would be more entertaining if he could just admit he's forgotten the name of the mother of his child. Anyway, each group is asked to come up with a list of questions they would like the class to answer.

WOMEN

Can we eat during labour? (Yes, a bit in the early stages.)

Can we video the birth? (Depends on your doctor. Some would wear a party hat if you asked nicely. Some don't because it could be used in court against them. You can't video a caesarean.)

Will the hospital run as normal on the religious day of worship? (Yes.)

I want hints to help me in labour. (We'll be covering that.)

When is it really labour? (That too.)

Tell us every single pain relief option. (Certainly.)

What about if it's an emergency this small hospital can't deal with? (We have facilities for a sick mother. A sick baby will be sent to a larger hospital by NETS ambulance – the newborn emergency transport service. We can look after the baby adequately until the ambulance arrives.)

Is there a modem link in the delivery suite because I'd like my overseas relatives to see the birth on the Internet? (That's a very weird question, but I'm too polite to say so.)

Can I have twenty-seven people in the room when I'm giving birth? (No. You're a fruitcake.)

Do men ever display the nesting instinct? (Frankly, no.)

MEN

How do we know when it starts? (We'll be covering this.)

What should we expect on the day? (Ditto.)

How can we prepare? (Ditto.)

What support can we give? (All this will be revealed.)

Do WE get any drugs? (Good one, Des.)

What is the man's role during labour? (Do whatever she tells you and be quick about it.)

What if we faint? (Keep up your meals and drinks during labour and sit down if you think you might faint.)

How to recognise signs of postnatal depression? (That will be discussed.)

What to bring and wear? (Ball gown.)

What to have ready at home? (Alcohol.)

What if the baby comes early and quickly? (Ring the ambulance and follow their instructions.)

Young Lorraine, who is actually a Melissa, explains that the first lesson will be on signs that labour isn't far off (maybe hours or days). Signs include the 'show', which is the mucus plug coming out (she says that it might be the size of a 50-cent piece on your undies, and possibly bloody and mucusy); and the 'waters breaking', which is about a cup of amniotic fluid leaking or gushing out when the membranes break (she says don't get it on the car upholstery because it rots it, so from thirty-five weeks I'll be sitting on a tarpaulin and four towels in the passenger seat of Des's precious van). I ask if it's true the waters smell of pickles. Melissa looks sideways and lets us know it's a sweet smell that's actually, ahem, like semen.

Other signs that labour may begin soon are: tummy dropping as the baby's head engages with the pelvis, nesting and cleaning, more Braxton Hicks practice contractions, increased vaginal secretions, pelvic pressure and heaviness in the groin, and a decrease in foetal movements.

Then Melissa points to a chart and explains the following parts of a pregnant woman's anatomy: the vagina ('If you didn't know where that was, you wouldn't be here'), cervix (the bit between the vagina and the uterus), foetus, and fundus (the top of the uterus). She explains that labour contractions begin in the fundus and the pain radiates down to period-cramp territory in the lower abdomen. Our bags should be packed by thirty-five weeks as thirty-seven weeks is considered 'full term'.

Melissa shows us a 'snib' for a newborn baby, which hits me for a six. It looks like what I thought was a pilcher. A pilcher, she says, is actually plastic overpants. I give up. Two hours of this and I'm ready for a whisky. Ready, willing, but not able.

info

what are the signs of early labour?

Even if you're feeling like pregnancy has gone on quite long enough, premature labour might be a bit of a freak-out as well. Always remember you're living in a developed country with a Medicare system. (If you're living near a major metropolitan centre, you should have the best available medical care for premmie babies; if you're in a rural or remote area, especially if you're an Aboriginal woman, that access statistically falls away dramatically.)

Labour is considered premature if it begins earlier than the thirty-seventh week of pregnancy. Early signs that you may be in labour are:

◉ cramps, like period pains, that may be accompanied by nausea, diarrhoea or indigestion

◉ increasing pain or feeling of pressure in the lower back

◉ unusual or persistent achiness or feeling of pressure in the pelvic floor, thighs or groin

◉ a watery or pinkish or brownish discharge, possibly preceded by the passage of the thick mucus plug (euwwwwww!) that has been blocking your cervix

☺ fluid from your vagina (your 'waters breaking'), which means the amniotic sac has ruptured and some amniotic fluid is rushing or trickling out.

late bleeding

Some light bleeding or spotting in the second and third trimesters is usually okay, but you need to have it checked out immediately by your obstetrician to be absolutely sure. Two uncommon conditions that cause bleeding late in pregnancy are placenta praevia and placental abruption.

placenta praevia or low-lying placenta

The placenta is attached to the lower part of the uterine wall, instead of the upper part, partially or completely blocking the way out. In the late stages of pregnancy, as the uterus stretches and the cervix ripens (becomes thinner and softer, ready to 'dilate' – open wide – enough for the baby to pass through during birth), a placenta attached to the lower uterus can become detached, causing painless bleeding. The risk of having placenta praevia is increased if you have uterine scarring from previous pregnancies or surgery, you smoke, or there's more than one baby in there. If the bleeding is severe you may need an emergency caesarean, but sometimes your obstetrician will adopt a 'wait and see' approach after mild bleeding.

placental abruption (abruptio placentae) or placental separation

Placental abruption is when the placenta comes away from the uterine wall too early. The amount of bleeding and also the amount of pain depend on how much of the placenta has come away. The cause is unknown, but it tends to be more common in women who have had two or more children, women with raised blood pressure, and smokers. Sometimes the problem resolves itself and the pregnancy continues as normal. Sometimes the birth must be induced; in serious, sudden cases a caesarean is necessary.

WEEK 30

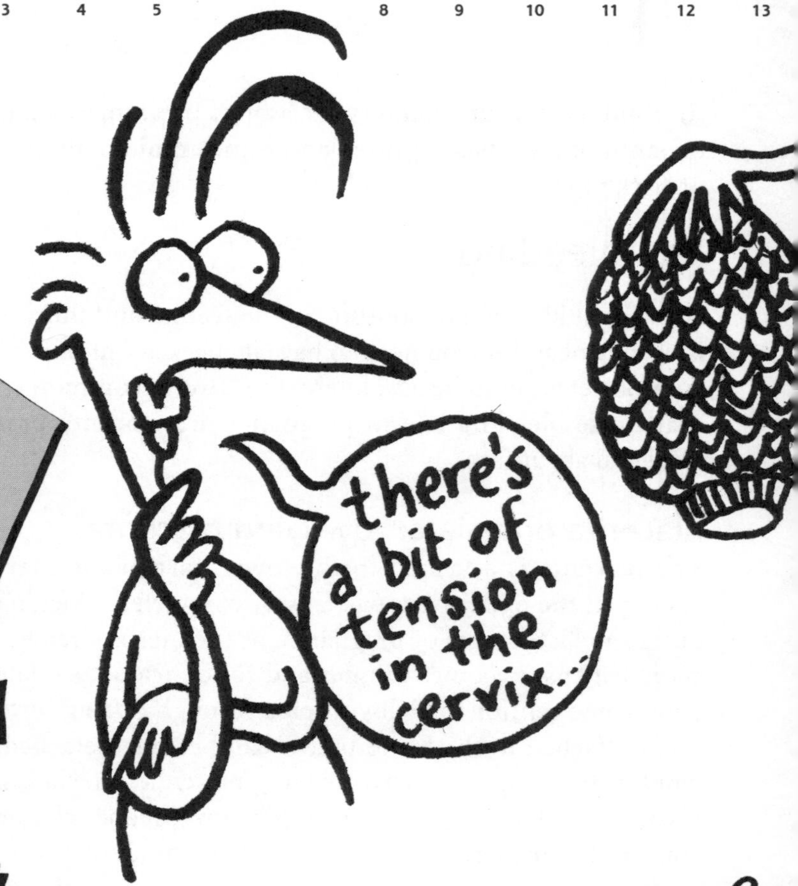

confronted with the knitted uterus

Average approximate baby length this week from head to bum

what's going on Your breasts are

STILL getting bigger. Will they ever stop? Yes. You might

be feeling Braxton Hicks practice contractions now,

although most people don't feel them until the last weeks.

Proper contractions last for 1 minute each, come at intervals of

5 minutes or less and go on for at least an hour, and then after

a while a baby comes out. So if that happens, you're probably

really in labour.

This week and the following three, the baby puts on

fat at a greater rate. The skin is still a bit wrinkled, so there's

room for the new fat underneath. The lanugo will start to fall out,

although a full head of hair may stay. The eyes are fully

open, but it can't be very interesting just watching all that hair

floating around. Baby hiccuping starts to get more violent: you

can feel the little jerks. The baby may be jiggled around by

the Braxton Hicks contractions. Weight: about 1.3 kilos.

Diary

Thank God I go to see Marg's baby, Gloria. It reminds me that there's a reward at the end of all this. Marg's full of advice about the change-table arrangement, the best pilchers, the best singlets, etc. I must start taking notes.

Also go to see Dr Herb.

He takes one look at me and says, 'It must be soon.'

'Soon!' I shriek. 'It's ten weeks away. I can't even begin to tell you what I have to get done before it arrives!'

There was a woman in the waiting room who'd come to give him a present. She had a 3-year-old with a narrow little face – this was the smallest and earliest surviving baby Herb had ever delivered. She came at twenty-three weeks and spent months in a humidicrib. Her mum was obviously madly in love with her little girl.

When Herb examines me, he smiles and says, 'Your baby is big and healthy. It's going to be the opposite of that one you saw in the waiting room.'

I hope this doesn't mean it's coming out at fifty-seven weeks.

Herb agrees I have put on a lot of weight, but says, 'Worry about it after the baby is born. Just don't eat junk food.'

All the skinny girls at work put on more than 20 kilos during their pregnancy and lose it again afterwards. You can't go on a weight-loss diet during pregnancy. You (well, all right then, I) can stop eating a Magnum a day though, which might help. I tell myself that it's usually more dangerous for a baby if I don't put on enough weight during pregnancy than if I end up looking like a pivotal protagonist in *Moby Dick: The Mini-series*.

For a fashion designer, I've got fanny-all to wear. But how selfish, I think. I'd better shop for the baby. (Besides which, shopping is no fun any more because after you've been walking for 15 minutes your feet feel like someone's been whacking them rhythmically with a baton for an hour.) I go to a posh shop and accidentally spend $277 on baby things like bunny-rugs and singlets – honestly I didn't buy anything flash at all. I become quite stupidly emotional over a tiny pair of socks for a newborn baby and start crying. Good God. Let's face it, I'm liable to burst into tears during a tampon ad.

Des is being a prince – well, a prince's servant – still doing all the dishes and cooking most nights. (He tends to cut things up into infinitesimally small pieces, but never look a gift dinner in the mixed metaphorical mouth, I say.)

Hired the removalists again to move more furniture around. Getting there. This weekend had better go and look for a change table, and that cot Uncle Stan said he'd pay for. More shelves being delivered. Des just stands back and lets it all happen, and occasionally shakes his head and mutters like one of the witches in Macbeth. At least I think he said 'bubble'.

Second week of childbirth classes. And tonight our special project is: Normal Labour. Melissa is slightly less perky. Perhaps she's been delivering babies for 36 hours.

Melissa gives us the old line about having faith in your body and the pain being part of a natural process. I can't help it, it sounds like a crock. While I have always thought childbirth was actually a design fault, it is strangely comforting to know that millions of women have done it.

What Melissa says is that the average for a first-time labour is 12–16 hours. The time is counted from the start of getting regular contractions. (Statistically, second and subsequent babies slither out after about 6 hours.) I'm still not clear about this 12–16 hours. It's roughly made up of 10–12 hours waiting for the cervix to dilate to 10 centimetres (first stage), and then say 2 hours pushing and shouting at people (second stage), as far as I can ascertain. After that there is a third stage of labour, when the placenta comes out, which nobody seems particularly interested in. If an injection of oxytocin is given this takes between 10 and 30 minutes. If it comes out naturally, it's usually under an hour.

Next Melissa produces from her handbag a very startling pink knitted uterus with a cream cuff on it, which represents the cervix. I don't know where she got the pattern. She says your waters can break at any time before or during the labour, even right at the very end. At first the contractions last for 20 seconds, like a period cramp. They increase from 20 minutes apart to 5 minutes apart. During the last bit of the first stage, the contractions are very intense and 3–5 minutes apart.

The second stage of labour is heralded by the 'transition' – when the cervix is almost completely dilated (about 10 centimetres): wide enough for the baby's head to fit through. Ow. Ow ow OW. The contractions are only 2 or 3 minutes apart and last for up to 90 seconds. This is usually the stage when women scream for an epidural and are often refused.

'If you're abusive we know you're nearly there,' says Melissa.

This sounds like a horrible stage when you can be shaky and vomit from the shock and stress, and you flake out for those tiny minutes between contractions.

At this point most of the men in the class move closer to their partners and take their hands. (You can tell they're thinking, 'Oh you poor dear', and then, 'Glad I don't have to do that bit.') They will not be so free with their fingers during the real thing: support people are advised that only two fingers be gripped by the labouring woman as any more fingers are easier to squish together, and even break. Support people are also advised to eat and drink and take rests.

After this stage, as far as I can see, a soft-toy baby comes out of a knitted uterus into a stuffed pelvis. Melissa advises us not to be too energetic in the early stages of labour before going to hospital as we'll need our strength later.

Apparently the very end of labour feels exactly like the urge to poo. Some women keep changing positions; some have their baby on all fours or a birth stool, or sitting up on the bed. Squatting is not something we do a lot of, so unless you're on one of those giant inflatable birth balls they have in some labour rooms it will probably be too much for your leg muscles.

This week was probably the perfect week to consider some of the mechanics of childbirth as I am just changing from major denial (well yes, I know I'm pregnant, but I don't think I actually want to go through childbirth) to major denial (look, I know I'm pregnant, but I really don't want to think about how this baby everyone keeps saying is so HUGE is going to get out – I feel like I'm going to give birth to a small apartment block).

Melissa says we can massage the perineum (the area in front of your anus) for weeks before the birth, but there's no proof this

is any use. Sounds like an excuse for being at yourself to me.
(Dr Herb's view is it's a complete waste of time.)

'Often we ask the dad if he wants to cut the cord,' Melissa says.
For some reason every woman in the class packs up laughing.
'Once the head is through, that's the hard bit done – unless
you've got a really big baby and then the shoulders can be
difficult.' Oh dear.

Melissa then talks about the third stage of labour, which
involves the expulsion of a large stuffed red stocking, with a veil
around the edge that makes it look like a giant jellyfish, and a
twisty grey dressing-gown cord hanging from it, which is the
placenta and umbilical cord. At this point Melissa admits that
somewhere she has a knitted breast as well. I hate to think what
her tea-cosies look like.

Then we watch two videos. The first one is narrated by a
serious bloke who says things like 'some of the joy and happiness
brought about by this happy event' and 'this stained mucus plug'
as if he were reading the Channel 10 news. This happy event
and the stained mucus plug are both brought to us by
somebody called Julie, who wears a yellow jumper until the
second stage of labour, when she changes into a mauve silk
negligee (bad move, really). At the hospital Julie wanders the
corridors like Lady Macbeth and then ends up panting,
which Melissa has said is not good so early in the labour. An
obstetrician turns up in a hideous patterned jumper and
holds one of Julie's legs while Scott, her husband, holds the
other. Being in labour is probably the only time a woman
wouldn't even notice this happening. Then the midwife squirts
some cold detergent on Julie's private parts, which Melissa says is
shocking behaviour as it gives Julie quite a fright. 'We like to give
you a quick, warm wash,' she says. The whole video is 15 minutes
long, which I think is a little misleading.

The midwife holds the baby back so it doesn't come out in too
much of a rush and tear Julie, and then the head comes out a very
grey-blue and turns slowly before the rest slips out. By about this
stage nearly every man in the room has gone into shock and half
of them have tried to crawl into their partner's lap – forgetting that,

with a seven-month pregnant woman, lap space is at a premium.

We watch a second video, starring a rather more hippie couple. (Why is it that in every picture, drawing and video to do with pregnancy and childbirth the husband has facial hair?) Anyway, this woman gives birth on all fours and then scoops the baby up as if she does it every day.

Neither woman needs stitches. As if.

Back at home poor old Des is squished into an area of the bed that's the size of an envelope. I waddle to the toilet about six times a night and have taken to having under-desk naps at work.

And the mood swings! Des never knows whether he's coming home to Medusa or Mrs Bunnikins.

One of the male models looks at me in the lift at work and blurts out, 'What happens to all that stomach . . . afterwards?'

'I'm giving it to the Salvos,' I reply.

info

premature birth

why does it happen?

About half the time, medical people don't know. Here are some possibilities:

◉ over-distended uterus caused by more than one baby, or too much amniotic fluid

◉ incompetent cervix (incompetent my foot – what a RUDE medical term; it just means that your cervix isn't staying tightly closed enough)

◉ early rupture of the membranes of the amniotic sac ('waters breaking')

◉ something wrong with the baby or the placenta

◉ the baby has died while still in the uterus (this is rare)

⑥ an IUD left in the uterus

⑥ the mother has a disease or malnutrition, or experiences a trauma (such as a car accident), or is overworked

⑥ the mother's and father's blood types don't mix ('rhesus incompatibility')

⑥ diabetic pregnancy

⑥ the mum is a young teenager.

how early is too early?

Any baby born before thirty-seven weeks is considered premature, or preterm. With specialist care, babies as young as twenty-four weeks can survive. By thirty weeks, there is a 90 per cent survival rate, and more than 80 per cent of these babies will be fine after a bit of special care. If there is enough warning, mothers are often given steroids to improve their baby's lung development.

special care

⑥ Premature babies used to be routinely delivered by caesarean section to prevent the possible damage to the baby's soft head that may occur during vaginal delivery, but recent studies show this is not conclusively safer if there are no other complicating factors such as pre-eclampsia, signs of foetal distress or breech birth (bum-first baby).

⑥ A neonatal paediatrician or neonatal registrar will be part of the medical team at any premature birth: in other words, a specialist or a doctor training to become a specialist in premmie babies will be there.

⑥ If your baby needs help with temperature regulation or breathing, it will be placed in an incubator or ventilator and taken to the hospital's intensive neonatal care unit.

⑥ Your baby's condition may be assessed using a test of responses at 1 minute and again at 5 minutes after birth, called the APGAR test.

◉ If the lungs are not developed enough, your baby will be given steroids or surfactant-replacement therapy, which uses an artificial protein in place of surfactant, a substance that normally completely coats the lungs in the last weeks of pregnancy to prevent them collapsing.

◉ If your baby can't take your breast milk, it will be fed formula through a tube. If your baby can take milk, you can express it: this is something positive you can do that will really help your baby's progress, even if you feel helpless.

◉ Premature babies grow and thrive better if exposed to massage, skin-to-skin contact with parents or carers (called 'kangaroo care'), soft music, recordings of heartbeats or the mother's voice, and water beds or hammocks that simulate movement in the uterus.

common premmie characteristics
Premature babies differ from full-term babies in a number of usually temporary ways.

◉ Obviously, premature babies weigh less than full-termers.

◉ They are small, red, wrinkly and frail, with relatively large head and hands.

◉ Their skin is pale, and blood vessels can easily be seen underneath because there is not much fat.

◉ There is a layer of fine hair (lanugo) on the body.

◉ Their motor functions, including breathing and feeding, are less efficient and their cry is not as lusty as that of a full-term newborn baby.

◉ They tend to be less expressive than full-termers – they sleep most of the time, and when they are awake they do not make much eye contact or respond to people talking to or touching them. They also tend to be irritable. Can't blame them really.

  See Premature Babies in 'Help'.

your record

What experiences have you had of childbirth?
Have you been to a birth? What was it like?

What videos and descriptions have impressed you
either positively or negatively?

what's going on

Hello stretch marks here, there and possibly everywhere! What a splendid mauve, perhaps an attractive eggplant colour, or is it hot pink? Mind your posture, as your tummy will be putting you off balance.

The baby can blink or close its eyes when a bright light is shone onto your tummy. There's a lot of brain action going on: receiving and sending lots of signals through the nervous system, maybe testing out the idea of thinking, possibly wondering how long it has to hang out in a hairy swamp. The baby's definite awake and sleeping times are still usually roughly the opposite of yours.

Weight: about 1.5 kilos.

WEEK

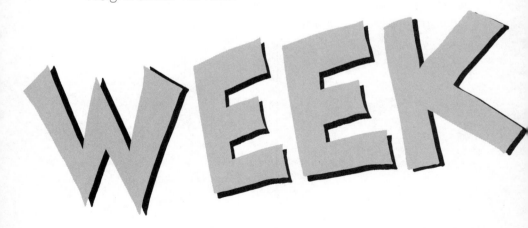

Average approximate baby length this week from head to bum

cm   1   2   3   4   5   6   7   8   9   10   11   12   13

31

Guard against madness —
DON'T IRON YOUR UNDIES!

16 17 18 19 20 21 22 23 24 25 26 27 28 29

DiARY

I'm a little breathless because my lungs are all squished up. Unfortunately this does not make me sound like Marilyn Monroe singing 'Happy Birthday, Mr President'; it's more like an over-exerted warthog. Also, I have a constant ache where the ligaments from the baby area extend down to the groin. Leg cramps keep waking me up at night at 4 a.m., and I can't get back to sleep.

Beck says it's probably not magnesium deficiency but a circulation problem and maybe I should walk shorter distances every day instead of 2 kilometres every second day. Maybe I get worse cramps during the nights when I don't walk.

During my walk today a huge truck pulled up at the park with rolls of cyclone wire in the back, and a big burly bloke in a reflective vest, Stubbies and Blundstones got down from the cab, walked around to the passenger seat and collected a 2-year-old girl with a Milly-Molly-Mandy haircut.

'Come on, darling,' he said. And they went to feed the seagulls.

It made me think that having children brings out the best kindness and the worst temper in us. And I hope it will bring out the best in me, not the worst. Or at least when it brings out the worst there will be someone else to take up the slack while I go and bite some telegraph poles.

Des and I spend an afternoon looking at cots. It's amazing – some of them even LOOK dangerous, having gaps that a rhinoceros could practically climb out of. Not much more to buy now, but it would be nice if the washer-dryer fairy paid a visit.

Never speak too soon about household appliances. Just after I write that bit I notice that the enamel is flaking off the toaster onto our toast, so no doubt I've been ingesting bits of plutonium or aluminium or something.

Then this creepy guy turns up to service the heater, which I thought should have a new fan because the old one sounded a bit like the Concorde landing. He opens up the front and says, 'It's a wonder you're not dead.'

'Pardon?'

'This thing's been leaking carbon monoxide. You could have

nodded off to sleep on the couch and never woken up. I'm surprised you're still alive.'

Well.

Finally manage to rustle old Pollyanna With Spanner out the front door, burst into tears and call Des, only to get his mobile. Damn, damn, damn, he is probably down the back paddock of the shop explaining succulents to some dopey businessman who thinks hydroponics is a grunge band, so I call the Poisons Information Centre, who put me onto the local women's hospital where FINALLY, just before I think I'll go mad, a woman in the drug information department explains that unless I have experienced the symptoms of carbon monoxide poisoning (severe nausea, severe headaches and severe lethargy and faintness) nothing will have crossed the placenta, and even if it has the likely result will have been a lack of oxygen getting to the baby, similar to what would happen if I smoked or walked around in the traffic all day, in which case the baby might be a little small.

'No,' I assure her. 'The general consensus is that I am having a baby approximately the size of Danny de Vito.'

'Well,' she says, 'nothing to worry about then.'

Phew.

It is really very uncomfortable now. Beck has prescribed a grab-bag of different supplements for me (which she hates doing) to try to bring down my fluid retention. Vitamin E, vitamin C, dandelion-leaf tincture (all at very precisely calibrated doses or it won't work), a complicated specialist herbal mixture that tastes like a petroleum byproduct with bats' ears in it, and I'm sure if she thought it would help I would have to hang upside down every 3 hours as well. Dr Herb just shrugs his shoulders and says he hopes it helps because he can't give me drugs.

Every now and then I forget I'm pregnant for a minute or two, and then the baby kicks or I have to move or something and remember. Des is being very sympathetic. I can't believe I have put on 17 kilos. From behind I look like two driver's-side airbags going off.

Go and buy some 100 per cent cotton cot sheets – very hard to find. Another pregnant woman and I both put a hand on the last set. We look at each other.

She says graciously, 'You take it, you're more pregnant than me.' Sisterhood!

'Most people,' says a Lorraine-like sales assistant, 'don't buy 100 per cent cotton because they have to iron the sheets.'

'Iron the sheets?!' I shriek. 'Are they mad?!'

Our third childbirth class: when to come to the hospital. Melissa says to come to hospital when your contractions are 5 minutes apart, the waters have broken or you're overwrought, but to ring first in case they've all stepped out for a daiquiri. No, to tell them what's been happening. Once you get to the hospital a midwife will inspect you before calling in your obstetrician.

Here are the main points I shall have to memorise.

False contractions are irregular, don't increase in intensity and usually go away if you lie down.

The waters breaking can be a tiny trickle or 1–2 litres of amniotic fluid coming out. Put on a pad. You're supposed to write down the time your waters break and note the quality and colour of the fluid. If there's a stain or blood in the waters, tell your midwife or hospital staff immediately, by phone.

Don't ring everyone and tell them you're in labour or they'll all be round to the house or turning up at the hospital or getting times wrong and starting accidental rumours. Don't play hockey – conserve your energy for the labour.

Everyone is on the edge of their seat. This is what we came for – a bit of a chat about the real thing. Mind you, I thought there'd be a lot more beanbag action, and a lot more practice breathing. Apparently it's out of fashion. I am so glad Melissa is not the type to say, 'Pinch your hand as hard as you can', each week to demonstrate the pain of labour. Because it's a bit like saying, 'See that wee dinghy? It's kind of like an aircraft carrier.'

Melissa says not to worry if you poo during labour, and you probably won't because diarrhoea is often an early sign of labour so you'll have got rid of all the poo before you deliver. Anyway, now that I've done wee on my own floor because my pelvic-floor muscles are so hopeless, I suspect I can poo on the hospital, no worries.

Everyone is rather surprised to learn a few things. No wonder the baby comes out with its eyes closed – otherwise the first thing it would see is its mother's . . . ahem . . . arsehole. Also, after the baby comes out there's an enormous gush of fluid: the banked-up amniotic fluid – and up to 300 millilitres of blood. (A 'post-partum haemorrhage' is technically more than 600 millilitres.)

At that point I thought things would be pretty much all over but I'd forgotten there's the third stage – the placenta comes out. (In order to demonstrate the placenta, Melissa drops the 'baby' on the carpet, which she promises not to do if she's assisting at any of our births.) And then the obstetrician will do a bit of classy embroidery on any tears or cuts. Melissa gives us the hospital's March stats: forty-five deliveries, twenty-two intact perineums. Yikes.

info

pre-eclampsia

what is it?
It used to be called pre-eclamptic toxaemia (if your mum had it, that's what it would have been called). It only ever happens in pregnancy, and it's diagnosed from a combination of signs and symptoms, including a rise in blood pressure; swelling of the ankles, feet, hands and face; sudden weight gain due to fluid retention; upper abdominal pains; visual disturbance; and protein in your wee.

Put your feet up!

Pre-eclampsia is a serious condition that affects up to 15 per cent of pregnant women, usually in the second half of pregnancy. Occasionally the onset will coincide with labour and, rarely, it can occur after delivery. The cause has still not been established.

Pre-eclampsia can interfere with the placenta, stunting the baby's growth and depriving it of oxygen. It can cause the baby to come early, and damage the mother's kidneys, nervous system and blood vessels.

Sometimes pre-eclampsia can get worse really quickly: symptoms (apart from fluid retention) may include persistent headache, blurred vision, 'seeing' flashing lights, upper or mid abdominal pain, irritability, nausea and vomiting. Women being treated for pre-eclampsia, if not hospitalised, should get emergency medical treatment at the onset of any of these symptoms.

Severe pre-eclampsia can escalate into eclampsia, which is a life-threatening condition for mother and foetus, but now extremely rare because of better medical monitoring. Eclampsia can cause convulsions, kidney failure and coma. Blood vessels in the uterus go into spasm and cut down the blood supply to the baby.

checks

Early detection and treatment mean pre-eclampsia is better managed, though it can't be prevented. Your wee sample and blood pressure are checked at each prenatal visit to the obstetrician or prenatal clinic, and you should tell your pregnancy carer about any puffiness or swelling. (Having only one of the pre-eclampsia symptoms, such as fluid retention, doesn't mean you have pre-eclampsia.)

You're more likely to get pre-eclampsia if you had high blood pressure before you were pregnant; have a family history of pre-eclampsia or high blood pressure; had or have kidney disease; have diabetes; have had or are having a multiple pregnancy; had pre-eclampsia in a previous pregnancy; are a teenager or an older mum; or the pregnancy is your first.

treatment

There is no conclusive evidence, but many people believe that good levels of calcium in your diet can reduce the risk of pre-eclampsia. Treatment for very mild pre-eclampsia may include bed rest at home or in hospital, changing what you eat, and careful monitoring of you and your baby. Tests may include blood and urine checks, monitoring of the foetal heart rate, and ultra-sounds.

If the condition progresses or is advanced when diagnosed, you'll need to go to hospital. You may need medication to wrestle your blood pressure into submission, and your labour might be induced, or you may have a caesarean, depending on whether you respond to treatment, the state of your uterus and how advanced the pregnancy is.

Sample

take-away caffe latte

Do Not get them CONFUSED...

WEEK 32

what's going on

Your lungs are getting stronger, although because of all the pressure you may feel breathless if you overdo it. You may be starting to get a bit sick of the whole pregnancy thing. It's uncomfortable being this big, you're running out of outfits and as for sleeping well – ha!

The baby's lungs are stronger too, but not fully ready to go yet. The baby is filling out with fat, although it still looks a bit on the skinny side. It might be upside down in readiness for the lunge to the outside world. This is pretty much your complete baby item, covered in vernix. If the baby was born now it would open its eyes and take a geek at the world (except it can't focus on much at this age and will look endearingly cross-eyed). Weight: about 1.7 kilos.

| cm | 1 | 2 | 3 | 4 | 5 | 6 | 7 | 8 | 9 | 10 | 11 | 12 | 13 |

OH MY GOD MY BABY'S going to BE A SCORPIO!

sorry Muncky

Average approximate baby length this week from head to bum

| 16 | 17 | 18 | 19 | 20 | 21 | 22 | 23 | 24 | 25 | 26 | 27 | 28 | 29 |

DiARY

I walk into Dr Herb's office.

'You look tired and bloated,' he says.

Charmed, I'm sure.

He says the insomniac sore legs when lying down are probably due to the fluid retention. He listens to the baby's heartbeat, asks if the baby's moving (is it ever: the Pikelet loves to rhumba all night long), and measures the length of the uterus.

'The baby's doing beautifully – you're doing brilliantly well,' he says.

It's very kind the way he does this sort of positive bit after he tells me I look like shit (in the nicest possible way).

There are no safe drugs for fluid retention during pregnancy, Herb explains.

'Why can't I take diuretics?' I whine.

'Two reasons. They reduce placental blood flow, and they can mask the symptoms of pre-eclampsia.'

Oh all right, smartypants.

He sends me round the corner to a pathology lab, where I get a blood test from a Lorraine to check if there's a high level of uric acid in the blood or my platelets are at all 'deranged' – both signs that I might be susceptible to pre-eclampsia. I quite like the idea of my platelets being deranged. I'm so responsible these days there should be some part of me acting like an idiot, but on second thoughts I can definitely do without pre-eclampsia. I have to come again next week because I'm retaining so much fluid Herb wants to keep an eye on it.

Week 4 of the childbirth class: Melissa's potted version of stuff that might happen that isn't your ideal plan. Forceps might be used if you're too tired to push any more, the baby seems to be staying put, you've been pushing for too long (1–2 hours), or there are signs of foetal distress. Usually you'll get an epidural first. I can see why when Melissa holds up a pair of forceps. They look like very upmarket, Italian, oversized salad servers from one of those designer shops full of stuff that people don't really need but has 'Alessi' written all over it. There are three types: rotator forceps (also known as Kiellands forceps), lift-out forceps and Neville Barnes forceps. I hope nobody ever says, 'This is a job for

Neville.' It never ceases to amaze me what men will name after
themselves.

Then there's the rather sophisticated-sounding ventouse, a
suction cup that they can stick on the baby's head and, well, pull
it out. (It's a vacuum in the sense of the plumber's mate, not the
type you do the carpet with.) Melissa sits there absent-mindedly
playing with the soft-toy baby on her lap. So far she's folded it in
half and is waving one of its feet past its ear.

Emergency caesareans are performed when a large baby is
stuck, the cervix just isn't getting any wider or the baby is really
distressed. Usually you'll get an epidural or a spinal block to numb
the lower half of your body. After a caesarean you get morphine
or pethidine – 'Hi baby! Mummy's reeeeally stoned!' Usually
you're on a drip for up to 24 hours and have a catheter for weeing
for up to 24 hours. The baby feeds as normal, and the dad,
another helper or a staff member does the nappy changes and
baths and stuff.

What about the bizarre-sounding 'induction' or 'inducement'
(as in 'He offered me an illegal inducement, your worship, and I
booked him for aggravated bribery')? An obstetrician may bring on
('induce') labour if you're more than one to two weeks overdue; if
your little bub isn't growing well; or if you have pre-eclampsia.
Melissa says she knows of a doctor who induced a baby because its
mother didn't want a Scorpio, and a doctor who refused to induce
a baby on the fourth of July for an American couple.

Then Melissa talks about stillbirth. Everyone in the room goes
very quiet. She says she doesn't want to talk about it, but she has
to because it does still happen rarely that a baby is born dead, or
is born with so many problems that it slips away from life a few
days later. She says that in the case of a stillbirth, the baby often
hasn't moved for a day or two before the labour. So always call your
obstetrician if you haven't felt the baby move for 12 hours –
although usually the baby's fine and just quiet, getting ready for
labour.

If a baby is stillborn, the hospital organises to have photos taken
and inked footprints on a card done, even if you don't want these
mementoes at the time. (One bereaved mum called after three years
to get hers.) Melissa's eyes fill with tears as she talks, and so do mine.

info

birth plan

what is it?

You write down all the things you want to happen during your labour. It's not a legal contract, but rather a memo of understanding between you and your birth attendants: it can cover whether you want an enema to start with, right through to who's going to hold the baby first.

It's also a starting point for discussion with your obstetrician or midwife about their usual procedure and about the policies of the hospital or birth centre, and about things such as playing the music of your choice during labour, family and friends being able to visit straight after the birth, and so on. You may not be able to have your own way on everything – this is the time to find out.

Discuss your birth plan with your obstetrician or midwife early, so that you're not still negotiating as the baby's coming out. The birth plan can be dated and signed by both parties to show that its details have been agreed upon Tuck a copy away in your handbag.

what's in it?

The following plan is a best-case scenario, but what if there are unexpected difficulties (induced labour, forceps delivery, emergency caesarean)? For example, if you have a caesarean you will probably want to keep the baby with you, not have it whisked away immediately for weighing and measuring, as this time can be very important for bonding with your baby. You will need your obstetrician to agree, so it's good to have it in your birth plan.

Your plan may be a long and detailed list of what you want to happen at every stage of your labour, just a letter to your obstetrician or midwife saying what you want, or a point-form list of the stuff you think is most important. It might include:

⊚ who will be there

⊚ what you'd like to have around you to help you feel more comfortable and relaxed, such as music, massage oils and photos

⊚ what clothes you would like to wear during the birth (hats and gloves are passé, and don't forget that anything that goes lower than your hips is likely to come off very second best in the stain department)

⊚ whether you want a tape recording, photos or a video of the birth, and who will be taking these

⊚ whether you want your pubic hair to be shaved or trimmed (not in a sexy heart shape, sadly), and whether you would prefer to do it yourself (you will have to look in a mirror to see what you're doing as your tummy will be in the way)

⊚ whether you fancy an enema – yes/no/only if the bowel is full at the onset of labour/not on God's green earth

⊚ how, and how often, you would like to be monitored – some foetal monitors inhibit walking around

⊚ whether you would like to be able to eat in the early stages and drink through the labour

⊚ whether you would have a catheter (a tube coming out of your urethra, which wee automatically flows from) – yes/no/only if you have an epidural and can't feel whether your bladder is full

❂ at what point you would like to be offered pain relief

❂ what your preferred pain relief options are

❂ what delivery position you'd prefer – squatting, sitting or on all fours perhaps

❂ whether you object to an episiotomy (a cut made at the entrance to the vagina to pre-empt the tearing that could make healing more difficult)

❂ whether you want to touch your baby's head as it 'crowns' (peeps out for the first time)

❂ who gets to lift the baby up first – maybe the baby's father, or you, or the obstetrician or midwife?

❂ who you would like to cut the umbilical cord

❂ whether you want to keep the baby with you until *you* decide staff can measure and weigh it – check if your hospital has a 'baby-friendly' charter that includes this as a policy

❂ whether you would accept drugs to speed up the normal delivery of the placenta.

pain relief options

Way before you're due, the following people will give you advice on pain relief: your obstetrician, your midwife, your partner; plenty of people who haven't had a baby; plenty who have; and a large man called Trevor who you meet at a leather bar.

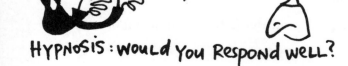

HYPNOSIS: would you Respond well?

The final decision rests with you. You can choose the pain relief you'd like for an ideal delivery, but accept that you may have to resort to, say, a caesarean. Having a back-up plan means that you won't have to make any spur of the moment decisions about pain relief during labour, if for example it lasts longer or is more painful than you ever expected.

non-drug methods

The following non-drug methods of pain relief are often suggested (for each of these, faith in the method will help – if you're sceptical now, you may be a lot more so when you're yelling):

⊚ acupuncture

⊚ reflexology (a form of acupressure massage of the feet)

⊚ aromatherapy – this is *not* pain relief, it's just dickering with the atmosphere

⊚ breathing and meditation techniques – these need to be learnt and practised before labour

⊚ massage – this also needs to be practised before labour by the person who will give it

⊚ moving around – keeping mobile can help take pressure off your back, as well as distract you from the pain; some women find that standing or squatting positions are much more comfortable during contractions and childbirth

⊚ hydrotherapy – a warm shower or bath will help to relax you; sitting in water can provide pain relief by supporting the abdominal wall and decreasing the pressure on muscles during contractions

⊚ localised heat – hot towels and heat packs can help mask pain and reduce muscle cramps and spasms

⊚ vocalisation – groaning, chanting or singing to 'release' pain, otherwise known as Just. Plain. Yelling.

⊚ transcutaneous electrical nerve stimulation (TENS) – a machine delivers a very low electric current to stimulate the skin through pads attached to either side of the spine, creating a tingling sensation. This current can block the pain signals coming from the uterus. This method only offers slight pain relief, but some women find it is enough, and it can be safely used throughout labour

⊚ hypnosis – if you respond well to hypnosis, you can reach a state of consciousness where you are aware of what is happening but don't perceive it as painful (but you would *really* want to have practised this one)

⊚ music (more dickering with the atmosphere, and be warned – a lot of people make elaborate birth tapes and end up throwing them across the labour room).

the hard stuff

Gas Gas, also known as inhalation analgesia, is nitrous oxide ('laughing gas') under various brand names, inhaled during contractions through a rubber mask. It is generally accepted that it eases the perception of pain, but doesn't provide a complete block. Some women find that just the distraction of using the mask helps to take their mind off the pain. Others find the mask claustrophobic (a mouthpiece may be available). Gas can be used safely throughout labour and appears to have very little effect on the baby. It makes some people feel sick and light-headed.

Epidural and spinal block Many women request an epidural. First, a local anaesthetic is injected into your back. Next, a fine, hollow needle is inserted between two vertebrae in your lower back, then a catheter is inserted via the needle, and anaesthetic is injected into it. The catheter allows epidural drugs to be placed in the right spot in the back to block pain, and the continued administration of pain-killers throughout labour and delivery if needed. The anaesthetic takes effect within a few minutes. The whole procedure usually takes about 30 minutes and must always be performed by an experienced anaesthetist.

An epidural goes into the lower back tissue that surrounds the sac containing the spinal cord and spinal fluid, whereas a spinal block goes directly into the spinal fluid and so works quicker (it is often used in a caesarean delivery when speed is important). Epidurals wear off after one or several hours depending on how much is used – they can be 'topped up' during a long labour. A spinal block is a one-off injection that lasts 1–4 hours.

These are the only methods of pain relief currently available that take away all perception of pain yet allow you to stay conscious. That's why epidurals and spinal-block injections are used for caesareans.

An epidural or a spinal block for a caesarean numbs all sensation in the abdomen and also affects the nerves in the legs, making them feel very heavy, and nerves in the bladder (so you'll probably have a catheter inserted in your bladder because you won't know when you're weeing). Epidurals and spinals used to block pain in labour without numbing the legs and bladder are now routine in most large maternity units.

Epidural anaesthetic is often used when women are in great pain, if the baby is in an awkward position (such as breech), if it's a multiple birth, or with a forceps or suction delivery. An epidural can sometimes make it difficult for you to push because you can't feel the strong second-stage contractions; but your doctor or midwife should be able to tell you when to push. Some people choose to let the anaesthetic wear off a little towards the end so that they can feel the contractions again.

There is very little risk involved with having an epidural or a spinal block administered by an experienced anaesthetist. Occasionally an epidural only blocks pain in part of your abdomen, but the anaesthetist can often fix that. Less than 1 per cent of women who have had an epidural report having a headache lasting up to a few days. Having an epidural or spinal block in itself won't affect your baby.

Narcotics, including pethidine   They used to give heroin in childbirth: pethidine is now the most common narcotic still on offer. Narcotics, usually given as injections during the first stage of labour, dull the sensation of pain by stimulating opiate receptors in the brain and spinal cord.

The injection takes about 20 minutes to work and it lasts 1–3 hours. Side effects can include headache, blurred vision, mood changes, feeling well away with the fairies, and nausea. If given in large doses, it may make the baby sleepy and affect its breathing – this is usually remedied by giving the baby a little oxygen or a drug called Narcan after the birth, to reverse the effects.

Local anaesthesia   The two most common forms of local anaesthesia given during labour are a pudendal nerve block, which involves an injection to numb the lower vagina and perineum before forceps or a vacuum instrument is used to pull the baby out; and perineal anaesthesia, injected into the perineum to reduce discomfort or, most commonly, to perform an episiotomy. Both types of anaesthetic take effect within a few minutes. Minimum doses are used so as not to affect the baby.

General anaesthetic   This is almost never used during labour, but is sometimes necessary or preferred for caesareans, especially in an emergency. Except in special circumstances, an epidural or spinal block is safer and better for mother and baby during a caesarean.

more info on childbirth

Childbirth Choices by Adrienne Bennett, Wendi Etherington and Daphne Hewson, Penguin, Ringwood, 1993.
Sets out your options and variations on a theme for your birth plan, including pain relief and birth attendants, and explains the usual stages of labour, things that might happen such as a caesarean, and a running list of 'myths' to do with pregnancy and childbirth. Australian.

Your Baby and the Birth Experience by Dr Gregory Fox, Wilkinson Books, Melbourne, 1993.

An easy-to-read explanation of labour and the medical procedures that may be involved. Good diagrams except for the 'alternative birth positions', which look like a stop-sign doing the hokey-pokey. Written by an Australian obstetrician, so it's a good guide to the prevailing medical thought.

All the pregnancy books listed in 'Week 2' have some birth info.

 Contact the Childbirth Education association in your nearest capital city.

W E E K 33

what's going on

You feel like there's not another thing that could be fitted inside you, not even a Mars Bar. Well, maybe a Mars Bar. Your navel is probably sticking out.

All the baby really needs now is more surfactant to coat its lungs and some more fat. It has an excellent chance of survival if it comes out now. As well as blinking, the baby is starting to learn to focus its eyes on close things like its own extremities and the umbilical cord. Weight: about 1.9 kilos.

DiARY I've been reading even more lists in books and hospital pamphlets about what to take to hospital: pillows, hottie and a birth ball; sanitary napkins the size of Bribie Island; every beauty aid known to woman-kind, including 'setting equipment' (one book apparently thinks you'll be giving yourself a home perm) and a mascara for that touch-up during a difficult second stage of labour. PLUS: clothes for the baby, including bootees (get out), bonnet (oh shut up), undershirt, sleeper with legs (what?) and bunting with legs (stop it); cameras for still photos and videos (no thanks); change or a phone card to ring people up ('Hello, I'd like to order a bunting. No, I *don't* know what it is.'); your admission forms for hospital already filled in; books and magazines; your address book and notepaper to write thank-you letters for the flowers and presents (don't they know all you'll want to do is sleep?); and while you're about it, possibly some occasional furniture, a blunderbuss, and, oh, maybe a kayak.

I've checked the hospital's policy on giving out info about the birth: luckily they refuse to tell anyone anything. Having confirmed her presence with the switchboard, the parents of my friend Fatimah drove straight to the hospital when she was in labour and tried to force their way into the delivery room while she was yelling at them to go away. Most unseemly. And I won't be leaving a message on the answering machine saying we've gone to the hospital. In fact I'm going to leave a message saying, 'I haven't gone to the hospital, I'm just not answering the phone. Do not call the hospital. Repeat, and this means you Aunty Peg, do not call the hospital. Leave a message.'

Another fluid-retention vigilance visit to Dr Herb to have blood pressure checked. The waiting room is an endless parade offering excellent people-watching opportunities. Today there is a very old man sitting in the corner sucking on his dentures so vigorously you can hear it coming down the corridor, and a couple who look straight out of the pages of Italian *Vogue*. Her: full, heavy make-up, hair done by the caring hands of a professional in the last 5 hours, Manolo Blahnik shoes, Armani suit, gold jewellery and diamonds the size of small mammals. Him: full-length suede overcoat, tailored suit, silk tie, designer specs, carefully cultivated two-day growth. Not a hair out of place, not a piece of lint. I can't imagine what they would do with a baby. Put it in a vase, maybe.

I have plenty of time to look around – and to babysit a 6-week-old bundle whose mother is in with Dr Herb. The Lovely Lorraine has gone off down the corridor to do something and has handed me a squirmy package who looks like she has nothing but disdain for the likes of my empty boozooms. Turns out she was halfway through a feed when her mum finally got to go in. Dr Herb is running about 2 hours late. Luckily I have taken some sketches and a report to work on.

When it's my turn, I climb up on the bed thing, which is so narrow it always reminds me of being on a ship (especially when I was feeling sick). Dr Herb gets out his tape to measure the height of the uterus and feels my stomach and starts laughing.

'My, it's a whopper,' he says.

Now, don't get me wrong. If I was on a fishing trip with somebody, or the boss was telling me about a pay rise, or an Italian sailor was taking off his strides in a sexual fantasy, the words 'My, it's a whopper' could be exceedingly welcome. When the phrase refers, however, to something that has to come out of your vagina, sometimes referred to amusingly as the birth canal in a pathetic attempt to make it sound bigger, like, say, the Panama Canal, well, it is a different kettle of episiotomies entirely.

Dr Herb's approach to the big-baby question is basically to wait and see what happens during labour. He says that ultrasounds have proven notoriously unreliable in judging whether a baby's head will fit through the middle of its mum's elvis. I mean pelvis. I suppose I had better read a bit more about caesareans, just in case. I have a mental picture of a whole lot of people with miners' helmets on, carrying coils of rope, peering up my fanny and shouting, 'Come out, you big bugger!'

Dr Herb also promises to refer me to a skin specialist who can remove the moles and skin tags that have gone berserk, but he says any mole or tag removal should wait until at least three months after the baby is born because they often disappear by themselves. (Not the babies, the moles.)

The fluid retention is really getting me down. I'm from a generation that has been taught (wrongly as it happens) that you can be somehow in control of your body – even change its essential shape by diet and exercise, or surgery. The feeling of being totally OUT of control – along for the ride, part of a biology experiment – is kinda disconcerting.

An uneasy feeling grows that David Attenborough is outside my house with a film crew, waiting to breathlessly narrate the next bit of my life. 'And now the Hermoine has only six weeks to go,' he whispers to the camera, as he crouches behind the hibiscus. 'Inside, she is groaning and puffing every time she lifts her enormous weight from the couch. She is now totally demented about getting the nursery set up, and if her mate, Des, does not perform the act of cleaning his crap out of his room by the agreed deadline of thirty-five weeks, she will eat his head.'

Des, fully appraised of the whopperiness of our offspring, has taken to calling it Gigantor instead of the Pikelet. I am running out of wry smiles.

My dreams are getting weirder and weirder. The night before last I dreamt that Des left me and took the furniture, and I forgot to ask him if he was interested in seeing the baby after it was born. Then last night I dreamt I had given birth and then one of the nurses (who were all dressed in pastel French maids' uniforms – a very sartorially satisfactory dream) said, 'There was another cord hanging out so we followed it back in, and it was attached to another baby, which has been hiding behind the uterus the whole time. So now you've got two.'

Week 5 of childbirth classes: Melissa devotes the night to breastfeeding. I must admit I have kind of blanked out about breastfeeding. After Melissa wipes the floor with my illusions and severely bashes up my expectations, I fully realise that if I breastfeed I must accept that for several months I won't be able to (a) sleep, (b) work, (c) speak, (d) twirl tassels in opposite directions while they are attached to my nipples.

It's just that apparently you have to feed the little blighters at least every 4 hours in the early days, and apparently you're supposed to be awake while that happens. I can't imagine who designed this system. No wonder women in some other cultures aren't allowed to do any work or housework or even get out of bed for the first few weeks after childbirth.

And apparently for the full benefits that everyone raves about (boosting the baby's immune system, annoying old fuddy-duddies who simply go gaga at the sight of a publicly bared bosom, etc.), you need to breastfeed for a minimum of three months.

Melissa drops a few hints: go to the loo and wash your hands before you breastfeed, and have a set-up next to your chair with a glass of water, phone, etc. on it. You see, I had imagined I could pop out of a long office meeting and whack the baby on a gland for, say, 7 minutes before handing it to a passer-by and rushing back in. But apparently babies can stay on for up to half an hour each side! And sometimes they want it and sometimes they don't! And it might not be the 7 minutes you choose! And you can't just fill them up when it suits you because it takes 2–3 hours to 'fill up' the breasts with milk again! Outrageous!

There are an awful lot of instructions about breastfeeding, but at least everyone now admits it can be really difficult. Plus Melissa is pretty sure that most of the midwives and lactation consultants (bet that looks good on a passport) at this hospital have their story straight, and we won't be plagued by seven different recommended methods while we're learning. Eventually ('they' say) you can whack a baby on your bosom upside down in the dark while riding a horse backwards side-saddle, but in the beginning it can be all rather laborious. Of course some people go at it as if they've been doing it forever.

When your breasts get engorged – have too much milk – they get really big and hard and painful, and that's when you get some cabbage leaves out of the hospital fridge and put one in each bra cup. (You may have to bring your own leaves if your hospital doesn't stock them.) Nobody really knows why it works, but I'd like to meet the person who worked it out.

The whole idea of expressing breast milk – pumping it out and putting it in bottles – which I'll have to do if I go back to work (or even leave the house at any point), seems damned weird. I can remember seeing rows and rows of dairy cows being milked and am starting to have visions of myself that are along the same lines.

We have reached the point with the fluid retention where the disgusting-tasting dandelion-leaf tincture I'm taking only goes so far towards keeping me distinguishable from a hot-air balloon. Now I just have to put up with it. Unless my blood pressure goes up as well, there's no danger to the baby. I can't find my Fat Boots. In the vague frame of mind I'm in, they'll probably turn up in the crisper. I specialise in sentences that are in search of an endi . . .

info

what to organise before hospital

◉ Go to prenatal classes, and do your reading. Labour and delivery are unpredictable, and it is very helpful if you and your partner or labour support person at least have *some vague idea* of what you might be in for.

◉ Write your birth plan (see info in 'Week 32').

◉ Organise child care for your other child or children: this may need to be available at a moment's notice – even in the middle of the night – so it's a good idea to have a first choice and a back-up. Make sure the kids are well briefed on the plan so they are not freaked out when they find you gone.

◉ Plan your transport to hospital; don't drive yourself. Avoid freeways if you can – they are hard to escape from when there's a traffic jam.

◉ Try to have nursery items and baby clothes organised by about now, just in case.

◉ Have a freezer stocked full of easy food, ready for the first few weeks at home. You could prepare soups, pasta sauces, quiches, pies, lasagnes or casseroles. Put it this way – you won't want to be plucking any chickens. When you go home your priorities will be (a) baby care, (b) sleep and (c) – there is no c.

⊚ Have some light, nutritious early-labour food, such as home-made chicken stock, beef broth or pureed fruit, in the freezer.

⊚ If you can afford it, arrange a house cleaner (friend, relative or agency) for the first few weeks at home, especially if you know you're having a caesarean.

⊚ Order nappy wash service, if you plan to use it – they generally only need a day's warning, but you may as well make a call putting them on notice while you have time.

⊚ Fit the baby restraint in the car, and practise buckling and unbuckling with a teddy bear. You'll need it to take the baby home.

⊚ Find out what labour aids your hospital maternity section or birth centre can provide during labour and what you might need to bring in yourself – does it provide tape players and aromatherapy burners, for instance? Always double-check, when ringing to say you're coming in, that whatever you need is still available just in case it's been booked by someone else.

⊚ When the time comes, phone your independent midwife, hospital or birth centre to tell them you're in labour and ask about when you should come in.

to take to hospital

Your hospital or birth centre will give you a list in advance of what it recommends you bring in for yourself and the baby.

NO: SILK STOCKINGS

WAR & PEACE Arthur Tolstoy

box 'o' condoms

YES:

GIGANTOR SANITARY PADS THEY'RE HUGE!

bag for labour

◉ Labour aids might include: music and a tape or CD; massage oil; birth ball; massage roller (or rolling pin or tennis ball); a spray pack for spraying water and an aromatherapy refresher; lip cream; plenty of food and drink for your labour support person or people (you don't want to have to do without them while they go out hunter-gathering) and sustaining snacks for yourself; warm socks with non-slip bottoms; glucose sweets or sugar-free lollipops; aromatherapy oils.

◉ Take something to wear such as a large T-shirt, giant-sized cotton shirt or cotton nightie. If you want to keep some semblance of being covered up during labour, go for a front-buttoning shirt (or back-to-front hospital gown) so you can have easy skin-to-skin contact and breastfeed your baby after delivery. Whatever you labour in is likely to get stuff all over it: whoever does your washing should soak blood stains in cold water before throwing it in the washing machine. You might also need a couple of pairs of dark undies and some pads to absorb leaking amniotic fluid while you're in labour.

◉ Pack toiletries – soap, shampoo, conditioner, toothbrush and toothpaste, moisturiser, hair elastics, hairbrush, hairdryer, shower cap – ear plugs, eye mask, and make-up if you want to joosh up a bit for visitors.

◉ The support person's clothes should be comfortable, not too warm, and easy to wash. If your support person is likely to be, for instance, giving you pain relief massage in the shower, they might also want to pack bathers, because hospitals do try to restrict the number of people running around in the nicky noo nar.

◉ Apparently some people who are into 'creative visualisation' look at a photo of their dog. Of course they're obviously insane.

a bigger bag for the hospital stay

⊚ Take a few packs of super-soaker sanitary pads – these are sold as maternity pads.

⊚ Include a few front-opening nighties, a dressing-gown, slippers, six pairs of black cotton undies. (It would be nice to have a clean nightie each morning and each night, and plenty of cotton undies – it's a leaky old time – so pack according to your helper's washing plans. Will the washing be done every couple of days, or not until you all get home?) Some hospitals provide a laundry service – your clothes will need to be labelled with your name. You can wear regular day clothes in hospital, but the combination of a sore, tender and tired body, the high temperatures at which hospitals are generally kept and the number of times you'll need access to the business end makes cotton nighties a practical choice.

⊚ Take at least two very firm nursing bras for supporting tight, engorged breasts, and nursing pads to soak up the leaking breast milk when it 'comes in'.

⊚ Pack going-home clothes for you (probably maternity clothes because your tummy will still be big); and for the baby – include a hat and a warm blanket if the weather's cold. New babies love to be wrapped up firmly because it's more womblike.

⊚ Take a newborn-baby-care book such as Robin Barker's *Baby Love* or *What to Expect in the First Year*, by Arlene Eisenberg and cohorts (see Baby-care Books in 'Week 43'), and a book of names if that debate is still dragging on.

⊚ Don't forget a wrapped present for your toddler so they feel central to the action. This is the beginning of a difficult time for them, and they will be nicer to the new baby if they think it's brought them a special present.

what's going on

From now on your baby will hog all available space and squash up anything silly enough to get in the way, like your lungs. If you do get breathless, sitting or standing up straight will help. So will taking it easy. If you're interested in going to childbirth classes but haven't organised this yet, you'd better make that phone call now. Lay in the 'layette' (baby's clothes).

Your body is starting to put the final touches to the baby: it's the finishing-school stage. From now on your bub is pretty busy practising sucking, breathing, blinking, turning the head, grabbing things (such as its other hand or the umbilical cord) and stretching out the legs – but there's not quite enough room to actually do that. Hence the jarring kicks you may feel. The baby's skin is becoming smoother and less translucent – more like the final skin colour.

Weight: about 2.1 kilos.

Average approximate baby length this week from head to bum

| 17 | 18 | 19 | 20 | 21 | 22 | 23 | 24 | 25 | 26 | 27 | 28 | 29 |

DiARY

It's really hard to find comfy positions. If I lean back, I get heartburn. If I lean forward, I'm not resting, I'm listing. If I lie down, I can't get anything done. If I don't lie down, the fluid retention reaches epic proportions. If I lie down, my lower legs ache. If I walk around, I aggravate an ache in my groin. At the start of the day my face is all puffy. By the end of the day my ankles are all puffy. I'm starting to feel like one of those ballpoint pens with the liquid in the side: if you turn it upside down all the liquid falls down and the girl's bikini top comes off. Now I can't even adequately describe a novelty souvenir writing implement.

Make the mistake of trying to buy a frock in a flash boutique with three mirrors in the change room. When I realise quite what I look like from behind, I have to sit down on it for a minute, in shock. And my arms look like the sort of arms that gigantic ladies get a few years after their wood-chopping days are over. Good grief.

I skitter between nausea and indigestion and faintness and wondering if that weird feeling is hunger.

This baby is a booter. I try to imagine what else it will be like when it comes out. Still trying to get past the thoughts of labour itself, and wondering how on earth I can get all my work finished before the Pikelet arrives.

Des finally cleans up his room but leaves all his water polo trophies on the mantelpiece. There is a rather tension-ridden scene with me trying to be diplomatic ('How would you feel if we put your trophies up in the living room?') and Des looking grumpy. Perhaps it is some deep-seated male displacement thing going on. Poor Des. He gets his own back by doing a load of new baby things in the wash (to make sure there are no manufacturing chemicals left on them) and waving a very tiny sock at me, which he knows perfectly well will reduce me to tears.

A tree in the backyard drops a big branch. A tree 'surgeon' (why not 'barber'?) comes and describes it jauntily as 'self-lopping', so of course now we have to cut down a perfectly charming lemon-scented eucalypt full of birds and expose ourselves to the scrutiny of approximately ninety flats in the block behind because we don't want it self-lopping onto the baby. And that will be $400, thanks. Honestly sometimes you don't know where the next bill is coming from.

Aunty Peg is now worried about dust in the baby's room.

'It's thoroughly dusted and vacuumed once a week,' I reassure her. Well, that's a lie.

You don't so much reassure her as send her fleeing to another fixation.

'There'll still be dust in there,' she warns ominously, as if the dust were somehow radioactive.

Then when I say I am looking for a woollen bunny-rug or shawl to wrap the baby in when it's cold, she starts in about that.

'I don't understand,' she says, muttering about heat stroke and meningitis and the fall of civilisation as we know it. 'Nobody I know wraps a baby in a wool rug. They might throw one onto the pram, but it's not for wrapping up.'

'Yes, okay,' I finally say. 'I'll just throw it on the pram, then.'

Oops. Just remembered we don't have a pram. Must ring Luke and Fatimah to claim theirs.

Buy some extra-large pyjamas to take to the hospital. Start to pack hospital bag. The top of the pyjamas doesn't even look like it will fit me now, and as they were mail order I didn't realise they were going to say 'Brand New Mum' on the pocket. How ostentatious. And I think that will be fairly obvious without anyone having to read my pyjama pocket. Especially because the bloke who designed the Brand New Mum's pyjamas didn't leave enough room for a not-yet-deflated tummy. You'd think someone in the fashion industry would know better . . . I must have totally lost my marbles: I could have got one of the seamstresses at work to run up a giant T-shirt in 4 minutes flat.

This gum nodule thing just above my front teeth seems to be getting worse. It bleeds profusely every time I brush my teeth and is clearly visible as a kind of bulge between two teeth. I have started to spit blood like a prize-fighter. The only book that mentions it is *What to Expect When You're Expecting*, which says it's called a pyogenic granuloma, or in the usual deeply reassuring doctor language a 'pregnancy tumour', which is actually

completely harmless and will go away right after the baby's born.
Which is not what my dentist says.

My dentist says (after inquiring whether the baby's father is my
boyfriend or my husband, a question obviously essential to dental
hygiene): 'It won't go away. I can just slice it off. It will bleed for
an hour or so and then be all right.'

Call me crazy, but I'm going to wait and see.*

Everyone is saying how beautiful Marg's baby is. I am starting
to feel a bit paranoid that our baby will have a head like a robber's
dog and there will just be polite silences on the subject.

I have been thinking about the birth plan and I've decided
that I don't want the baby to come out the vagina, and I don't
want a caesarean. I may have to do some more research. Perhaps
it can come out of an elbow.

My pants have started curling down my tummy like a roller
blind.

I'm too busy to have a child.

Walk to work and get completely exhausted. Business lunch
follows. Try to be sparkling and feel like I'm mentally swimming
in custard.

Miss my appointment with Dr Herb as he is out delivering a
baby somewhere, and I can't face the waiting room banked up
with trillions of tired women so I wag.

I am SO huge out the front that close friends can't help just
patting and rubbing my tummy – like I'm a Buddha – for luck.
I don't mind. People have started to ask 'How long to go?', and
'Are you excited?' (some kind of code word for 'utterly terrified',
perhaps).

The last childbirth class: by this stage all the people in the class
who were going to loosen up have loosened up. Only two couples
haven't lost their quiet, stunned-mullet approach to everything.
One woman keeps looking at her partner as if he's a ghastly
apparition and she's suddenly realised she's tied to him for the
rest of her life.

The picture I'll take with me is of women bulging in the
middle, with their hands crossed over their bulge and their male

---

* The book was right.

partner leaning towards them. The woman who wanted her birth on the Internet, and her husband, the filthy show-offs, arrive halfway through the class, with their baby! It came two weeks early, on the weekend, and they're still high. Melissa confides that she doesn't let parents come if they've hit the baby-blues stage. You don't want a brand-new mother sobbing and falling about a class, I suppose.

Melissa shows us two videos of couples with new babies. The men all work away from home and the women at home. The couples talk about lack of privacy and personal space, their relationship as a couple, tiredness, guilt, coping with a distressed and needy baby (the gist seems to be that 'this too shall pass'). And there's footage of a woman with twins: she looks a bit like someone has hit her on the back of the head with a rubber cricket bat. You would, wouldn't you?

Melissa talks about having an unsettled baby. New ones sleep 16 hours a day, but after a few weeks or months they can cry for a few hours a day no matter how well fed and clean and cuddled they are. This is often in the early evening and is known as 'arsenic hour'.

We gallop through some different things to settle the baby, how not to expect much from your sex life until at least after the six-week check-up (one man mishears and shouts 'Six years?!'), contraception (twelve condoms at once, thank you), services available if you get into trouble with feeding, sleeping or crying, and baby safety.

Revelation: one woman in the class asks, 'Shouldn't you have the baby checked out by a paediatrician before it goes home?' Melissa says yes, most parents do. I haven't even thought of this. I guess the obstetrician is a mother specialist, not a baby specialist.

info

labour

You might or might not notice the early signs of labour. If you do, rest and eat – labour could start any time and you need to conserve your energy, though the Real Thing may still be up to a few days or even weeks away.

When your contractions start, they may be 'pre-labour', sometimes called 'false' contractions. These are quite bearable – more uncomfortable than painful – and irregular, and go away if you move around, lie down or have a bath. It's often difficult to tell the difference between 'pre-labour' and the 'latent phase' of the first stage of labour (during which the cervix dilates 3–4 centimetres), so don't hesitate to telephone your midwife, the hospital or birth centre, or your obstetrician to describe what's happening and to find out whether to stay at home or go straight to the hospital or centre.

Call your hospital or obstetrician immediately if:

⊚ when your waters break, you notice a green or dark stain in the amniotic fluid; this is meconium – the baby's first poo – which can be a sign of foetal distress

⊚ you have bright red bleeding, which may indicate a problem with the placenta

⊚ you feel or see the umbilical cord in your vagina, which is called cord prolapse. This is an emergency. Ring an ambulance, open the door, then kneel down with your bottom in the air and head and shoulders down to take pressure off the cord until the ambulance arrives. (If you can, get someone else to make the call and open the door.)

When contractions start in earnest, they will usually:

❺ be regular

❺ get stronger

❺ last for longer

❺ come closer together

❺ be increasingly tough to cope with.

Time their length and frequency and give this information to your obstetrician or midwife, or the hospital or birth centre.

The 'average' labour *for a first-timer* goes something like this:

❺ first stage – the cervix dilates to 8–9 centimetres (average 8 hours)

❺ first stage transition (second part of the first stage) – the cervix dilates to about 10 centimetres (can be 3–5 hours)

❺ second stage – build-up to pushing, then the baby is born (average 2 hours)

❺ third stage – the placenta and any other bits no longer needed are expelled (about 10 minutes after the birth if oxytocin is given, up to an hour if delivered naturally).

Gosh, that sounds neat. In reality your experience might be radically different.

When you arrive at the hospital or birth centre, or when the midwife or obstetrician arrives at your homebirth, you'll have a medical examination, which will probably involve:

❺ checking your blood pressure

❺ checking a urine sample

❺ checking your temperature and pulse

❺ a feel up your vagina to see how dilated your cervix is

❺ electronic monitoring of the baby's heartbeat, usually done by placing a belt around your tummy, which is attached by wires to a machine that prints out when your uterus contracts and also records the baby's heartbeat. The monitor is often removed after a set time (for example, 20 minutes) if there seems to be no problem. The heartbeat can also be checked for briefer periods with a stethoscope.

Make sure the midwife makes a note of your relevant health details or special needs.

Ideally things will now proceed according to your birth plan. But any unpredictable turns will have to be dealt with as they arise.

first stage

For some people the latent phase of first-stage labour – the first 3–4 centimetres dilation – is barely perceptible; others experience intense backache and painful contractions. For some it happens quietly over a long time; for others it may all happen in just a couple of hours of full-on labour. Contractions may last 30–35 seconds, and could be regular or irregular – anywhere from 5–20 minutes apart. You'll probably be at home and may even be able to sleep through some of this phase. Rest as much as possible and have some of the light snacks you have ready in the freezer. It can help to have warm baths, if your waters haven't broken, and you should keep timing your contractions.

All the following advice may fly out of your head, so get your birth support person to read it well before you might need it so that they can remind you.

By the time you're well into the first stage, you'll probably be in hospital and looking to your coping strategies: massage, TENS machine, relaxation techniques, breathing techniques. Not to mention drugs. Remember to wee frequently: the area is feeling such intense sensations from labour that you mightn't notice you need to wee. Stay as mobile and upright as possible. Try out different labouring positions for greatest comfort. Stay hydrated, taking ice chips, juice cubes or sips of water.

Try to rest completely and relax between contractions, and not expend energy anticipating the next one. Use positive visualisation and psyching techniques, such as concentrating on a mental picture of a flower opening; focus on the positive goal of seeing your baby; chant 'This will end', whatever. Clenching everything up can hinder the progress of labour, so with your partner or labour support person's help use whatever it takes to go with the flow. If you can't stand the pain, or if this phase has gone on for a long time and you've had it, feel free to yell 'DRUGS!' around about now.

first stage transition

This is generally considered to be the most challenging time of labour. Contractions are strong and getting stronger, lasting longer – 60–90 seconds – and coming at shorter intervals. Sometimes there's no time to rest between them, and you're probably exhausted. You may feel hot or shivering and cold, or alternate between temperature extremes. You may be nauseated or vomiting, and feeling overwhelmed or unable to cope. You may feel totally pissed off.

At the end of this phase your cervix will be fully dilated, and you'll be ready to start pushing. If you've hung in there without drugs, your support person can remind you that you are nearly there, that you'll have your baby very soon, and you can hit your support person. If you have the urge to push during this phase, before the cervix is fully dilated, you may be advised to blow or pant instead.

second stage – pushing and delivery

About a third of labouring women have a resting, or 'latent', phase at this point before their body starts urging them to push the baby out – the active phase of the second stage. The go during this phase is to listen to your body when it comes to pushing. Contractions will still be 60–90 seconds long, but may be further apart (2–5 minutes), so you can rest between them. No need to pop the capillaries in your eyeballs or hold your breath beyond the point of comfort or turn purple. Using lots of shorter moments of bearing down with each contraction is less stressful to the baby, and makes it easier for the pelvic floor to relax, than one big, breath-holding push, like the ones you see in the movies.

This more relaxed approach may make the second stage a bit longer than if you use the push approach, but is probably less stressful for you as well as the baby. During this phase you might be making some deep guttural grunts and moans, which many other pregnancy books seem to think will embarrass you. You'll be far too busy to be embarrassed. You might also push out a poo during this phase. No big deal.

All being well, babies are not oxygen-deprived during this phase; they're still getting oxygen from the placenta.

Actual, honest-to-goodness birth There's more panting as the baby's head crowns and pushes against the perineum. You'll be asked to try not to push but instead to relax the pelvic floor, aiming to slow down the last bit to avoid tearing or the need for an episiotomy. You may be offered a bird's-eye view of proceedings with the help of a mirror: this is a fascinating prospect for some, and horrifying for others. You choose.

Mums often describe the sensation of the baby's head emerging as stinging, burning or intense pressure. A midwife may 'support' the perineum and anus (apply pressure from the outside to counter the bulging). This can help make it less painful. After the head emerges, the baby rotates so that its shoulders line up with the widest part of your pelvis and the little body slithers out. Hello there! Finally meeting and holding your baby is an indescribably awe-inspiring, emotional and happy time. (Or not, of which more later.)

third stage: the placenta and membranes expelled

You may be so engrossed in your new baby, you don't notice the third stage. The uterus continues to contract, causing the placenta to come away from the wall, taking with it what's left of the amniotic sac as it detaches; further contractions will push the placenta into the vagina, from where it can be pulled out, or pushed out with another contraction. The contraction of the muscles of your truly amazing uterus also seals off the blood vessels at the site of detachment. The placenta comes out more quickly if an injection of oxytocin is given to speed up contractions.

The placenta is inspected to make sure it has been delivered whole. You'll be checked to make sure you don't have post-partum haemorrhage ('post-partum' means after delivery). It's diagnosed when the blood loss is 600 millilitres or more; the usual loss is less than 300 millilitres. It happens to about 5 per cent of mothers.

The 'fourth stage', hardly ever mentioned in the textbooks, is stabilisation and getting acquainted with your baby, enjoying skin-to-skin contact, keeping your baby warm, the baby having a red-hot go and first drink at your nipples, the standard reflex and observation tests on the baby done by a doctor or midwife, clamping of the umbilical cord, and any sewing up of the perineum.

You May Need Bigger Shoes

WEEK 35

what's going on

That baby is taking up stomach space – smaller meals more often are easier to digest. You're probably finding it hard to get your shoes on and off. Wear slip-on shoes unless you need the ankle support of lace-ups. You've probably gone up a shoe size as well, especially in width, maybe permanently. Try to walk a bit every day until the baby arrives. To reduce the swelling in your feet and ankles, stand on your head a lot. Or at the very least sit down or, preferably, lie down and put your feet above the level of your heart as much as possible. (This can be especially effective in getting yourself extra room on public transport, particularly if you shout obscenities as well.)

Toenails are in. The fingernails may be poking over the end of the fingers. Your baby would fail that test they do at the start of netball games, and can scratch itself. Weight: about 2.3 kilos.

Average approximate baby length this week from head to bum

Diary

Help, it's going too fast. I'm not ready but I'm sick of being pregnant. Bunty, who does the accounts at work, says she lost 15 kilos at the birth, including the weight of the baby, and I must say THAT'S an attractive proposition. I'm wondering how long my legs will carry me. I weigh myself at a pharmacy and it says I've put on 7 kilos in five days. God, I hope those scales are faulty. I'm terrified of getting on the scales at Dr Herb's.

Before I leave the pharmacy the assistant thrusts into my hands the special chemist's show bag to encourage me to come back and buy baby stuff there. You get your nursing pads (colostrum-and-milk-soaker-upperers), five nappy liners (whatever *they* are), twelve thick baby wipes, a disposable nappy, a sample of cocoa-butter moisturiser, a pamphlet on same, a booklet about safety, and a copy of *Practical Parenting* magazine with the cover line 'I gave birth in a petrol station!', which I don't think has enough exclamation marks, and what's practical about giving birth in a servo I'd like to know.

I take an inventory of stretch marks. Several red-purple stripes on the underside of each breast, and on each hip a bunch of marks that looks as if a hand held me too hard on each fleshy part. Nothing on the tummy itself, which has stretched more than anything. What gives? Me.

Yet another visit to Dr Herb for the fluid-retention check.

He measures the height of the baby, gives it a feel and says, 'Oh God.'

First 'My, it's a whopper' and now 'Oh God'. If this goes on he'll be singing 'Oh What a Beauty! Never Seen One as Big as That Befoooooore!' on my next visit. For some reason I feel resigned rather than horrified. I suspect his tactic is to soften me up and get me used to the idea of a boombah bambino.

I show him the birth plan and he reacts to each point.

Will you induce at the due date? (No. I'll let you go ten days over.)

Ideally I would like to avoid either a vaginal birth or a

caesarean. However, there do not seem to be many other options. (Ha ha. By hook or by crook the baby will come out.)

The labour will be attended by my independent midwife, Miss Beck, who will probably prescribe herbs and supplements after the birth. (Fine.)

I would like to be kept informed of what's happening. (Yep.)

I would like to avoid monitoring that might 'tether' me to the bed, and an epidural, if possible. Des is particularly concerned about the possible side effects of an epidural, but understands it might not be avoidable. Anyway it's my decision. (It certainly is.)

I would like to avoid an episiotomy, but would rather be cut than tear if necessary. (Although sometimes an episiotomy is unavoidable, we will try to avoid it. Actually it's better to tear naturally unless it looks like you're going to tear down to the bowel or up to the clitoris, or shatter the whole area, which is hard to repair.) (Me: That's enough. Fine. That's quite enough chat about torn clitorises for one day.)

I don't want gas, would rather take pethidine. (You should try the gas, and see if it works.) (Me: No way – haven't you seen that movie *Blue Velvet?*, where Dennis Hopper has this mask on and . . .) (No.)

My Major Fears, in order, are:

1 possible neurological damage from epidural. (About the same chance as getting hit by a jumbo jet, unless you already have a history of trouble, such as multiple sclerosis.)

2 episiotomy. (You and I will just keep in contact throughout the delivery.)

But generally we agree: whatever it takes to get a healthy baby out with the least amount of damage possible all round.

While Herb is checking my blood pressure, I remark that it

doesn't seem to be within the laws of physics, but I appear to have put on another 4 kilos. At least Dr Herb's scales say I'm 3 kilos lighter than the chemist's did. I think I'm going to explode. This means I have put on 20 kilos!!! I'm not eating crap – in fact I'm not eating a lot at all. It's spooky.

Dr Herb says don't worry, I'll probably put on another 5 kilos before I give birth. I am absolutely flabbergasted.

'It's not humanly possible,' I say.

'Don't forget,' he says, 'you can lose 12 kilos just at the birth, and all the fluid over the next couple of days. Of course you can actually puff up after the birth as well. You'll lose it. It's easier to lose the weight that's not junk food.'

I don't tell him I have at least three Magnums a week.

Marg has given me a book called *The New Age Baby Name Book* by Susan Browder. Could its names be worse than some of the suggestions from friends so far, including Hezekiah, Ringo or Bluey if it's a boy. And if it's a girl, geographical names such as Deniliquin, Adelaide and what's next, Grand Canyon? How about fabric names such as Chiffon, Polly Esther and Tencel?

I guess I have to remember that I come from a family that has definite trouble with names. My grandmother named her three daughters after whatever household item she was holding at the time she went into labour: Peg, Bobbin and Rose. (Thank God she was gardening for the last one and not cleaning the loo or Mum would have been called Toilet Brush.)

There's some very good advice in the book, which you would already know unless you were completely brain dead, such as: if you have twin boys don't call them Pete and Repeat because the joke will wear off. It mentions a man in America who became a circus clown (natch) whose real name was Oofty Goofty Bowman. Des and I are thrilled and immediately rename the Pikelet Oofty Goofty.

According to *The New Age Baby Name Book*, in some cultures they name kids for what time of the day or night they arrive. Luckily this has not caught on here, where not many children are called Sparrow's Fart or Half Past Three. And you can use the

Ghanaian language to call the child after the day of the week it was born on. Young Wednesday from the Addams family would have been called Ekua.

You can also use any unfamiliar language to name your baby after a certain characteristic. What is the Burkina Fasoese for 'reluctant to mow the lawn', I wonder.

The book goes so far as to advise using the name Caimile from the Umbundu people of Africa, which is a sort of code for the proverb 'A tree bears fruit, the fruit falls to the ground, a family has children, and they all die'. How jaunty. And it suggests pinching some Native American even if you're not, such as Helkimu meaning 'hitting bushes with seed beater'. I think it would be better to wait and see whether the child grew up to be interested in whacking bushes before putting that kind of pressure on.

I don't think Yuttciso is going to catch on. It means 'lice thick on a chicken hawk'. The book says American names that have fallen out of favour include Minnehaha, Amorous, Ham, Lettuce and Bugless.

The book has also translated some names from their original Celtic meanings. Calvin Klein, for instance, means 'young, small, bald man'. And Mary Tyler Moore means 'bitter, dark-skinned roofer'.

But the handiest idea of them all is just to combine the names of the parents. For example, if your names are Mal and Trisha, you can call the kid Militia. Or, say, if your names are Louise and Arnie, you can call it Loonie. It's easy. Paul and May Ling? – Appalling. Bathsheba and Matthew? – Bath-matt. And in our case, Hermdes. Sounds like some kind of dangerous chemical.

I have learnt that we should only ever try out our suggested names on a few friends. There'll always be someone who doesn't like the name you choose because there was a girl at their kindergarten called that who used to put Clag in their hair. Or it was the name of the first man who dumped them. Best to just hit them with a fait accompli after the kid's born, and they'll have to put on a brave face and get used to it.

more info on baby names

The New Age Baby Name Book by Susan Browder, Warner Books, New York, 1987.

An unintentionally hilarious, American list of absolutely insanely stupid names you could give your child, as well as some definite possibilities. Good for seeing names from different cultures. It ranges from Agnes to Zaim, meaning 'brigadier-general' in Arabic.

Names For Australian Babies by Sarah Davis, Penguin, Ringwood, 1998.

I checked whether it has Bluey and it has Blue. Must be pretty comprehensive.

info
caesarean delivery

A caesarean section operation is a surgical procedure to take the baby out of the uterus through your abdomen. It's usually called just 'a caesarean' or 'a caesar'. A standard caesarean is considered to be a very safe procedure when performed by a specialist in a good hospital. But it is not a walk in the park. A caesarean is major surgery. (The way some people blithely refer to it, you'd think the baby just came out of a handy zipper.)

how common is it?

Depending on several factors, your chance of having a caesarean might be a lot greater than you think. Up to one in four Australian babies end up being delivered this way. Read up on it because it might happen to you, even if you've had a 'perfect' pregnancy.

what happens?

During a standard caesarean, you'll have the top half of your pubic hair trimmed or shaved, and then you'll be put on a hospital trolley and wheeled off to the operating room. In this very brightly lit room all the medical staff will wear shower caps, face masks and protective smocks, and so will your support person. An intravenous (IV) drip will be put into your arm, then you'll be given an epidural injection (or spinal-block injection if speed is necessary) by the anaesthetist (explained in Pain Relief Options in 'Week 32') to numb the lower half of your body. As well, a catheter tube will be put into your urethra for the wee to flow into a bag. A screen will be put up between you and your tummy, but a mirror can be angled for you to watch the operation if you're that way inclined.

A nurse or doctor will swab the lower part of your tummy with antiseptic. Your obstetrician will make an incision just above your pubic hairline, usually horizontal and about 10 centimetres long. Then the obstetrician will cut through layers of fat and muscle to the uterus wall, cut open the uterus and pull the baby out. You may have some sensation of pulling or pressure but should feel no pain.

It all happens very quickly: the baby is generally born 5–10 minutes after the first incision. The baby will be shown to you and then will be fully examined by a paediatrician standing by in the room. (The baby might also have mucus sucked from its tiny airways.) If the baby doesn't need to be taken away for special care, insist on a long cuddle and first breastfeed straight away. Measuring or baths are not important enough reasons to separate you and your baby at this crucial time, but many hospitals take babies away to suit their policy, not you.

You might be too preoccupied to notice what happens next, but usually you'll hear some gurgling, slurping noises when the amniotic fluid is suctioned out. The placenta and membranes, and the swabs, are removed, then you are stitched up. This can take quite a while because it's not just one row of stitches, it's seven different wounds to be sewn, including layers of skin, fat, muscle, and the inner and outer walls of the uterus.

why would you need one?

A caesarean can be elective: you 'elect' to have one on the advice of your obstetrician and make a hospital appointment. Or it can be emergency surgery performed unexpectedly and suddenly when a problem develops during labour. In the case of an elective caesarean, you have to weigh the pros and cons of setting a date rather than waiting for the spontaneous onset of labour before having the operation. These can be discussed with your obstetrician and midwife.

If you want to avoid having a caesarean, talk to your obstetrician, but remember that there's never a guarantee you won't have one.

The basic criterion for a caesarean is whether it will be less of a risk to the mother and baby than a vaginal birth. In some cases the decision is very clear cut, in others it's more open to interpretation. Some reasons why you might end up needing a caesarean are:

❻ you have a medical condition such as pre-eclampsia or eclampsia (see info in 'Week 31')

❻ you have diabetes and must deliver early, but the cervix isn't ready

❻ active genital herpes (the baby may catch the herpes from sores as it comes through the vagina)

❻ the baby is sick or isn't growing properly

❻ the baby is in an awkward position – perhaps sideways, which is known as the 'transverse lie', or bum not head down, which is called the 'breech position' (though many obstetricians will agree to try first to deliver a breech baby in the normal way)

❻ the baby's head seems to be too big to fit through its mum's pelvis; this is technically called cephalo-pelvic disproportion (CPD)

◎ placenta praevia (the placenta is positioned over the cervix)

◎ placental abruption (the placenta comes away too early)

◎ an overdue baby in a deteriorating uterine environment

◎ the umbilical cord is 'prolapsed' – coming down into the vagina, possibly cutting off the baby's circulation if the baby's head is against the cervix

◎ the baby's lowered or erratic heartbeat during labour indicates it is distressed or in danger

◎ failure to progress during labour.

recovery from the surgery

Probably the first thing you'll notice when you're in the recovery room or back in your own hospital room is that you're still hooked up to the IV drip and doing wee into a bag through a tube, which will continue for up to a day. There will be a very nice drug coming through the IV drip, probably morphine or pethidine. You might be hungry, but you won't be allowed to eat or drink anything until your bowel shows signs of post-operative activity (okay, farting), at which time your IV can be removed.

Over several days your pain relief is likely to be reduced in strength. Don't skimp on relief, and ask the nurses or midwives for it if they miss your due time or you are in pain. It's important not to be in pain whenever possible.

See or call your natural therapist about any vitamins and minerals that may help recovery. Make sure they're approved for lactation and by your doctor.

Get up and move as soon as humanly possible. Immediately you can feel your legs again, start flexing and rotating your feet, and doing leg bends in bed. Get out of bed and go for a walk as soon as you're allowed to. It won't be a brisk hike, mind you. It'll be more of a small shuffle round the bed. Soon you'll be going down the corridor and back. Make sure someone goes with you because you'll be a bit woozy.

Early mobility will help you to avoid complications such as

pain from gas, difficulty weeing and blood clots in the legs. And it's amazing how quickly you start to feel better once you are mobile. But DON'T OVERDO IT. Do only half as much as you feel you can, even if you're sure you can walk around the whole block on day four. Discipline yourself to increase the exercise a *little* bit each day, otherwise you'll get overtired and set back your recovery.

Laughing, coughing and sneezing in bed are less painful if you bend your knees and support your scar with a pillow. If you're standing up, bend over and put your hands over the scar. Avoid constipation, as it will be painful. If it gets to dire proportions (four to five days without a poo) your doctor can prescribe an anal suppository.

Your tummy will look as if it's in the earlier stages of pregnancy for a while. It will be sore, but on the plus side there will be no stitches in your fanny and you can sit without pain.

Your hospital stay will be longer than for a vaginal delivery – up to a week, depending on hospital policy and how you feel. Don't be swayed by friends or staff – if you want to go earlier or stay longer, discuss it with your obstetrician and do the best thing for you, not for some bureaucrat's government policy guidelines on bed allocation based on funding cuts. After you go home, any sign of infection such as oozing or pus from the wound should of course be reported to your obstetrician.

Full recovery is generally longer term than for vaginal delivery – it's about six weeks until everything is healed up and several more weeks before you're up to full pre-pregnancy exercise capabilities. And of course it is harder to look after a baby and recover from major abdominal surgery at the same time. You will be very tired, and your body will be in shock for longer. Remember that recovering from a caesarean is comparable to convalescing after a serious car accident: go easy on yourself.

The double burden of looking after a baby and recovering from surgery can lead to feelings of depression and some women believe they are 'failures' because they have not had a natural birth. Having a caesar, though, doesn't necessarily mean you'll have negative feelings about the birth – not least because it may have saved your life or the baby's.

You're usually told not to drive until your six-week check-up (mainly because it hurts to brake so you may brake more slowly than usual), although some doctors believe it is safe after about three weeks; if you do drive before six weeks, check with your insurance company that you are covered. You're also usually told not to reach above your head to get things down from shelves or do any similar activity, or lift anything heavier than your baby, before the six-week check-up. The rules for taking things easy still apply: only do half of the exercise you think you could do, and keep it gentle.

more info on caesareans

Childbirth Choices by Adriene Bennett, Wendi Etherington and Daphne Hewson, and **Your Baby and the Birth Experience** by Dr Gregory Fox (full details and reviews in 'Week 32').

Both these books cover caesarean deliveries in detail.

what's going on

You're tired. You've probably got sore feet, fluid retention causing swollen everything, and tingling fingers; and you could be breathless or dizzy. If you're really lucky you might even faint. You'll probably visit your obstetrician every week from now on. You may get stabbing pelvic pains or aches – like a 'stitch' – which are probably the pelvic ligaments loosening up. The baby's head may be down low in the pelvis and can bounce up and down on your cervix giving you 'shocks', particularly if you sit down too quickly. This doesn't necessarily mean that the baby is 'engaged' (in position and ready to come out head first). You should begin to feel movements every day, even if it's only a little leg wave.

Those new lungs are still not completely finished. The baby has put on lots of fat. If it hasn't turned upside down already, it may be about to. (If it's still the wrong way up by the time labour starts, you may have a breech birth – meaning bum first.) Weight: about 2.5 kilos.

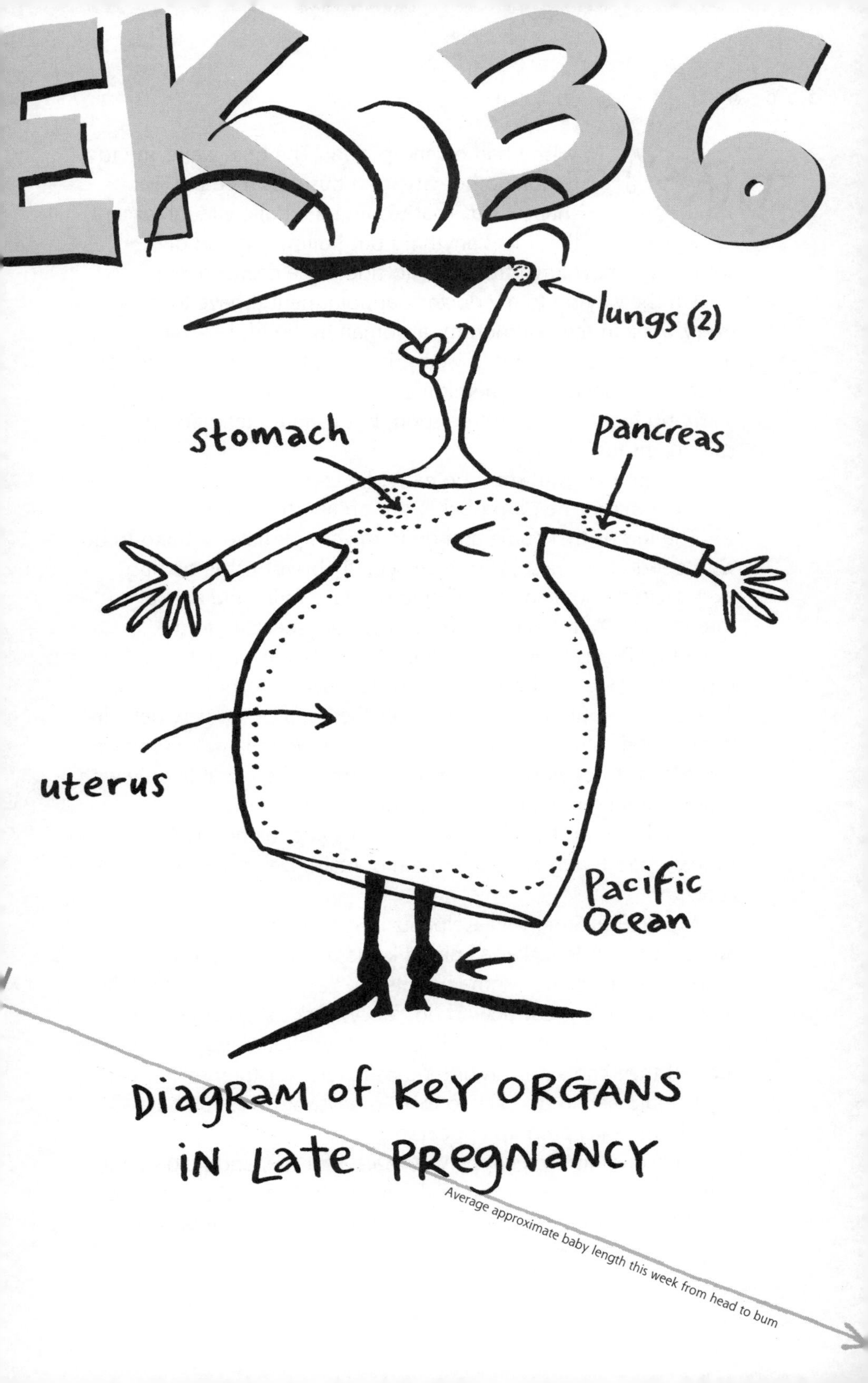

EK 36

lungs (2)

stomach

pancreas

uterus

Pacific
Ocean

DIAGRAM OF KEY ORGANS
IN LATE PREGNANCY

Average approximate baby length this week from head to bum

DiARY Wish I had given up work. The boss wants me to fly to another city for a business meeting. Fat chance. Ha. That would be a hollow laugh except that I feel anything but hollow. Instead of waddling, I now lurch from side to side like a drunken Yeti.

On the way up to my doctor's appointment (I have to go every week in the last month), a woman in the lift tells me she had a 1-hour labour and not to worry, it doesn't even hurt. I think she might have been at the pethidine cabinet. Dr Herb says I'm still 'carrying high' so it won't be soon, but I should read about caesareans just in case.

'I'd bet that you won't go early,' he says.

He reminds me I'll probably put on another 5 kilos.

The lumps that come and go in my armpit have nothing to do with deodorant, he says. They're actually breast tissue getting over-excited about soon having to produce milk, and are called 'breast tails'. Which sounds like a stripper's specialty to me.

Aunty Peg is making cushions (don't ask me why). Uncle Stan is ringing up to see how I'm going. Just had a horrible vision of Aurelia and Aunty Peg meeting over the head of the new baby in the hospital. Must warn Uncle Stan to keep Aurelia away until we come home. Keeping Aunty Peg away would be possible only with a very cunning plan and some Semtex.

Finally surrendering to the inevitable and taking on the role of Muhammad trying to escape the mountain, Des is sleeping on the couch.

My old pal Simon Weaselpantz has scoured the country fêtes and sent the little tacker a knitted koala and a knitted bunny rabbit. Thank heavens some people are keeping up the old skills. Women used to know how to do 'fancy work', showing-off sewing, crochet, knitting, tatting and heaven knows what else. Now they're lucky if they know how to order a caffe latte for themselves. Can't say I would like to go back to the old days, but nice to know somebody is keeping up appearances.

Jill is organising a nappy wash cartel for me, and helping me compile a data base for the birth announcements. We've got two versions ready to go, one that says Eddy and one that says Pearl.

I think that's all the options covered. I've been thinking about the pros and cons of having a boy or a girl. Boy: won't be so bombarded with 'you're ugly' messages from advertising and film and TV. Girl: will probably find it easier to talk about emotions and be slightly less likely to play noisy war games on the roof.

Although, truth be told, it's impossible to really imagine what it will be like when this baby is OUT. The baby-being-IN thing and the getting-the-baby-out thing just take up so much brain space.

The worst thing about being this pregnant, except for being uncomfortable and sort of nervous (could go any time from now), is that if you have someone to cuddle it's an exercise in geometry. It's impossible to get really close with a third person stuck way out there in the middle.

info

late babies

why are babies late?
Your baby is not likely to arrive at precisely midnight on the 266th day of pregnancy. So if it isn't early, it's going to be late (der). We don't know exactly what makes a woman's body go into labour, but it's now believed that the baby, when ready to be born, somehow releases hormones or prostaglandins or a greeting card or something that doctors don't know about yet. This unknown

signal triggers the softening of the cervix, ready for it to dilate and let the baby through, and contractions of the uterus.

Only about 5 per cent of babies are born on their given 'due date'. About the same number arrive more than two weeks early or two weeks late. Traditionally babies of first pregnancies have been more likely to be 'overdue' than subsequent ones. If you go beyond two weeks overdue the doctor will probably induce the birth as the placenta might start to deteriorate.

how long can you go?

Up to forty-four weeks with careful monitoring, although most obstetricians and midwives don't like to leave it that long. Beyond forty-two weeks of pregnancy, babies are at increased risk of foetal distress during labour, inhaling their first poo, and as the placenta starts packing up, the baby could even die. Some of the most common methods of checking that an overdue baby is okay are:

⑥ your obstetrician examines you to see whether the cervix is ripe – if it is not, it may be an indication that the baby is not ready to be born yet

⑥ you keep a 'kick chart' to monitor how much the baby is moving

⑥ the baby's reaction to sound or vibrations is tested

⑥ electronic monitoring of the baby's heart rate to make sure it is not distressed

⑥ an ultrasound to help estimate the baby's size and the amount of surrounding amniotic fluid.

induction methods

Prostaglandin Prostaglandins (which are like hormones) are found naturally in the uterus; some prostaglandins stimulate contractions at the beginning of labour. A synthetic prostaglandin gel or pessary (like a large pill) put on the cervix can ripen it and trigger labour. It usually takes a number of doses, sometimes spaced over more than one day, before labour starts, but it is one of the least intrusive and most effective methods of induction.

Artificial rupture of the membranes (amniotomy) A plastic hook called an amnihook (sort of like a crochet hook) is used to break the membranes of the amniotic sac. Often it is enough just to brush the hook against the membranes, but sometimes it will have to be inserted to make a small hole. It usually doesn't hurt at all. Once the membranes have been broken, labour usually follows quickly as the baby's head is no longer cushioned by amniotic fluid so descends, putting pressure on the ripe cervix and encouraging it to widen. Breaking the membranes also triggers the release of prostaglandins, which help to speed up the labour process.

Artificial rupture of the membranes is a very effective method of induction on its own if the cervix is ripe, and the contractions afterwards should be no more painful than normal. Amniotomy is often used during an otherwise normal labour to speed things up, and also if an electrode needs to be attached to your baby's scalp to monitor its heartbeat.

Oxytocin A synthetic form of oxytocin (the hormone that causes the uterus to contract) is given through a drip to increase the strength and regularity of contractions. The membranes will probably be ruptured as well. Contractions brought on by oxytocin are usually stronger, longer and more painful than normal, so pain relief drugs are often used during labour.

Other methods:

◉ acupuncture or acupressure – often a course of a few treatments over a few days – which must be performed by a trained specialist

◉ some homoeopathic remedies can be used to help ripen the cervix – again these must be prescribed by a natural therapist experienced in pregnancy care

◉ nipple massage – gently massage one nipple at a time (massaging both nipples at once has been shown to cause foetal distress), either by hand or with a warm, moist cloth, alternating nipples every 15 minutes for three periods of up to an hour each day, which can stimulate uterine contractions and ripen the cervix

◉ semen is rich in prostaglandins, which ripen the cervix – the easiest way to 'administer' it is by having sex with, well, frankly, a man

◉ orgasm results in several strong uterine contractions; it is thought that these, combined with sexual arousal, can stimulate prostaglandin production

◉ keeping moving – keeping upright and moving will allow a little extra pressure to be exerted on your cervix by your baby's head, which may stimulate ripening, but remember not to overdo it

◉ visualisation – some people believe that the power of suggestion can affect the body. If you're good at this sort of thing, try to relax and visualise the birth (leaving out any bits that make you anxious). Some women have found that watching films of babies being born triggers labour (remember all those stories about *Three Men and a Baby*?).

characteristic features of late babies
Late babies often look a bit different from those born on time.

◉ They are sometimes described as looking 'overcooked' because during their extra time in the uterus they lose fat from all over their body, and their skin becomes red and wrinkly and may 'crack' as the waxy coating of vernix disappears.

◉ They tend to have longer fingernails and more hair.

◉ Although often skinnier, they keep growing in the uterus so they are larger all over than babies born earlier.

◉ They are generally more alert than babies born earlier.

◉ A longer time spent in the uterus may result in a greenish staining of the skin and umbilical cord by meconium: in very post-term babies these stains will be yellow.

your record

What labour issues do you feel really strongly about?

How do you feel about medical intervention?
What if it becomes necessary?

What have you included in your birth plan?

what's going on

Your bosoms may have developed a mind of their own and be leaking for no apparent reason or when a baby cries. (Any old baby will do.) The stuff is the colostrum, which will give your newborn baby protein and antibodies in the few days before your milk 'comes in'. The baby can't tumble around so much because it's run out of room, but the kicking and whacking can have a real force when they do happen. From here on in, try to be strict about getting as much rest and sleep as you can. Labour and recovery are much easier if you are well rested.

The baby isn't doing much except putting on more weight. The tiny lungs are getting ready to work on their own. The baby has a firm hand grip and is swallowing about 750 millilitres of amniotic fluid a day. Weight: about 2.7 kilos.

wet spots!

Average approximate baby length this week from head to bum

Diary — Dr Herb says, 'Don't have the baby on Saturday.' He is going for his motorbike licence. He says his helmet is very black and racy. I say if I do go into labour he'll have to come, but he can wear his helmet.

'It's part of my mid-life crisis,' he says cheerily.

It is a measure of the serenity of Dr Herb that this statement doesn't make me nervous in the slightest.

'Does your wife just laugh at you?' I ask.

'Yes she does, actually.'

I am not astonished.

Dr Herb is still convinced that the Pikelet won't come early, but on the due date or later.

'Is it engaged?' he asks.

How would I know? All I can report is that it appears to be wearing Doc Martens and doing Irish dancing on my cervix.

I have been overcome by an ineluctable torpor. In other words I lie on the couch and watch 'The Bold and the Beautiful', and it is pointless to try doing otherwise. My priorities are all changing ('Stuff all of you at work! And the horse you rode in on!'), I am consumed by stupidity hormones, and can't seem to call people back.

I hear from Aunt Zelda, the adventuress, now settled in Botswana, who sends me a tiny card with twelve teensy buttons sewn onto it, each half the size of a little fingernail. 'A decent aunt would have made these buttons into a three-piece Lafayette or something. I've had them for twenty years,' she writes. I am somehow pleased she doesn't know the difference between layette and Lafayette: neither do I.

I hit the wall and give up work. I had planned to work until the first contractions, but something has happened to my brain. I was working too hard for contemplation, and my mind was demanding space. So of course what always happens when you stop working? I get a cold.

I buy some lollies to put in the labour bag for energy and eat them all by 3 o'clock. I have written down the phone numbers of the hospital and Des's work and Dr Herb, but if I don't pin them to the inside of my underpants I'll probably lose the lot.

Beck asks am I bonding with the baby? 'As much as I can with someone I haven't met yet,' I think. Other mums have warned me there might be an ambivalent fog descending after the birth. We'll see.

Nausea. Walks not. Horizontal. No verbs in sentences.

info

your newborn baby

Newborn babies can look pretty weird. Yours might have the following:

⑥ blood and creamy vernix all over it (premature babies have more, late babies may have hardly any)

⑥ puffy, bruised or squinty-looking eyes

⑥ a puffy face

⑥ a head that looks elongated or cone-shaped because it's been squeezed through the pelvis and vagina – this will normalise, often within hours, although it can take up to a couple of weeks (the bones have spaces between them called fontanelles so that they can squish up during childbirth; these harden within a few months and become one thick skull)

⑥ an unfocused, sometimes cross-eyed gaze; at this early stage a newborn can only focus on something very close, like a nipple in front of its face

⑥ a swollen lump on the head, caused by the ventouse vacuum

⑥ temporary indentations on the face or head or pointy-headed look from forceps

⑥ lanugo on the body – the downy hair is often on the shoulders, the back, and the face around the hairline (with more if the baby is premature) – which usually rubs off within a few weeks

⑥ small pimple-like white spots on the face called milia, which are caused by temporary blockages of the sebaceous glands

⑥ red blotches (often called 'stork marks' because they look as if a stork has held the baby in its bill) (yeah, right) on the back of the neck at the base of the skull, the forehead and/or the eyelids, which are caused by little veins close to the skin – they will disappear after a year or so and only reappear with heat and stress, such as tantrums, during childhood

⑥ 'Mongolian spots' – bluish-grey patches on the back, the buttocks and sometimes the arms and thighs, which are more common in Asian and darker-skinned babies; the spots will fade away

⑥ other birthmarks (see a paediatrician if you're concerned)

⑥ big, swollen baby genitals and breasts, a discharge from the nipples, or even some blood from the baby vagina, due to a temporary oversupply of oestrogen

⑥ testicles that may not yet have 'descended'

⑥ a bruised bum and very swollen genitals, if it's a breech-birth baby

⑥ jaundice – more than half of all newborn babies become 'jaundiced' (yellow) about three to four days after birth, but the baby's liver should soon deal with this pigment, caused by the breaking down of unneeded red cells, and only a very small percentage of babies need treatment with sun or ultraviolet lights to come good. Have any newborn jaundice checked by your doctor: although it's rare, severe jaundice accompanied by other symptoms (including floppiness or spasms) can mean a severe health problem.

routine medical stuff
The APGAR test will be performed to assess the baby's health.

Named after its originator, Dr Virginia Apgar (oh my God, something's named after a woman), it's also an acronym for the things that are checked:

⊚ appearance (colour)

⊚ pulse (heartbeat)

⊚ grimace (reflex)

⊚ activity (muscle tone)

⊚ respiration (breathing).

In each category 0, 1 or 2 points are given, and a score of 7 or more is considered to be good. The test is conducted 1 minute after birth and again 5 minutes after birth. A very low score will mean emergency medical care is needed.

It is common to suggest that all babies be given a vitamin K injection very soon after the birth as a preventative measure against haemorrhagic disease of the newborn (HDN). (If you're having a homebirth, check whether the midwife will give it.)

A full weigh, measurement of length and medical check will include the test for congenital dislocation of the hip (CDH), which can be corrected during the first three months using braces or a harness to stabilise the legs while the hip joint develops.

The Guthrie or PKU test, routinely done two or three days after birth, involves a blood sample being taken from the baby's heel and is a screening test for the disorders of phenylketonuria, hypothyroidism, cystic fibrosis and galactosaemia, all of which are best caught early for treatment.

things you mightn't know

⊚ Some newborn babies don't have tears when they cry until they are 1–3 months old.

⊚ The eye colour a baby's born with may change before they're a year old. Despite what many people say, not all babies are born with blue eyes, especially dark-skinned ones.

⑥ Newborn babies often develop sucking blisters in the centre of their top lip.

⑥ The first poo, meconium, is like something out of a horror movie; thick and sticky, it looks like extruded, green-tinged tar, but once your milk 'comes in' gives way to the characteristic little-baby poo: yellowish and liquidy, with curds. This can come out at high velocity kerrrrrr-SPLAT!, and you quickly learn to be ready at nappy change time to intercept a stream with the corner of a nappy. (And baby-boy wee can also travel quite a distance at short notice, in a large arc.)

⑥ The early-baby wee may contain crystals that can make it look reddish. Disposable nappies have absorbent crystals that some-times 'escape' and look like tiny glass bubbles.

⑥ The stump of the umbilical cord drops off in about a week or two, and the hospital midwives will show you how to take care of it in the meantime.

⑥ There is no medical reason for having baby boys circumcised, except in extremely rare cases. Cutting the foreskin from the glans of the penis involves a terribly agonising and deeply shocking ordeal and a painful recovery (babies are too little to be given anaesthetic). Few doctors will do the procedure. Some parents insist on it for religious reasons.

hearing tests

Many hospitals now do hearing tests on newborn babies – ask if you can get one before you go home. Ear experts say that, to give kids the best chance of learning language and to speak, deafness should be detected as early as possible: ideally in the first weeks or within two months, but certainly within six months. If you couldn't get a newborn test at the hospital, check with your obstetrician at your six-week visit, or with your GP or baby health centre nurse, to find out where you can have your baby's hearing tested.

your record

List of possible names:

Girl	Boy	Either

what's going on

The nesting urge is likely to be at fever pitch. Many women find themselves scrubbing underneath shelves and may have to be restrained. Don't do anything that involves standing on a chair or a ladder, no matter how much you feel that dusting the curtain rail is crucial to life as we know it. You might have aches and pains caused by your ginormous uterus. A gentle walk should help.

The baby is technically 'full term' – that is, fully developed – as it enters this week, although most doctors say forty weeks is full term too because that's the typical length of a pregnancy. Most of the lanugo has fallen out, but the baby's still covered in vernix. About 14 grams of fat is laid down each day from now on. The baby probably has a bowel full of meconium in a rather disgusting-looking hard rope of greeny-black stuff. Once the baby's out and starts on milk, the poo will be much more liquid. The baby still moves every day, but not very far. Weight: about 2.9 kilos.

WEEK 38

Average approximate baby length this week from head to bum

DiARY Take Des to see Dr Herb, who says reassuring things about gigantic babies not necessarily being a problem because their mums' pelvises can handle it. Some of them simply pop out of their mothers singing a sea shanty, I'm sure. But he says he'll induce ten days or so after the due date if I'm still lying around doing my walrus impressions. I inquire politely about which weekends he's not on call, and promise to keep my legs crossed until he comes back on duty. The only time I can sleep properly is between 8 a.m. and noon. Luckily I don't have to be anywhere.

Because it's all a bit bloody exhausting. Have taken to not returning phone calls and living in my dressing-gown. Wish I hadn't agreed to go into work once a week. Hard to exercise. Starting to think more about the baby coming home, and in deep denial about childbirth itself. (Surely it couldn't hurt that much. Maybe I could just buy a baby from a nice shop and avoid the whole thing.) I'm trying to focus on the advantage of having a big baby – it'll be more robust and less scary. Hang on a minute. All the advantages will come when it's out, and it's not out yet.

I try to think about what kind of person the baby will be, but get grumpy and tell Des off for putting the wrong things in the fridge, when it was really me all the time and I'd forgotten and maybe this is some kind of weird pregnancy Jekyll and Hyde thing, or maybe it isn't and . . . Anyway, whatever. I'm all nested out. The house is getting untidy again, but I can't be bothered cleaning it. At least I know that Des will make the house spotless before I bring the baby home because otherwise he knows I would have him killed.

Even more chemists have started thrusting show bags at me full of pamphlets and sample-sized stuff. Heartburn lozenges, nappy rash lotions, pads for bleeding, pads for incontinence (oh GOD), ads for safety seats and equipment, safety hats, safety pants, safety bootees, lures to get you into Toys 'R' Us, and 400 different kinds of disposable nappies. They certainly give the impression that children are (a) dangerous and (b) moist.

info

your body after the birth

immediately afterwards

After the birth of your baby, you might feel shivery and shaky, ecstatic, exhausted, sore, empty, blank, numb, sleepy or wide awake: whatever you feel is okay, and certainly won't be unprecedented. (At least one woman has taken the first look at her baby and said, 'Where did that come from?'.) If you've had an epidural, you may still have a wee catheter in your urethra and an IV drip in your hand.

Putting the baby to the breast as soon as possible after birth helps stimulate the uterus to contract and to squeeze out the placenta. Your new baby might not be hungry yet, but it's nice to meet a nipple anyway.

in the following days

Bleeding (the lochia) The lochia – the discharge of blood, mucus and tissue from the uterus – will continue for two to six weeks after the birth. It is kind of like having a period at first, with some clots. It changes to a pink or brownish colour and ends as a yellow-white discharge.

⊚ Take plenty of maternity pads with you. (Because the cervix takes a while to close and tampons can cause infection, you can't use them until your first real period after the birth, and that could be months away if you're breastfeeding.) You can use the new, ultra-absorbent, thin pads if you like, but the extra padding of the thicker maternity pads might make sitting more comfy.

⊚ Tell your obstetrician if you have very heavy bleeding, the discharge has a yukky smell or the bleeding suddenly gets bright red. Also tell the obstetrician straight away if you haven't bled at all since giving birth.

'Afterpains' 'Afterpains' usually occur for a few days or more after you have given birth, as your uterus contracts back towards its normal size. It's quite common to feel afterpains during breast-feeding.

Haemorrhoids and constipation

⊚ Labour and delivery can give you haemorrhoids, a distension of the blood vessels at the entrance to your anus. Try not to strain when having a poo, even if you're constipated, because it will make the haemorrhoids worse. Some people don't poo for a few days, especially after a caesarean, and you might need help.

⊚ If you have haemorrhoids, ask your obstetrician, midwife or the nursing staff about icepacks and ointment for relief.

⊚ You may also need to eat more fruit, vegetables and cereals for fibre, and drink lots of water. See the hints on how to avoid constipation in the info in 'Week 8'.

Your poor sore fanny There will usually be 'some level of discomfort in the perineal area', as doctors say, after a vaginal delivery, ranging from bearable to excruciating; you may need some pain relief for a day or two after delivery. If you've had an episiotomy or tear, the midwives in hospital will show you how to look after the stitched area so that it heals up well, and the site will be regularly checked for infection.

◉ Regular baths or hip baths with salt or *very diluted* (10 drops per bath) tea-tree oil can help the healing process.

◉ Wash stitches gently, even just with water, two or three times a day.

◉ Dry the area well after bathing and give yourself some pants-off airing time if possible.

◉ Don't dry stitches with a hairdryer unless you have a cool setting – some people numb the area with ice or drugs and then scorch themselves with a hairdryer that's too hot or too close. It might be better to wave a paper fan or a handy copy of the *New Idea*.

◉ If your stitches are sore and itchy, try dissolving a teaspoon of bicarbonate of soda or salt in warm water, then sitting in it after a wee.

◉ Try leaning forward (with your hands reaching towards the floor) when you wee so that wee doesn't get onto the stitches.

◉ Splash out (so to speak) on some thick, soft toilet paper.

◉ While having a poo in the first couple of days post-delivery, you might find it more comfortable if you support the perineal area firmly with a pad or wad of toilet paper.

◉ Avoid constipation by keeping your fibre intake up and drinking plenty of water.

◉ Don't sit on a rubber ring – it will direct more blood to the area, creating more pressure.

◉ Sit on a rolled-up towel or with a pillow under each buttock.

◉ Fill a condom with water and freeze it, and then pop it in your knickers.

◉ Apply salt poultices to the area.

◉ Ask your doctor to prescribe anti-inflammatories or pain-killers that won't be transferred to the baby in breast milk.

◎ Take vitamin C for healing. Ask your natural therapist or independent midwife for doses or follow instructions on the bottle.

◎ Pelvic-floor exercises will stimulate circulation in the area and assist in the healing process. The first few times the area will feel very tired and trembly, and you may have some numbness, but do as many as you can as soon as you can.

◎ Attack any urinary infection quickly by taking an alkaline powder, so that weeing doesn't sting the wound.

◎ Most doctors say no bonking until the six-week check-up at least – possibly *after* the six-week check-up would be better (*during* might be considered a little inconsiderate).

your record

What are your feelings about breastfeeding?
Are you determined to do it? How long would you
like to breastfeed for? What if you can't?

SOME STRETCH MARK ZONES
(ARROWED)

EEK 39

what's going on

The cervix gets softer and thinner, ready to open wide enough for a baby's head to come through. Any time from now it could release the mucus plug, which will end up on your knickers and is a sign that labour could start within hours. The uterus is still practising contractions; in fact that pesky Mrs Braxton Hicks may be visiting rather too often and possibly confusing you about whether it's actually labour or not. You are probably completely fed up with being pregnant and have forgotten what your feet look like.

Your baby's genitals at this point have been over-excited by all your extra hormones and will be very large indeed in comparison to the rest of the body. They will return to a more seemly size a few days after the birth. Overall, the baby's growth slows down this week in preparation for birth.

Weight: about 3.2 kilos.

Average approximate baby length this week from head to bum

diary

Latest inventory of body changes: gigantic, veiny boozoombas with brown nipples; new, brown, flat moles on them, and heaps of skin tags under each one; huuuge tummy; purple, stripey stretch marks on bosoms and hips. And I can't see my legs or pubic hair. For all I know they've been stolen.

I know why whales beach themselves. THEY JUST CAN'T BE BOTHERED ANY MORE.

Having a baby is a preposterous proposition. How can this huge, hard thing possibly come out of a vagina? I hear about a woman whose first words after labour were 'What a completely shocking thing to happen.' I've also heard so many stories about people looking blankly at their newborn baby and wondering what on earth to do with it. I'm determined not to panic if I don't bond straight away.

I ask Marg, 'Is it like an out-of-body experience?'

'No,' she says. 'It's a get-out-of-my-body experience.'

I still can't tell what my body wants – am I hungry, tired, nauseous, getting a cold? I have no idea. Walking is hard now, the damn groin pain never goes away: those ligaments must be under so much strain the anchor points are constantly stressed.

The word 'deliver' is sexist, says one pregnancy book, because it indicates a male doctor does the work of 'delivery'. Bollocks. The mum's delivering – just like a postie with the mail. How about 'de-mummed', or would the mum be 'de-babied'? One person has already asked if I have been 'unsprogged'.

At this week's visit, Dr Herb looks exhausted – he's been up all night delivering babies. I didn't sleep much either.

'Is anything worrying you? Is there anything you want to ask?'

'No. Except don't go off duty, and did you get your motorcycle licence?'

Turns out he didn't do it a fortnight ago, so now he's going for the test this Saturday.

'I want to roar up next to some of the other doctors at the lights and see the looks on their faces,' he says. (Apparently the other doctors were shocked when he shaved off his beard. They sound pretty easy to shock. Maybe he should just start cross-dressing.)

People are so different about babies. Attitudes range from the clucky to the disbelieving, through to distaste and secrecy.

I told my accountant, 'I feel stupid and tired.'

She was horrified I'd said it aloud. 'Don't tell anyone!'

There is a conspiracy of working mothers to hide the effects of pregnancy and motherhood so as not to be discriminated against.

I look up 'pregnant ladies' on the Internet and the first eleven matches are hardcore porn sites.

info

feeding your new baby

You may as well read this now because you won't feel like reading it straight after your baby's born! It's hard to think past labour at the moment, but when it's over you'll be preoccupied with your bosoms.

Breastfeeding is the best way to feed because breast milk is perfectly designed to nourish your baby with all the right nutrients and supply antibodies to boost the baby's immune system, which formula milk can't deliver.

BaBy's fAvouRite View

In the past, babies were weaned onto plain old cow's milk, which wasn't very good for them, being designed for calves, not human babies, but now infant formulas are specially designed to give as many of the nutrients in breast milk as possible. Formula still runs second, but it's a much better second than it used to be.

breastfeeding in the first days

◉ For the first few days after birth the baby will be drinking the creamy yellow pre-milk, colostrum, which is specially designed to nourish a baby and provide it with antibodies before it gets the milk. Most babies will lose a bit of weight until the milk 'comes in', and then start to gain again.

◉ At first breastfeeding might be painful, especially if your baby is having trouble latching on properly (latching on is often called 'attachment') and chomps on the nipple or can't seem to stay 'on' and suck. The baby needs to take most of the areola as well as the nipple in its mouth and the nipple goes to the back of the mouth. Different mothers and babies find different feeding positions suit them best. Use your time in hospital to get as much help and advice from the staff as you need. Or ask your independent midwife.

◉ If you're having problems breastfeeding and feel that the hospital staff have done all they can to help you, or don't have the time, or are giving you conflicting advice, ask them to get the hospital's lactation consultant, or a private consultant, to come and see you.

◉ When your milk comes in (usually after three or four days), you can expect your breasts to feel full and hard. The staff or your own midwife will be able to give you advice on how to ease this, such as expressing a little milk before each feed and applying hot washers or cabbage leaves. You might need a cream to keep them supple: lactation consultants recommend different things, from pure lanolin, which you don't have to wipe off before the baby drinks, to paw-paw ointment. You don't need 'tough' nipples, you want pliable ones.

◉ You might be asked if you can feel your milk 'coming in'. This is like a shiver, a prickle or even a stabbing pain in each breast, though sometimes you don't feel it for days or even weeks after the birth – or ever – but the 'let down' of your milk will be happening before each and every breastfeed.

◉ If you can, try to let your nipples air dry after feeding. Exposing them to very mild sunlight for short periods (3–5 minutes) will dry any excess moisture, and the ultraviolet light helps them to heal.

hooray for bosoms

Because breast milk is so fabulous for babies, because it helps you to bond with your baby, and because it's on tap and free of charge, it's really worth persevering if you have initial trouble breast-feeding: very few babies and mothers can get their act together straight away. The thing to remember is to try to relax (I know it's hard at the time when you've got a hungry, crying baby and you can't get it to 'attach' properly). Take a deep breath and lower your shoulders. It takes time for you and the baby to learn breast-feeding together. A middle road could be expressing your milk and putting it in a bottle to give your nipples a rest. You can also supplement a low supply with formula. Even managing six days or six weeks of breastfeeding is a big bonus for your baby. And if it really doesn't work, you have a fine back-up with formula: your baby will not starve. So give it another go.

It's more convenient to get the feeding sorted out before you leave hospital, than at home. Ask to watch another mother feeding her baby if you like. Quite often you'll get conflicting advice from hospital midwives about how to hold the baby and how to position yourself while you feed. If it's all putting your head in a whirl (you'll be madly sleep deprived, which doesn't help), choose to listen to ONE of them – call in the lactation consultant, for example, and don't be swayed from their advice if it's working. Choose someone who clearly likes babies, is encouraging and gentle, and takes the time to help you, sit with you, watch your technique and try different ways to help. (Don't choose anyone who grabs your breast in one hand, the baby in the other and brings them together like a clash of cymbals.)

The Australian Breastfeeding Association (formerly the Nursing Mothers' Association of Australia) has trillions of booklets, pamphlets, videos and books available to help you solve a bewildering array of breastfeeding problems and can be a marvellous support. I suspect if you want to breastfeed a Down syndrome baby upside down in an igloo, there'll be a pamphlet on it.

If you become a member of the association they also have local area co-ordinators who can give you advice. But remember, the association is passionate about breastfeeding under almost any circumstances. If you want HOW advice rather than WHY advice, get a trained lactation consultant or specific video or book from the association relevant to your problem. Ask for practical advice, not just encouragement to continue breastfeeding. The association member around the corner may be able to encourage you, but may not have the special skills to help.

You may find that in their zeal for breastfeeding, some people gloss over the real problems you're having, with the advice 'Just keep trying'. If you think breastfeeding is 'taking too much out of you', it probably is – don't accept that this is 'nonsense' or inevitable: get some nutritional and coping advice. If you're finding it impossible to juggle work and breastfeeding, don't just accept that 'Many other women do it and you can too': make sure you get practical help on how to continue.

See Breastfeeding in 'Help'.

not breastfeeding

If the worst comes to the worst and you can't breastfeed your baby or breastfeeding is not for you, it's nowhere near the end of the world. The way people go on about it, you'd think not breastfeeding was the equivalent of making the baby drink gin and wheeling it across freeways during blizzards in a war zone. Plenty of bottle-fed babies grow up to be strapping, robust, healthy adults. Look at the adults around you. Look at the kids around you. Can you tell who was bottle-fed? Course you can't. Many other factors affect a child's development and immune system, including the amount of chemicals in an environment, access to fresh, healthy food, and exposure and building up a resistance to germs.

It would be lovely if you could breastfeed, but you can't. Instead you can enjoy the relaxed feeling of bottle-feeding your baby while making eye contact, and the freedom it gives you because you can always get somebody else to feed the baby if you'd like to go out for an hour or so and have an affair with a

couple of firemen. Now crank up the steriliser, tweak those teats –
not those, the ones that fit on the bottle. And get on with it.

A midwife or your baby health centre nurse (who will visit
you after the birth courtesy of your local council and who you'll
visit regularly after that) can help you with all the stuff you need to
know about sterilising equipment and storing and heating bottles.

Stuff to tell nosy people
'I have an illness controlled by medication, which mustn't be
passed through breast milk to my baby.'

'Both my nipples blew off during a wind storm.'

'I have an antibiotic-resistant form of infected bosoms, and
either of them could explode at any moment.'

'It's easier to get the gin into a bottle.'

'Both my bosoms were removed years ago.'

'I can't breastfeed, and I don't want to talk about it. Gosh,
that's a lovely blouse.'

'So far five lactation specialists have told me I'm one of those
women who just can't breastfeed. In the old days I would have
had a wet nurse.'

'Oh, just BUGGER OFF.'

what's going on

This is the magic week when your baby is 'due', unless somebody has cocked up the dates. But this is based on averages, so don't expect to give birth on the due date. If you do, it is simply showing off.

The baby is rounder and fatter and probably ready to be born. It is now about 200 times heavier than it was at twelve weeks. Boys are often bigger than girls. Weight: about 3.5 kilos.

WEEK 40

DIARY

I'm due. And I am nothing but a limbo-living, dimply-arsed, stoned giantess. When I go to see Dr Herb the women in the waiting room who are only a couple of months pregnant look at me with very contemplative expressions: 'Surely I couldn't get THAT big', I hear them saying in their innermost thoughts.

Des has suggested we change the name of the baby to Godot, and I am like a cat waiting to have kittens, prowling around the house looking for a good cupboard to give birth in – or tidy up. I'm finding it harder to drink Beck's herbal uterine tonic concoction – I'm just sick of it, but I persevere because she says I have good uterine tone, which I am immensely proud of, it being the only part of my body which HAS ANY TONE.

Obsessed with the idea of labour. Someone reminds me of Kathy Lette's description of a post-caesarean vagina as 'honeymoon fresh'. If I didn't laugh I'd sob m'self silly. It's also becoming clear to me how many pregnant women worry about pooing during labour. I'm just surprised your lungs don't come out your bum considering all the pressure.

Have left a message on the answering machine saying nothing's happened yet. People ringing and asking all the time. All the ones who are already mothers say, 'Good luck', 'Take the drugs' and 'You're not going to try and have a natural birth are you?'.

Uncle Stan turns up on the doorstep dressed like a Hollywood B-movie costume designer's idea of a part-time pimp: opaque, yellow-lensed, concave, wraparound sunglasses, ankle-length leather jacket, high-heeled boots and grey beard. I try not to stare. Aurelia is always waiting in the car, usually taking advantage of the mirror on the inside of the passenger sun visor.

He hands me a bunch of organic chokoes and remarks casually that he and Aurelia are going on holiday next week to a commune.

'So', I venture, 'you won't be here when the baby's born?'

'Leave a message on the answering machine!' he cries gaily as he heads for the gate.

Family support. What would you do without it? Get along all right, is my guess.

My dream birth: I am lying on a sexy, dusky pink satin-quilted four-poster bed reading a magazine full of photos of gorgeous clothes I could afford that would look quite nice on me (I *said* it was a dream) when a man in a leopard-skin suit comes past with a cocktail trolley on wheels full of excellent cakes, bottles of attractively coloured alcohol, an icebucket and some syringes.

'Martini?' he inquires politely.'Or would modom care for an epidural?'

Just at that moment a perfectly charming baby pops out of my vagina.

'Ow,' I remark, absent-mindedly. 'Why, thank you, I'll take a gin and lime. And a small colostrum for my new young friend.'

Just in case this doesn't happen, Dr Herb has scheduled me to go into the maternity hospital next Monday at 5 p.m. to have my cervix annointed with a prostaglandin that mimics the one in the body that basically says, 'Lady, start your engines for labour'. I have to stay in hospital, and they might put some more in the next morning. Then I should be able to start on my own without the oxytocin drip, although in some cases the membranes have to be broken by the doctor if the waters don't break by themselves. This is scary.

Had a problem sleeping last night, thinking about bringing a baby home, and caesarean, and pain . . .

Beck's given me acupuncture twice to try to move the baby along a bit, and I've taken some tiny homoeopathic pills. The baby finally 'engages' (goes into firing position) after two days of this. So TIRED. Some anxiety attacks, but mostly sort of numb.

Everyone is ringing up saying, 'Has anything happened?'

'NO!'

info

your hospital stay

Staff midwives will be assigned to you in hospital. Their job is to take care of you as you recover from the birth. They are also there to help you learn how to feed and look after your baby. Ask them anything you want to know, and take full advantage of their time and knowledge. Most women spend two to five days in hospital after giving birth, and often seven after a caesarean. You can ask to be discharged when you feel ready to go home, providing you and your baby get the all clear from medical staff. If you feel you need more time in hospital – either because you're still not feeling a hundred per cent or because you don't feel ready to cope with the baby on your own – talk to your obstetrician or midwife and explain that you need to stay a couple of extra days.

exercise

If your hospital offers postnatal exercise or physio classes, try to get along. It's a good way to get into an exercise routine that you will hopefully continue in the weeks after you get home, it will help your body recover, and moving about should help you to feel less stiff and sore. (Actually you probably won't have the time or energy for exercises for a while. If you do, that's great. If you don't, don't beat yourself up about it. But do go to the classes so that when you get a minute, you'll know what to do.)

food

⑥ Nutrition and beating hunger are important issues for breast-feeding. Ask your lactation consultant, hospital dietician, independent midwife or natural therapist for suggestions.

⑥ It may be nutritionally sound, but hospital food is usually, at best, pathetically boring. Get friends to bring you decent food such as fresh fruit. Most wards have a fridge and access to a micro-wave so you can have a stash of your own.

visitors

⑤ Don't feel obliged to see everyone who wants to check out the baby while you're in hospital. Make the most of this time when your meals, cleaning and other needs are being taken care of by other people to recover from the birth and to prepare yourself for when you go home.

⑤ If you like, ban all but a few close friends and family from visiting for the first few days so you can rest and spend time with your baby.

⑤ Visiting hours are not as strict as they used to be, but you can pretend that they are, or choose a hospital where they are. If you don't want people dropping in outside the set hours, enlist the help of the nurses and ward staff.

⑤ If you have a phone, you can ask the switchboard to take messages for you so that you can ring out but the phone doesn't go all the time.

❺ Ask people to phone you before they come to visit. If you're too tired or don't feel up to seeing anyone, you can ask them to come another time.

❺ If flowers get in the way and cause allergies, ask people who are coming to visit you not to bring them. Instead have one or two close friends bring you a small bunch to brighten things up.

time out

Some hospitals encourage new mums to go out for an evening with their partner or another companion, leaving the baby in the care of staff. This can be a real treat, but you may find your first separation from your baby just makes you think about the baby non-stop. If you don't feel like it, don't go.

paperwork and other nitty-gritties

Birth notice   You might want to write a paragraph for the classifieds in the newspaper and keep that edition for the baby when they grow up.

Registering the birth   This should be done as soon as possible after the birth, once you've got the name sorted out. Your hospital should give you a form, or you can get one from a post office. The date by which you are legally required to register your baby's birth varies from State to State, but it's usually within a month or two.

If you're not sure what involvement the father wants with the child, or the father isn't around, get legal advice from a community legal centre or your own lawyer about whether to put his name on the certificate. It's quite okay to leave the father bit blank if you need to. Don't let anyone write 'unknown' or anything judgemental for the kid to read when they grow up and get a copy. If you're not happy with the birth certificate when it is mailed to you, you can have it altered.

Registering for benefits   If you haven't already, call your nearest Centrelink office about any government benefits you may be entitled to, such as the sole supporting parent's benefit.

Health cover Usually a baby is automatically added to Mum's Medicare card when she fills out forms in hospital. It could be very useful to also add the baby to Dad's card. This makes it easier for either parent to take the child to the doctor, and either card can be used as a form of identification. (Many airlines will not let a child travel with an adult unless there is proven guardianship, and they may not tell you this rule until you're at the airport.) Adding the baby to the dad's card requires a Medicare form, the bub's birth certificate and the signatures of both parents.

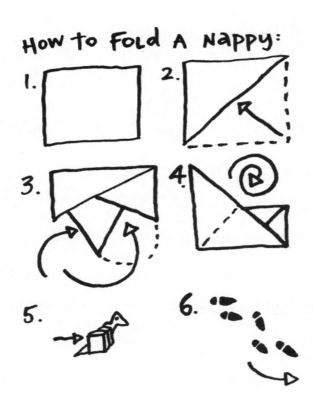

How to Fold A Nappy:

what's going on

If your pregnancy has been 'average' (forty weeks long), your baby is out in the world and perhaps sleeping off the shock. After your baby is born a whole bunch of hormonal activities happen, quite suddenly. Your body expels the placenta, which has been pumping out huge quantities of hormones. Suddenly you're bereft of the 'happy hormones' and getting a boost of hormones such as prolactin to help breastfeeding. Your body looks less pregnant, but your tummy is still very big. You're bleeding from the vagina as the body expels all that nice uterine surface the baby needed. Your body is recovering from the massive shock of childbirth – whether natural or surgical. Give yourself a break. Don't do anything but recover and be with your baby.

The baby may have some characteristic newborn marks, such as 'stork marks' (red, rashlike shapes on the forehead, eyelids and/or back of the neck) or temporary marks from forceps. More than half of all newborn babies develop a yellowy tinge to the skin and eyeballs, called jaundice – it's no big deal. Your baby is sucking colostrum because your milk probably won't come in until day 3 or 4. The bub will be down a bit from its birth weight before the breast milk kicks in. Don't worry about this: too much scientific measuring and talk of weight-loss percentages can be freaky – lost weight in those first few days is expected in all babies and the loss can be made up in just a few days.

WEEK 41

pleased to meet you

DiARY

It's time. We drive to the hospital, with the bag neatly packed with all the things we'll need for labour, to meet Herb for the prostaglandin-on-the-cervix induction, feeling nervous but excited. Luckily Maternity isn't busy so we get our own room with a double bed, which Des bounces on. Sleep! Can't imagine it myself.

In the morning, when contractions will probably start, I'll ring Beck and tell her to come in sporting her best midwifery hat.

Dr Herb comes into our room wearing a lovely suit and some Issey Miyake aftershave on his way to a film evening with his wife, and puts the gel on my cervix. What a charming bedside manner he has – he chats away about something else and one could almost be at a dinner party if he didn't have his hand up your pooncey.

A nice Lorraine-y midwife arrives in a white jacket and navy pants and puts a piece of electronic equipment on wheels next to the bed and attaches a belt around my tummy. This is the monitor. It continually rolls out a graph of any contractions and a graph of the baby's heartbeat, which is usually up around 150 beats a minute. Des and I start to play cards, pretending that we can keep our mind on Snap! instead of all the machinery.

A long time later I write this: Suddenly I noticed that the baby's heartbeat had dropped to 80 beats a minute and the graph line was plunging down like a sheer cliff face. And so began the worst 2 hours of my life.

Des tried to reassure me that it was probably normal, but when the midwife came back she got a look on her face I never want to see again and rang Dr Herb, who, it transpires, was just reaching for his first angel-on-horseback hors d'oeuvre at the film preview. Within 15 minutes he was back in the room, looking at the graph.

'I'm just going outside to consult with someone, and I'll be back in a moment to tell you what we're going to do,' he said calmly.

Left alone, Des and I held hands and tried not to look as frightened as each other.

'He's going to do an emergency caesarean. I guess Beck's not going to make it in time,' I thought suddenly.

Herb came back in and sat on the bed, and held my hand
and said – oh dear, I still can't write these words without crying –
'Your baby is distressed, and if it's this distressed because of a little
Braxton Hicks contraction, we won't risk going through labour.'

Behind the scenes an anaesthetist, a paediatrician and another
obstetrician were rushing in from their homes or elsewhere in the
building. They took Des away, which was awful, and they quickly
wheeled me out on one of those cold, gleaming trolleys and into
the white, shining operating theatre, where there were people with
blue paper masks, shower caps and gowns. ('Nice to see some
fashion co-ordination,' I thought, ages later. At the time I wasn't
thinking much at all, I was just frightened.)

The anaesthetist put an IV drip in my left hand, and then gave
me a spinal-block injection into the lower back, with me curled in
a foetal position while a nurse held my hand. It was really scary
staying perfectly still so he didn't get the wrong bit of the spine.
As the anaesthetic started to work, Dr Herb came back in with the
hospital midwife, a paediatrician, the other obstetrician and –
thank God! – Des, who looked like he was playing an extra in 'ER'.
They put up a blue fabric screen over my chest so I couldn't see my
tummy. Everyone fussed around behind the screen for a moment.

'Let me know when you start,' I said to Dr Herb.

Everybody laughed.

'We've been in for 3 minutes,' he said.

When I looked up at the huge light with the flat globe cover,
I could see the reflection of my insides, yellow and pink and
purple. These were the things I was thinking: 'Please let my baby
be all right', 'Thank God I live in a First World country', 'Thank
God I'm not having a homebirth', and large stretches of blank that
probably had something to do with shock.

'There's your baby coming out,' said one of the nurses, taking
a Polaroid photo.

'Is it Eddy or Pearl?' I asked.

'It's Eddy!' everyone chorused.

And suddenly Herb held up a silent, purple, slimy creature
with a screwed up, tiny little face and a smudge of dark hair. A sob
caught in my throat as I reached out and gently touched my baby's

leg with the back of my hand. I didn't know if any other contact would hurt Eddy or be the wrong thing to do.

Instantly he was whipped away to a table by the paediatrician and the midwife, who started to check everything.

'He's got all the right things in all the right places,' said the paediatrician.

And then Eddy started to cry. All the experienced people in the room broke into huge smiles.

'That's a good cry,' they said simultaneously, and you could feel the relief in the room.

The two obstetricians were doing their downstairs needlework on what Des would later refer to as 'the tummy smile': my curved red scar. The paediatrician, the midwife and Des whisked out to go and do tests on Eddy. For some reason I told Des through my tears – I couldn't stop crying – not to let Eddy out of his sight. (As if he was going to duck out to the pub for a few coldies.) The obstetricians finished and went away, and two nurses wheeled me next door into the recovery room and gave me a lemonade icypole, and there I stayed for about an hour, drugged out of my mind and not really believing it had happened, and wondering where my baby was.

When finally I was wheeled back into our room, there were Des and Eddy. I was really worried that Eddy was all right, but I didn't feel an immediate surge of overwhelming love. Mostly relief that he was okay, and confusion about how to get him on the breast for a snack of colostrum. Eddy just looked tired and tiny, and slept a lot. And guess what? He wasn't even a whopper: 3.6 kilos. Damn. All the rest was Magnums.

info

coping when you get home

getting organised

◎ To stop people dropping in at all hours, insist that friends and relatives call before visiting or set aside particular times (say certain mornings a week).

◎ If friends or relatives offer to help with cleaning, cooking or shopping, ACCEPT IMMEDIATELY!

◎ There will be days when preparing dinner will seem impossible or unbearable. Prepare for these by cooking extra, large batches when you make things that can be frozen such as soups and casseroles. If friends and relations offer to bring you meals, ACCEPT IMMEDIATELY! Keep take-away menus from a few decent local places.

◎ Instead of flowers and fancy baby accessories, ask friends to contribute to getting you a nappy service for the first month or so – you'll have enough to cope with without spending hours soaking and washing dirty nappies. Instead of lots of outfits, ask a couple of friends to buy bibs. You'll soon find out why: much easier to whip on and off than change a whole sicky outfit.

◎ If you can afford it, get a cleaning service in for a few hours every one or two weeks so that the basic housework, such as cleaning the bathroom and kitchen, is always done.

◎ If you can't afford a cleaning service but can't stand being in a messy house, just keep one room tidy. This will give you somewhere to relax or see visitors.

◎ If you live by yourself, try to organise a roster of friends to come by each day for the first few weeks so that you can have an uninterrupted half hour to take a shower or bath, sit down without the baby or get out of the house briefly.

looking after yourself

◉ Ask someone you trust to look after your baby while you do something relaxing such as going for a walk or seeing a friend.

◉ Try to get out of the house every day to help keep yourself sane. If you're going somewhere like a shopping centre, check out the parents' facilities and whether there are lifts or flat escalators. If you have to negotiate a lot of stairs, you may be better off with a baby sling than a pram.

◉ Try to get time each day to do your postnatal exercises (especially the pelvic-floor ones) – you'll find you have more energy for them in the mornings. If you enjoy exercising with other people, a postnatal class after a few weeks will also give you a chance to talk with other new mothers.

◉ If you have a partner, make time to go out alone with them, even if it's just for coffee.

◉ Make sure your partner understands that most women don't feel like flinging themselves into chandelier-swingin' rumpy pumpy for a few weeks at least. It might be nice to break this more gently than placing a sign saying 'Off Limits' over your fanny.

◉ Use the time when your baby is sleeping during the day to have a nap or relax. Put your needs ahead of visitors, housework and other chores.

◉ Don't pretend you're coping if you're not: share things with your partner or friends.

◉ If you feel you need more help than you can get at home, consider spending some time at a family-care centre (see Parent Services in 'Help'), where experts can give you advice on feeding, settling and looking after your baby, as well as giving you a chance to rest and take time out from household chores. You can go each day or stay over for a few days, and many centres allow partners to stay as well.

a crying baby

Small babies often cry for mysterious reasons. Here are some tips to stop your baby crying if they are not hungry, tired, hot, cold, wet or in pain from wind, a nappy pin or whatever else you've checked for:

◎ curl up together in bed in a warm, dark, quiet room, tummy to tummy for maximum skin contact

◎ try a warm bath and baby massage (some babies hate both until they're a few weeks old) – ask a midwife or baby health centre nurse for a demo; basically, be gentle, use any sort of oil you can eat, and stop if it makes the baby cranky

◎ rock with your baby in a chair

◎ play soothing music (you might feel like a dill but sing to your baby – anything soothing, even if you have to make it up – and if you 'can't sing', your baby won't notice)

◎ walk up and down a hall about 5,000 times with the baby over your shoulder

◎ try to distract the baby by holding them level with your face and nodding your head, while making a (pleasant) noise or grinning – this can give them such a surprise that they forget what they were crying about

◎ go about your business with the baby in a sling

◎ try an approved dummy for newborns

◎ accept there's nothing you can do, and get someone else in to hold the baby while you walk around the block.

 See Crying and Parent Services in 'Help'.

getting your baby to sleep

⑥ Ask your baby health centre nurse how you can recognise when to put your baby down to sleep, and if you need a 'routine'.

⑥ Try to get into a settling routine when your baby is due to go down so that they start to associate certain things with relaxing and going to sleep. You might use sounds (singing, music or even rhythmic noises like the washing machine), movements such as rocking in a chair or baby hammock or being carried close to your body in a baby pouch, massage, a ride in a pram or car, or a warm bath. (A car is an expensive habit to get into and not great if you're exhausted.)

⑥ Use a dimmer switch or soft lamp to feed by at night-time, and avoid talking to or stimulating the baby or they'll think it's play time.

⑥ Overtiredness is a common cause of crying, and paradoxically can make it harder for the baby to get to sleep. A baby can seem 'hyped up' when they're really overtired. Soothing methods that involve walking, rocking or singing to the baby may end up stimulating them more, so that it is harder to get them to sleep. Instead, try stroking your baby's head or tummy, patting its back rhythmically, or make soothing hushing sounds.

There is a comprehensive explanation of babies' sleep patterns, and suggested routines, in the sequel to this book, *Kidwrangling: The Real Guide to Caring for Babies, Toddlers and Preschoolers*.

and the rest

For all the other stuff you'll worry about such as wind, vomiting and weird-lookin' poo, see your baby health centre nurse, peruse 'Help', and always have a baby-care book on hand (see Baby-care Books in 'Week 43').

 See Sleeping and Parent Services in 'Help'.

BABY HEALTH CENTRES

Somewhere near you is a baby health centre. You may not have noticed it, but it's about to become a very important landmark in your life. Depending on which State or Territory you're in, it may be called a mother and child health centre or maternal and child health centre or infant-something-mother-something. The baby health centre nurse will ring and make an appointment to visit you at home in the first days after you get home with your baby (your hospital or home midwife should alert your local council, which gives your name and number to its employee, the nurse).

After that first home visit, you will regularly go to the health centre for appointments with the nurse to check on your baby's general progress and how you're going too, to weigh and measure your baby, and to answer your inevitable questions about baby care. You should be able to ring the nurse or a back-up at any time of the day or night. Nurses are generally really supportive and helpful with any problems or queries you have. (If you have a personality clash or a problem with a nurse, remember it's important to go to another nearby centre, instead of just giving up.)

Baby health centres usually run immunisation programs, and can put you in touch with parents' groups, mothers' groups and playgroups. The nurses are trained to pick up any problems you may not have noticed. Centres are good places to find pamphlets or posters about local toy libraries, babies' and children's activity groups, and services and information available on common problems people have with kids' health or behaviour, plus community notices about second-hand clothes or equipment and babysitters.

Baby health centres are absolutely vital to mothers and babies in those early weeks and months. Many councils, looking for ways to run their services more cheaply, are cutting back the available hours of nurses and health centres. You can protest about this to your local council, State or Territory and federal politicians.

 See Baby Health Centres in 'Help'.

your record

Scribble down everything about your labour. I know
you don't believe it now, but you will forget!

YOUR UTERUS IS SHRINKING

what's going on

Your uterus is slowly shrinking, contracting each time you breastfeed, or a little more quickly if drugs are administered to shrink it because you're not breastfeeding – it will be back to its right size in about six weeks. Your muscles and ligaments are all adjusting to the loss of relaxin. Retained fluid may still cause puffy ankles and sore joints, especially the knees, and the problem may stick around for some weeks.

Your baby will be starting to grow at a very fast rate. Sometimes it will seem as if you can see the difference in a day. Your baby can't see very much because their eyes only focus on things within 30 centimetres, and probably isn't smiling yet: this can make a baby seem very passive and not much fun. But before you know it they'll be staring at you with eyes on full-beam, and within about five weeks you'll be seeing gorgeous gummy grins.

WEEK 42

Diary

I'm writing all this down later, as the week after Eddy's birth is a hideous haze of drug-addled fatigue and incomprehension. I know I'm supposed to say it was a wonderful, joyous time full of relief and the tinkling laughter of well-dressed parents overwhelmed with a sense of achievement, and that sort of palaver, but it was a bloody nightmare.

Poor old Eddy, the least experienced of us all in the ways of the world, was plonked into a room with two sleep-deprived, deeply gobsmacked parents, one of whom was on drugs and a trolley, wired up to a drip and in pain, and the other of whom didn't have any bosoms. Not that we weren't happy to see Eddy. But I kept looking at him through a veil of pain-killers that seemed to deaden brain feelings as well as pain.

I just couldn't connect Eddy with who used to be inside me, especially because he had been taken away when he was born and I lay there outside the operating room for all that time in a surreal state – not pregnant, but without a baby. At first he just didn't feel like mine – maybe it was because we hadn't gone on the journey of labour together, and I hadn't felt him being born. Maybe it was because of the drugs or the shock, or because having a real live baby actually felt hyper-real.

Eddy looked exactly like Des without the 5 o'clock shadow. He had fists that could be gently opened into small starfish, and mother-of-pearl fingernails, and a very serious expression. He was so tiny and lovable, and so mysterious and passive. It felt like we were constantly doing things TO him – trying to breastfeed him, changing nappies, wrapping and unwrapping him. His vulnerable 'littleness' made me feel very protective and scared at the same time.

Des was in shock for days afterwards, I think. He kept trying to make everyone cups of tea and explain footy to a very deadpan Eddy. We spent ages looking at Eddy's little face, wondering what he was thinking. 'Probably "get me another bosom",' said Des.

The daytime midwives were mostly wonderful, especially the ones who would change the sheets and help tidy up the room. If I had my time over, I would have asked Aunty Peg or Jill or someone

to help every day – it's just not something you can usually do
yourself, especially after major surgery.

Eddy's bed was a plastic tub on a trolley that they'd take away
to the nursery at night when I got completely exhausted. And then
the night midwives – oh my God, the night midwives. Two were
brilliant. The rest were more trouble than they were worth. I got to
dread pressing the button for help at night because a midwife
would bustle or burst in, cross from being drawn away from the
nursery, or just cross.

They would gruffly grab Eddy with one hand and my breast
with the other and bring them together with the force of
somebody applauding heartily. After this tense-making and
confronting behaviour, often accompanied by barked instructions,
they would push down on my shoulders and command, 'Relax!
You're supposed to enjoy it!', or pull me into a position a previous
midwife had insisted was completely wrong.

One night midwife was so bad we held our breath when she
came into the room. Literally bursting through the door like
Cranky Bart in a bad western movie, she stomped across to turn off
the call button and jabbed her finger at the wall so hard she
injured herself.

Shaking her finger and glowering, she stood over us and
asked, 'What do you want?'

'My pain-killer was due an hour ago,' I said.

She reached into her pocket for the tablet, slapped it into my
palm and stomped off again. 'Just call if you need anything,' she
snarled, and slammed the door.

Yeah, right. Maybe if I were on FIRE.

One night I went up to the nursery to get Ed back and I could
hear him crying. I looked at this little sobbing creature in one of
the sprung hammocks they use to settle babies, and leant in and
cradled the baby to me. The crying stopped immediately and I
cuddled and soothed for a moment, then turning to take him back
to my room I happened to notice from the wristband that I had
picked up the baby of Rabbi Fierstein and his lovely wife, Rachel.

I turned to a midwife who had come over to see what I was
doing. 'Oh my God, I've got the wrong baby', I said.

'Yes.' She smiled at me as if I were a complete maniac.

I slunk into the other nursery room where Eddy was happily listening to a lullaby and whisked him off to my room, feeling like an idiot and an unfit mother who couldn't even recognise her own baby. No wonder all the babies have name tags attached.

I'm pretty sure it was the Rabbi and Rachel, dressed in full Orthodox gear, who met Des in the corridor one morning and were rather arrested by the sight of Des's gigantic pyjamas covered in a cheerful print of rubber ducks. Des's hair was sticking out to the side as if he were in a stiff wind, and the arm of one side of his glasses had snapped off, giving them a rather jaunty, 45-degree slant.

'Wow,' said Des.

Rachel averted her gaze, and the Rabbi just nodded as if something he had long suspected had been confirmed.

After about three or four days of Eddy waking up to be breastfed every 4 hours, a feed which would take about an hour or more each time, I hadn't had more than 2 hours or so of sleep in a row. And as a person who needs 9 or 10 hours sleep a day, this was taking its toll. I did what I always do when I'm tired. I cried and cried.

It just felt like I couldn't cope, couldn't function with the immobility and pain and feeding the baby, if I didn't get some proper sleep. If they took Ed away to the nursery, they would bring him back when he was really hungry and screaming his head off – so he would be all worked up and unsettled and harder to feed and full of wind afterwards, which meant more crying.

Anyway, it all culminated in me weeping uncontrollably after a bumbling attempt to feed Eddy with razor-painful nipples (one had a crack nobody could see except me) and watching a couple of midwives taking my baby away and telling me to sleep as they closed the door of my room behind them. I was almost hysterical thinking, 'What's the point of sleeping? It will only be two and a half hours at the most! I may as well stay awake and go mad.'

And then I said to Des, 'They're all standing outside my room saying I can't cope and I've got postnatal depression. It's not the blues, I'm just overtired!' (Not to mention a touch paranoid.)

Well, they sent for a private lactation consultant, who turned up looking starched and sympathetic, and I decided if I was paying this woman for a consultation I would just listen to her advice and ignore any conflicting info from each shift of midwives. (By this time I was wearing a rather firm maternity bra as my bosoms kept swelling up like cantaloupes.)

This turned out to be the best move to make because it meant I could continue to ring her up for help when I got home from hospital. AND what's more, she could see the nipple crack. Well, she said she could.

So many people are getting rushed out of hospital even before their milk comes in properly, and get into trouble when they arrive home with nobody to help. As far as breastfeeding goes, the only advice that you ever get is people saying 'persevere', in different ways – this doesn't always help if you don't know HOW to persevere.

I rang Beck nearly every day I was in hospital (a whole week) to tell her how tired and incompetent I felt. She sent in vitamin B, herbal tonics and stern instructions to get out into the fresh air.

Eddy just lay wrapped up in a bunny-rug looking at everything as if he were trying to memorise it. 'Well, mate,' I said to him, 'I'm sure I'll get better at this caper.' Eddy presumably was thinking 'I'd like some more of that bosom business, if it's all the same to you, Leaky.'

info

postnatal depression

what is it?

Most women experience what is known as the 'baby blues' – feeling weepy and sad – often on about day 4 after giving birth when the 'happy hormones' go and the prolactin kicks in for real milk production. For most women these blues only last a few days, but some

find that the depression stays, or returns, and gets worse. It's hard to decide where the baby blues end and postnatal depression (PND) begins, so figures for new mothers experiencing PND vary from one in ten to more than half of all new mums. Recently there has been some research into the incidence of PND in the partners of new mothers, with early findings suggesting that it could affect some men in the same way.

what causes it?

No one knows why PND affects some women more than others, but hormones seem to be the main culprits. Oestrogen and progesterone levels drop rapidly after childbirth, which may trigger depression in a similar way to fluctuating hormone levels causing PMS (pre-menstrual syndrome). There's some evidence that it runs in families.

The following are all recognised as contributing factors in PND and logical reasons why you may feel down.

◎ Exhaustion – childbirth wears you out; so do visitors and trying to follow any kind of schedule once you have a baby. One of the reasons for exhaustion is that your volume of blood has suddenly been cut by 30 per cent so a lesser volume is reaching your muscles than they have become used to, making them tire easily and feel weak. It takes a few weeks for your body to readjust to this. Sleep is one of the first things to suffer once the baby is born, and if you are depressed you can suffer from insomnia so you're unable to take advantage of even the ludicrously short sleep periods available to you.

◎ A traumatic birth – this can cause shock and disappointment.

◎ Frustrating or bad hospital experiences – you might feel you need to get away from all the prodding, the unfamiliar cramped surroundings and the artificial air.

◎ Anxiety about coping – going home can seem overwhelming and terrifying when you think about how much you have to do, especially if you have other children to look after.

⊚ A sense of failure – this can arise from feeling unable to cope with all the things you think you 'have' to do to be a good mother; disappointment if the birth didn't go according to plan; or feeling that you have somehow failed as a woman if you are having problems feeding and settling your baby. In reality, almost EVERYONE has a problem at some point.

⊚ A health problem – most new mothers will suffer from at least one following the birth: backache, fatigue, mastitis (infection of the milk ducts), painful episiotomy stitches, massive sleep deprivation. Feeling physically unwell adds to depression.

⊚ Ennui – after spending nine months on the high of anticipating seeing your baby for the first time, you may find yourself feeling underwhelmed by them. It is quite common to think that your baby is less than gorgeous or scintillating company until you have had time to bond emotionally. Tiny, new babies are very passive – there's none of the cooing, extended eye contact and sticking their heads up out of flower pots we associate with babies (and greeting cards) for a few weeks or months yet. The guilt you experience when you feel bored by or distant from your baby only adds to the depression.

⊚ Loss of individual identity – before the birth, everyone is focused on the pregnant woman and how she is feeling, and afterwards many women feel that they are less important to their family and friends as all attention is on the baby. You may feel as if people have stopped seeing you as an individual and now see you only as a 'mother'.

⊚ Perfectionist or anxious approach to life – PND appears more in people who tend to worry or are perfectionists. Many women feel disappointed in themselves if they have always dealt with things to exacting standards in their professional and social lives and suddenly feel unable to reach that level of 'perfection' in motherhood.

⊚ Subsequent pregnancies – PND is more common in women who already have children. Having to look after older children as well as a new baby is likely to place even tighter constraints on the time you have to yourself and to get enough rest. It can be scary wondering how you'll cope.

◉ Loneliness – if everyone you know is busy with their own lives and yours revolves around the baby, you may feel as though you are missing out on 'life'.

◉ A feeling of being trapped in this lifestyle for the rest of your days – 'Why on earth did I have a baby?'.

Signs and symptoms:

◉ the blues and the feelings listed above persist for more than a couple of weeks

◉ sleeplessness and/or lack of appetite

◉ low self-esteem

◉ confusion and/or panic attacks

◉ sadness

◉ feeling 'flat'

◉ feeling angry or aggressive towards yourself or your baby

◉ feeling wildly out of your depth.

strategies

◉ Set up a support network of family, friends and professionals – accept help from others rather than feeling as if you have to prove you're capable by doing it all yourself. Remember that in sensible cultures babies are looked after by an extended family or even a whole tribe of people from the moment they're born. We weren't meant to do it alone.

◉ Look after yourself – use the time when your baby sleeps to rest instead of catching up on all the things you think you should have done such as the housework; treat yourself to things that help you feel pampered and relaxed, such as a massage or haircut.

⑥ Get some fresh air – gentle exercise such as walking or yoga, with or without the baby, is calming and releases energy. Try to spend a little time each day realising it IS day, and not just sleeping, eating and feeding the baby in a twilight, indoor world.

⑥ Get together with other new mums – contact the women in your childbirth class or join a postnatal exercise class; or ask the local baby health centre about the new-mothers' groups.

⑥ Ask your GP to rule out a thyroid problem that could cause similar symptoms to PND.

⑥ If you feel your depression is severe or that you cannot cope any longer, ask your doctor to refer you to the postnatal depression unit of a hospital, or to a residential parenting centre. Lots of people find this really sorts them out.

⑥ Spending time at a parenting centre can be especially useful if you feel you need help with better techniques for feeding, settling, dealing with crying and so on. Being able to leave your baby in the care of professionals to have some time to yourself or to catch up on sleep should also help you feel better. (See under Parent Services in 'Help'.)

⑥ If you are staying overnight, many parenting centres allow partners to stay too. There can be long waiting lists (up to about 4 weeks) for a place in most of these units, so don't put it off until you're completely barking mad and at the end of your tether. If you have private health insurance, you can go to a centre attached to a private hospital. Ask your baby health centre nurse for a recommendation.

⑥ Be aware that your partner, if you have one, might also have the blues. They might benefit from counselling or special help as well, and it's a good step for the baby's sake too.

⑥ Some women find progesterone supplements useful.

 See Postnatal Depression in 'Help'.

your record

Write down your first impressions of your baby:
who the baby resembles, colouring, characteristics,
temperament, whatever.

How are you feeling ___ weeks in ?

Hospital/home visitors	Presents or flowers

what's going on
You're tired. You're still trying to get breastfeeding to be smooth and easy for both of you. Your body has started to heal. You're trying to cope with visitors as well as looking after the baby. You're in a dreamworld. FORGET THE BLOODY HOUSEWORK.

You'll find that the tiny outfits that fitted in the first week of hospital start to get too small (the baby's outfits, not yours). Your baby's eye colour may be changing, and the baby hair might be falling out, to be slowly replaced by a new lot. After another couple of weeks the shrivelled, stumpy bit of umbilical cord will come away from the navel and you'll see what your baby's tummy button looks like. The hands will stay curled in fists for a few weeks yet. Length and weight? Oh who cares. Forget the statistics for a minute. Every day

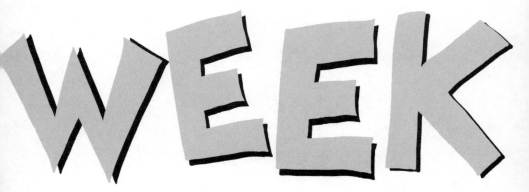

your baby's getting closer to becoming a social being who sleeps more and doesn't cry so much (although the amount of crying reaches a peak at about six weeks old). So every day you're getting closer to the time when you can get some more sleep. Live in the moment, as babies do. Forget about what you have to do tomorrow or next week. Take it one day, even one hour, at a time, sister.

43 falling through the days

DiARY

The only thing that really helped me to get a grip on the blues was getting home into an environment with fresh air, and the chance to sit outside even if I felt like a zombie and was not at all sure what to do with a tiny baby. It was kind of comforting having the hospital midwives nearby, but nothing like being at home. Besides, I could always ring them.

I was so tired in those early days I thought it would never end. I cried towards the end of every day when fatigue started to overwhelm me. We discouraged visitors because rather than offering help, so many seemed to need attention. The visitors who were really helpful were the ones who would pick up the baby or otherwise make themselves useful around the house.

Aunty Peg has forgotten about tiny babies. I remember that Peg didn't get hold of me until I was 3 months old, when Mum died – so she's all at sea with such a small bundle as Eddy and convinced that every snuffle means malaria, cot death or convulsions.

All at once I felt lonely, but too tired to make the effort to reach out to friends. It seemed like I was living in a fog of fatigue, robotically waking, feeding the baby and trying to sleep again; like some kind of demented wet nurse on Valium. Beck told Des to make me go outside for a walk in the afternoons so at least I would feel like I knew which was day and which was night, and that there was an outside world. This helped a lot.

Eddy was sleeping in the pram every night because he seemed so TINY in the cot – until this morning when Des goes in to see him and this weeny, supposedly immobile baby has wiggled his way to the top end of the pram and is millimetres away from sticking his head down into a dangerous gap. This gives us a big shock, so we drive to a baby equipment hire joint and get a hammock suspended from a spring on a large frame that looks like it used to be gym equipment. This is the most brilliant decision we've made and we can bounce him to sleep. They had these hammocks in the nursery for premmie babies.

Every time I think about how I told everyone I'd start work part-time in eight weeks, I'm overwhelmed with stress and anxiety. I've got to try to go with the flow. Eddy is waking up every 4 hours, which is not too bad compared with some babies, but I am still absolutely stonkered from lack of sleep. Not only do you have to live day by day, but sometimes hour by hour, without looking forward or back.

Marg described the first few weeks as 'falling through the day', and she had her sister and mother to help. Des and I don't have any help, but at least there's two of us. Even so we're lucky if one of us has had a shower by nightfall and somebody can make the dinner. For a while there the washing machine and dryer seemed to be going all day long and there were mountains of nappies . . .

Why didn't I think of it before! We've swapped to disposable nappies and are using the cloth ones as essential, all-purpose shoulder drapes, wipes, bum cleaners and nummy folded surfaces for the change table. Eddy sleeps up to an extra hour or two at night with a disposable nappy on, and I decide he might as well be more comfortable in the daytime as well.

There is a certain guilt in this, and we expect to be raided by the Baby Police or the Environment Squad at any moment. I listen to a caller who rings up a radio station and says that women who use formula baby milk and disposable nappies are 'lazy'. About 100 people rang and said they'd like to kill her. Hurrah! I do feel guilty about the environment, so I've joined the Australian Conservation Foundation in Eddy's name.

Breastfeeding is easier than it was at the beginning, but Eddy still has a lot of trouble attaching, especially to the left nipple (which is odd because it has always been his father's favourite). The scar and pain from the caesarean make everything harder, including finding a good position for breastfeeding. I need two pillows to balance him on, and how to feed him insouciantly and – arrgghhh – in public is a complete mystery to me.

His 'wind' is still bad and he cries and cries inconsolably after all the daytime feeds, really screaaaaaaming in the ear of whichever parent is holding him: it's extraordinary how loud a baby can yell. It's so hard not being able to take the pain away, and hard to remain patient with the crying. Yesterday I found myself raising my voice in frustration and saying angrily, 'Shut up!', which is about as useful as saying, 'Act your age', and as soothing as a lovely death-metal song. Luckily I get hold of myself, stop raising my voice, and just end up crying as well. I read Robin Barker's small book called *Crying* over and over, and what the other books say about it as well. But nothing really helps. I just have to keep saying, 'This will end, this will end.'

I ring the Nursing Mothers' Association's local contact and ask, 'How do I tell, when the baby cries 3 hours after a feed, whether he's hungry or there's something else wrong?'

'Just feed him when he cries,' she says.

'But it may be too soon and he isn't hungry,' I reply, knowing full well from experience that if I feed Eddy after 2 hours he'll projectile vomit. Which, by the way, is such an extremely shocking moment it makes you draw your breath in and open your eyes really wide like an English pantomime actor called Dame Chortlepants.

'Some women feed their babies every hour,' she says.

'But how do they do that without going mad?' I ask.

'Oh,' she says airily, 'they just do.'

How very marvellous.

I'm supposed to be doing all these exercises to help the post-caesarean body, but I might as well be told to read a couple of novels a day – there is just no time at all. And when there is, I'm afraid I need to be horizontal, usually with ear plugs in, my head under the pillow, an eye mask on, dreaming of getting stuck into a bottle of whisky.

early outings

Baby excursions in the first few weeks can be a tad gruelling, and you should never feel you have to go anywhere. It's good just to take your time at home, gradually getting to know your baby, apart from going for short walks in the fresh air, or sitting in the park.

One of the worst things about the early forays out the front door is that you are giving your first public performances as a new parent. Heaps of new mums cry with frustration the first few times they try to collapse that damn new pram into the car or get off a bus with a baby AND some shopping. After a few days they can do it backwards and upside down in the dark with one foot. It's just a matter of practice.

BaBy BaG

If you're still getting the hang of changing nappies, breastfeeding and working out why the hell your baby is crying, going out can be a bit stressful. Also, the virtually full-time nature of new-baby care doesn't change just because you're out. Your baby will still need to feed, be burped, have their nappy and maybe clothes changed, be settled down to sleep, feed some more, sleep – or whatever happens at home – while you're trying to have a cup of tea, stay awake and sound intelligible, or get home before dark.

Don't worry: it gets easier every time.

so what's in the bag?

The big bag that all parents haul about with them contains whatever you need to change and feed the baby. Its exact contents alter as the baby grows older, reaching peak capacity during toddler years, when it includes all nappy-changing equipment plus sundry snacks, drinks, security blankets and can't-leave-the-house-without-Binky-type toys.

The newborn-baby bag will need to contain:

⊚ nappies (pilchers and pins or snappy fasteners, if you use cloth) – usually 3–4 depending on how long you plan to be out

⊚ 1–2 changes of outfit in case the going-out clothes get poo on them, which is more likely if you have cloth nappies

⊚ a surface to change the nappies on – some bags have a built-in change pad; if yours doesn't, a bunny-rug with a folded nappy on

top or a waterproof-backed change sheet on the floor works just
as well

❺ whatever you use to clean your baby's bottom at change time:
a small container of water or small bottle of nappy change lotion,
and some cotton balls, or a packet of baby wipes

❺ nappy rash cream, which forms a barrier between wee and
skin

❺ a few plastic bags to bring dirty nappies and clothes home in –
re-using supermarket bags is ideal, but check they're not ripped,
and tie a knot or two in them for safety until you use them (then
tie them up firmly again) in case another baby or a toddler gets
hold of them

❺ bunny-rugs or muslin squares to wrap the baby in, depending
on the weather

❺ sun hat if it's hot, cap or hat if it's cold

❺ a couple of clean cloth nappies to drape over the shoulder of
anyone holding the baby as a vomit guard or chin wiper

❺ a couple of toys suitable for little babies – because newborn
babies see mostly contrasts rather than colours for the first six
months, black and white toys are good, and they also like those
plastic rings in a chain that you see dangling on prams, which
pharmacies sell

❺ bibs if you are already using them

❺ sterilised bottles of freshly made up but cold formula with
protective sterilised caps if you are bottle-feeding, kept in an
insulated bottle carrier. Better still, take the right measurement of
cooled boiled water in a sterilised bottle (with a sterilised cap on)
and add formula from a sachet to it (follow sachet instructions)
while you are out, then heat it up. This prevents bacteria forming.
Never take bottles of hot formula out and never try to keep them
hot. Bottles should be drunk within an hour of being heated.
Formula sachets are more expensive than bulk formula, and check

the instructions because you may have to make up a larger amount than your baby usually drinks.

Special hint: even if you prefer cloth nappies and a water wash at home, you may find it more convenient to use disposable nappies and commercial baby wipes for excursions.

The main thing about the big bag is this: have it packed and ready to go at all times. Getting around sleeping, feeding and changing times and actually out of the house is a finely tuned exercise in time management. There is no time for delay while you hunt about looking for things to put in the bag. The exception to this of course is if you are bottle-feeding, in which case you need to take freshly prepared bottles in an insulated bottle carrier.

To have the bag ready, you need duplicates of nappy change lotion, or wipes and barrier cream – probably in smaller, more portable-sized containers or packages than you would buy for use at home. You also need to remember to restock the bag when you get home from an outing. Get used to bringing it in every single time in case the car goes away with it, or you need to restock before you go out in the car again.

As well as the big bag, you may need somewhere portable for the baby to sleep. You can take a bassinet (the body of some prams converts to a basket, which is handy for visiting), or a quilted baby bag, or a lambswool, or a woven baby basket. You can let the baby sleep in the pram if you keep an eye on it all the time. If you set the baby up on the floor, don't forget to draw everyone's attention to this, so the baby doesn't get trodden or sat on. If it's a short visit, newborn babies can be just as comfortable sleeping in their parents' arms as anywhere. Be very aware of other people's toddlers and pets as a potential danger: they may not be used to babies or take any notice of warnings.

You can wear your baby in a pouch as a charming fashion accessory, with optional vomiting feature, so long as the baby is not going to be in a smoky environment, and someone can help you when the baby gets too heavy.

Leaving the house gets easier when feeding and sleeping turn into something resembling a routine. About when they're asking for their first pocket money, maybe.

IMMUNISATION

Immunisation is not compulsory in Australia, but the medical profession and the government strongly recommend it. Australia has very low rates of infectious diseases, and medical authorities say that to maintain this all kids should be immunised. Most child-care centres and schools ask to see children's immunisation records when they enrol; you can get your official record from the Australian Childhood Immunisation Register on 1800 653 809.

Kids who haven't been immunised are usually sent home if there is an outbreak of any of the illnesses that immunisation protects against. Some children will still get the diseases they've been immunised against, but the risk is far less after immunisation.

You can get 'scheduled' immunisations at your baby health centre or from your local doctor for free. There are routine vaccinations for diphtheria, whooping cough, polio, measles, mumps, rubella, chicken pox, pneumococcal disease, tetanus, *Haemophilus influenzae* type b (Hib), hepatitis B and meningococcal C. Sometimes several are given in one 'cocktail' injection. There are also optional and travel vaccines that may be not on the official schedule and not covered by Medicare.

Common side effects following immunisation are minor fever, soreness where an injection has been given, nausea and irritability. These should not be too severe or last for very long. Some of the newer vaccines are showing far fewer side effects. Some very rare side effects of vaccines can include convulsions, brain damage and death, and anti-vaccination activists point to these as unacceptable risks. Another view is often held by those of the older generation who remember the days before vaccinations when thousands of babies died from whooping cough or measles, and several kids in each school had polio and started wearing the callipers and using the walking sticks they'd need forever. A very large percentage of parents in Australia choose to have their children immunised.

Immunisation schedule   Check with your GP or baby health centre for your schedule. Sometimes they adjust the recommended schedules, so keep in touch with your GP or paediatrician as your child grows. Usually there are injections, including vital booster shots, scheduled for when the child is 2 months old, 4 months, 6 months, 12 months, 18 months and just before primary school starts, with a final top-up of some things at about 15 years old or before they leave school.

Helping your baby through it   Also find out from your GP or baby health centre what side effects to look out for after particular injections. Don't worry – the injections are no big deal. Usually babies just look horrified and accusing for a moment when they get them and cry a little until they're distracted, perhaps by a breastfeed or a bottlefeed.

The whole rundown on immunisation for kids up to the age of 5 is given in the sequel to this book, *Kidwrangling: The Real Guide to Caring for Babies, Toddlers and Preschoolers.*

 See also Immunisation in 'Help'.

and by the way . . .

⑥ Say it loud and say it proud: IF THE CHOICE IS BETWEEN SLEEPING AND THE HOUSEWORK, SLEEP.

⑥ If a certain book or person is making you feel guilty, avoid them. (I burnt Penelope Leach's book in the backyard when I read in it that a 'clever' mother shouldn't have to get up more than once a night if she juggles the times of feeds and anticipates her baby's crying at night. You may think it feels bad and wicked to burn a book. It felt FANTASTIC.)

⑥ After a few weeks your bosoms will stop being so hard and full before each feed, and stay much floppier, but they are actually producing more and more milk for your growing baby. Don't assume you're running out because your bosoms are softer between feeds: your body's just getting more efficient. And it's common for one breast to produce more milk than the other – or be easier for the baby to 'draw on'.

⑥ If you have committed yourself to other projects and you find that looking after a baby is harder than you thought, try to get out of everything you can, if you can, without damaging your work prospects, or decide which prospects you're prepared to sacrifice. Or find ways to get more help with the baby.

⑥ Show friends and family how they can help. Many people, not only blokes, will be feeling inexperienced and tentative, and scared of hurting a small baby. Show them the way, and everyone will have a better time.

⑥ If your baby screams blue murder when you do the bath thing, avoid the stress. It can be much more restful to get in the big bath together and cuddle while you wash, or to just wash bits of your baby with a flannel. And you don't have to do it every day.

SUDDEN INFANT DEATH SYNDROME (COT DEATH)

The cause of SIDS is not known. Basically what happens is that the baby stops breathing. Eighty per cent of SIDS deaths happen in the first six months. SIDS is now far less common. There is continuing research and a general agreement on how to lower the risk.

1 Sleep your baby on its back, never the tummy. Newborn babies who tend to vomit can be firmly propped on their

side with some rolled-up hand towels on either side, or tucked in firmly with a bunny-rug, so that they can't roll onto their back. Ask the hospital midwives to show you, if you're unsure. Roll the baby's head to the side if that is comfortable.

2 Don't smoke when you're pregnant or during your baby's first year, or allow anyone to smoke in the house or the car where the baby is.

3 Don't cover your baby's head when they're sleeping or have soft toys, bumpers or bedding such as doonas and pillows in the cot or bassinet, which could cover a tiny head while sleeping.

After about the age of 6 months, babies may stop sleeping in exactly the position you place them in and put themselves into all sorts of positions (bum up in the air is a particularly entertaining one). Some older babies roll onto their tummies during sleep, and by this age they should be able to move themselves if they get into any breathing trouble.

A few younger babies who are always placed in the same position to sleep may develop a flattened or unusual head shape. In most cases this does no harm and 'fixes itself' before school starts. Current SIDS research still indicates babies should be put to sleep on their backs, but you can change the head positions for each sleep, from face turned to one side, then to the other, then to looking straight up. (If your baby always seems to turn its head to face out into the room, you can alternate putting the baby at different ends of the cot, so their head isn't always in the one pozzie.) And if your baby's head seems to be oddly shaped or crooked, have it checked out by a paediatrician for your peace of mind.

 The SIDS and Kids organisation in your State or Territory has more detailed info (see Grief and Loss in 'Help').

BABY-CARE BOOKS

Baby Love: Everything You Need to Know About Your New Baby by Robin Barker, Pan Macmillan, Sydney, 1997.

Top of the list. Australian midwife and early childhood nurse, Robin Barker brings a no-nonsense but kindly aspect to the genre. This is a big, thick, reassuring book, not so much for reading straight through as for looking up what you need at the time: info on sole parenting, premature babies, choosing baby products, breastfeeding, bottle-feeding, worries, how to look after the baby, what to expect from a baby's development, sleeping and crying. Takes parents through, step by step, until the baby is a year old.

The Baby Love Guide to the First Three Months by Robin Barker, Pan Macmillan, Sydney, 1998.

A small, handy Reader's Digest version of the relevant section in Robin Barker's 'bible', *Baby Love*.

What to Expect the First Year by Arlene Eisenberg, Heidi E. Murkoff and Sandee E. Hathaway, Angus and Robertson, Sydney, 1998.

The American trio back again with the sequel to *What to Expect When You're Expecting*. Another beauty, again adapted for Australia, with relevant resources and a good index. A month-to-month guide that's easy to quickly check as the baby grows. One to keep and read when you need to. And when you're finished with it, you can use it as a doorstop: it's a whopper.

The New Parent: The Essential Guide for All First-time Mothers and Fathers by Miriam Stoppard, Dorling Kindersley, Australia, 1998.

Beautifully laid out, with a double-page spread for each theme, the book covers many aspects of pregnancy and then gets onto the business of baby arriving, baby's first day, what happens to the mother's body after birth, how to look after a baby in the first weeks. Info on breastfeeding and bottle-feeding, and how to put on a nappy, bath and dress the bub is well illustrated and short and simple, but this book isn't much good to you if things don't go according to plan. There's a handy section on how the average baby develops at each stage.

The Australian Baby and Child Care Handbook by Carol Fallows, Penguin, Ringwood, 1998.

Lots of hints on everything from what kind of equipment to buy, breastfeeding, dealing with tantrums and crying to fun ways to keep kids occupied and what to expect from child development.

Your Baby and Child: The Essential Guide for Every Parent by Penelope Leach, 3rd edn, Penguin, London, 1997.

This Englishwoman is kind of the new Dr Spock. Ms Leach is a research psychologist and mother of two who writes a meticulous account of what to expect during the child's development and your part in it. What sometimes gets up people's noses is that Leach's picture of a happy parent and child cooking together and constantly and merrily playing useful and fun games is an unattainable one for busy parents, especially if they have other children, or anything else to do. But as one stay-at-home dad says, it can be good to know what's the best thing from the toddler's point of view, even if you can't always deliver. You'll find most parents are divided into Leach haters or devotees.

How to Stay Sane in Your Baby's First Year: The Tresillian Guide by Cathrine Fowler and Patricia Gornall, Simon and Schuster, Sydney, 1998.

The Royal Society for the Welfare of Mothers and Babies began in 1918 with a brief to organise childhood and maternal services in New South Wales, when so many babies died of simple things caused by ignorance and poverty. It's now a number of linked organisations called the Tresillian Family Care Centres, which help new parents with everything from the 'baby blues' to specific problems with breasfeeding or bottle-feeding, sleeping, crying and feelings of frustration. The book contains well-presented, practical ways of dealing with each of these issues, and info on average baby development, introducing solids, travelling with a baby, common baby illnesses, safety, and child-care options. Each section has a few useful points to sum up called 'The Bottom Line'. Has a great list of support services in Australia and New Zealand.

Babies! A Parents' Guide to Surviving (and Enjoying!) Baby's First Year by Dr Christopher Green, Simon and Schuster, Sydney, 1998.

By the media-saturating author of *Toddler Taming*, it's a quick look at most aspects of the first year, including bonding, solid foods, babies' temperaments, average sleeping and feeding times, common baby illnesses, safety, grandparents, and your post-baby 'sex life'. Includes a useful list of the average milestones for a baby. You may have heard Dr Green's Irish accent on TV, but he lives here and the book is Australian.

Who'd be a Parent?: The Manual that Should Have Come with the Kids by John Irvine, Pan Macmillan, Sydney, 1998. (Also **Coping with the Family: A Guide to Surviving Your Kids from Babies to Teenagers; Coping with Kids; and Coping with School.**)

Who'd be a Parent? covers all sorts of common kid problems, from anger management for parents to bad dreams, aggressive kids, tantrums and throwing up in the car. Dr Irvine is an Australian doctor working with kids who need help with behaviour and learning.

Coping with the Family includes lists of suggested solutions from real kids and real parents for all sorts of problems, including jealousy, coping with teasing, having needles at the doctor's and kids who are teased at school for being gay. A very entertaining read – especially the suggestions from kids!

Children's Symptoms: The Quick Reference Guide to Identification and Treatment, Including Essential First Aid by Dr Bernard Valman, Dorling Kindersley, Sydney, 1998.

A medical look at recognising symptoms, assessing the next step (straight to bed or off to the hospital?) and likely treatments, by a London paediatrician. All aspects have been checked by Australian and New Zealand doctors, and the book is endorsed by the Australian and New Zealand Medical Associations. Flow charts are designed to help you diagnose problems and identify causes and necessary action. Then there's a bunch of typical problems from warts and bronchiolitis to head injury. Many of these are illustrated, as is the first-aid section.

The Penguin Guide to Family Health by Dr Frances Mackenzie, Penguin, Ringwood, 1999.
Includes a comprehensive First Aid section.

Pamela's Natural Remedies for Babies and Children by Pamela Allardice, Random House, Sydney, 1997.
NOT designed to be used instead of going to the doctor, this is a natural approach to baby massage and massage oils, nappy rash treatments, insect repellents for toddlers, soothing aromatherapy, and natural approaches to the less serious baby and childhood complaints such as gummy eyes and soap allergies. If the condition doesn't respond quickly, as they say in the classics, seek medical advice.

For specific books on sleeping and crying see the relevant entries in 'Help'.

forever after... (diary)

A number of months down the track I look back at those first weeks and wonder how anyone does it without going completely mad. Before I had Eddy, when people used to talk about 'lack of sleep' I thought of it as an inconvenience – like staying up too late and having a bit of a hangover. Now I can see why they use sleep deprivation as a method of torture. Good old Ed is finally sleeping for 8 hours straight a night.

'We got a good one, la la la,' sings Des.

I can't remember a thing about being pregnant but I still look about six months 'gone'. You know how they say you automatically lose weight when you breastfeed? Nup. And you know how they say you'll lose it when you stop breastfeeding, instead? Not me. Took me about nine months to feel robust again after the caesarean.

I breastfed for three months, then my endometriosis problem started again and I had to go on the Pill. And the Pill goes through into breast milk and that's no good for Ed. Sadly, he no longer regards my bosoms as something special, but don't get between him and a bottle of formula. He loves the stuff, and he's thriving on it. He also likes to 'chew' rice cereal, severely distressed parsnip and the tags on all his soft toys.

Some friends have disappeared over the horizon, but I've made new ones at 'sleep school' (where we learnt what a routine was) and among other mums. Thank God for the childless pals who still ring and ask me out. I've hired someone to come and look after Eddy when I'm working part-time from home. Eddy chats away happily in baby language to himself and everyone else, and we've weathered our first ear infection (which crept up and king-hit us while we were waiting for the much-warned-about teething that happened later than most people expect). I'm afraid gummy old Ed is a little backward in the teeth department. At least he's a gifted vomiter or we couldn't hold up our heads at playgroup. (And he's a champion dribbler, I'll have you know.)

Sometimes I just want to stop the clock and have a week off. Sometimes it's fascinating, sometimes it's dead boring. Sometimes

I yearn for a few hours just to myself and yet sometimes it's so lonely. And then there's that moment when he smiles and laughs and reaches out for a cuddle and I think it's the most gorgeous feeling I've ever had.

I suppose the next thing I know Eddy'll be crawling, and going to school, and designing a titanium spaceship, or cooking a dinner party for six. But until then there's a lot of cardboard books about duckies to be read, a lot of ludicrous baby hats to be worn, a lot of walks in the park to be had, and a lot of hurtling round the backyard being a fairy-seeking missile. And there's a little indent on the back of his neck that's just perfect for kissing, and if you whisper 'Oofty Goofty' in his ear he might giggle again. So. If you'll excuse me . . .

The End. (And just the beginning . . .)

HeLP

The contact details for organisations may change. When in doubt, try Telstra services, State and Territory government departments, and women's information services for help.

BABIES' HEALTH PROBLEMS

Many babies are born with health problems, ranging from a routine, temporary problem to a serious and dangerous one requiring intensive care and very hard decisions.

You will be able to derive some comfort from knowing that Australia has some of the best-trained and most dedicated hospital midwives, doctors, paediatricians, specialist surgeons, hospital social workers, and counsellors in the world. Keep pushing until you feel satisfied that everything that needs to be done is being done, and vote for and put pressure on people who you believe put medical care as a high priority.

Immediately there is a problem, take notes or bring a friend to take notes of your conversations with doctors and other relevant people – it can be a time when shock causes everything to go in one ear and out the other.

There are several parent support groups for specific conditions such as Down syndrome and spina bifida. Ask your doctor or see under Women's Hospitals or Women's Information Services in this section for a starting point.

BABY HEALTH CENTRES

Call directory assistance or phone your local council. (We'd tell you to look in the phone book but the position of the listing keeps changing.) Centres may have different names in different States and Territories – for example, infant health centre or maternal and child health centre. Most centres have an after-hours number you can also call – ask your baby health centre nurse about it.

BODY IMAGE

Pregnancy changes a body. You may find these changes confronting, or worry about not losing weight after the baby has arrived. If body image is making you depressed or confused, both these books provide a better understanding of the issues, and offer some practical solutions.

If Not Dieting, Then What? by Dr Rick Kausman, Allen and Unwin, Sydney, 1998.

Real Gorgeous: The Truth About Body and Beauty by Kaz Cooke, Allen and Unwin, Sydney, 1997.

BREASTFEEDING

Australian Breastfeeding Association (ABA)

The ABA has seven-day-a-week breastfeeding help lines staffed by trained counsellors. Can put you in touch with your local nursing mothers' group. Also has a gerzillion special pamphlets, and videos to buy or hire, on every aspect of breastfeeding you can possibly imagine.
website: www.breastfeeding.asn.au
Help Lines:

ACT	(02) 6258 8928
	(also southern NSW)
NSW	(02) 9639 8686
Qld	(07) 3844 8977
	(07) 3844 8166
SA and NT	(08) 8411 0050
Tas	(03) 6223 2609 *(south)*
	(03) 6331 2799 *(north)*
Vic	(03) 9885 0653
WA	(08) 9340 1200

ABA Lactation Resource Centre

Has an amazingly comprehensive collection of videos, books and other resources that can be sent or borrowed nationwide. Also has a catalogue of great baby and child products, and you can support their good works by buying through it.
1818–1822 Malvern Rd
East Malvern, Victoria 3145
(03) 9885 0855
email: lrc@breastfeeding.asn.au

La Leche League

An international breastfeeding support group.
website: www.laleche.org

◎ For private lactation consultants, and hiring breast pumps, see under Breastfeeding Support Services in the Yellow Pages.

Breastfeeding: A Beginner's Guide.

A video with lots of helpful hints on how to start breastfeeding, how to interpret baby's gestures, what to expect in terms of flow, and other useful business. The video is available from Tweddle Child and Family Health Service, 53 Adelaide St, Footscray, Victoria 3011. Call (03) 9689 1577.

CONTRACEPTION AND TERMINATION

Surgical termination is available in most States and Territories of Australia up to a certain stage of pregnancy, usually before twenty weeks, but up to twenty-four weeks if the foetus is severely malformed. You will need a referral from a GP, obstetrician or family planning clinic (see Family Planning Clinics).

It's not widely known, but there is another option. Australian women can ask their doctor to prescribe emergency contraception (the misnamed morning-after Pill) within 72 hours of unprotected sex. You take two of the prescribed Pills with an anti-nausea tablet, wait 12 hours and repeat. This means that if an egg has been fertilised, it will not implant in the uterus – in effect, the pregnancy will not have started – or ovulation may be delayed and fertilisation prevented. Many doctors will not tell a patient about this method unless asked. If your doctor refuses to prescribe what you need, go to another one or a family planning clinic without delay.

An 'abortion pill' called RU 486 is available overseas, but not yet in Australia because of conservative politicians. It has also been used quite successfully as emergency contraception and has fewer side effects than the contraceptive Pill. Australian women who feel they must terminate a pregnancy are only offered surgery.

CRYING

If your baby's crying is driving you crazy, don't just try to put up with it. Contact your doctor, closest women's hospital or major hospital and ask for help. Services ranging from phone advice to day visits and live-in programs are available at parenting centres, and private and public hospitals. See also under Parent Services, and Sleeping, which can be a related problem.

AUSTRALIA-WIDE

Tresillian
(02) 9787 5255 *(24 hr)*
Freecall 1800 637 357 *(24 hr)*

Karitane
(02) 9794 1852 *(24 hr)*
Freecall 1800 677 961 *(24 hr)*
Call to get the number for your nearest unit. The 24-hour phone service will help identify if the cause of the crying is of a physical nature – for example, teething or reflux. These organisations also provide live-in and day care. See Parent Services for further details.

Lifeline
Freecall 13 11 14 *(24 hr)*

Child Abuse Prevention Services (CAPS)
CAPS counsellors offer support and advice to parents and carers on any parenting issue.
(02) 9716 8000 *(24 hr)*
Freecall 1800 688 009 *(24 hr)*

Family Support Services Association
Call for your nearest local contact.
(02) 8512 9850

Crying by Robin Barker, Pan Macmillan, Sydney, 1998.
   A little, comforting, simple book on ways to tackle the problem.

EXERCISE
VICFIT
Fitness and pregnancy information and accredited courses.

Level 2, 232 Victoria Pde
East Melbourne 3002
(03) 9412 4311
website: www.vicfit.com.au

Exercise in Pregnancy.
   A video and book that educate trainers, gym staff and pregnant women about safe exercising and nutrition in pregnancy are available from Human Kinetics, phone (08) 8277 1555.

FAMILY PLANNING CLINICS
Sexual Health and Family Planning Australia
Provides medical advice and prescription, information and counselling on a range of issues such as women's health, sexually transmitted diseases, contraception, pregnancy care and pregnancy termination. Call for details of your nearest centre.
ACT
Level 1, 28 University Ave
Canberra City 2601
GPO Box 1317
Canberra City 2601
(02) 6247 3077
email: shfpact@shfpact.org.au
website: www.shfpact.org.au
NSW
328–336 Liverpool Rd
Ashfield 2131
(02) 9716 6099
website: www.fpahealth.org.au

NT
Clocktower Centre
Dickward Dve
Coconut Grove 0810
(08) 8948 0144
email: admn@spwnt.com.au
Qld
Family Planning Queensland (FPQ)
100 Alfred St
Fortitude Valley 4006
(07) 3250 0240
email: inquiries@fpq.com.au
website: www.fpq.com.au
SA
Shine
17 Phillips St
Kensington 5068
(08) 8431 5177
website: www.shinesa.org.au ▶

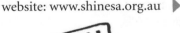

Tas
Family Planning Tasmania
PO Box 77
North Hobart 7002
(03) 6228 5422
Freecall 1800 007 119
email: info@fpt.asn.au
website: www.fpt.asn.au
WA
Family Planning Western
Australia (FPWA)
70 Roe St
Northbridge 6865
(08) 9227 6177
Freecall 1800 198 205
email: tif@fpwa-health.org.au
website: www.fpwa-health.org.au

Vic
Action Centre Family Planning
Victoria (for teenagers)
94 Elizabeth St
Melbourne 3000
(03) 9654 4766
email: acaction@fpv.org.au
and
Family Planning Victoria
(open age)
901 Whitehorse Rd
Box Hill 3128
(03) 9257 0121
email: fpv@fpv.org.au

FEEDING (SOLIDS)

I know it seems as if your baby will never be big enough to eat solids but in four to six months' time you'll be mashing up stuff for the little tyke to shove in their mouth/ear/nose. (Strike out the most conventional option.)

Your baby health care nurse and each book on baby feeding will have a different opinion on everything from what to feed the kid first and when you can introduce certain foods, to whether to offer solids before, during or after a bottle.

Maybe the easiest thing to do is to choose one book or direction and then stick to it unless it doesn't work, and in that case, be flexible. (For example, cross your fingers and try the opposite.) In the meantime don't worry – your baby won't starve to death if they miss a few solid feeds. Milk is still the most important thing at this stage. Here are some books.

The Baby Love Guide to Feeding by Robin Barker, Pan Macmillan, Sydney, 1998.

Pocket-sized, condensed version of Robin Barker's advice in her big baby-care 'bible', *Baby Love*, which starts with the first breastfeeds, or even bottle-feeds, and then gets onto solids. For quick and easy, rough and ready advice, when you haven't got time to read a lot and the baby's driving you mad, on matters ranging from sore nipples to a baby who refuses to eat with a spoon.

Australian Baby and Toddler Meals by Robin Barker, Pan Macmillan, Sydney, 1998.

An excellent, large-format book with a great layout that has user-friendly, simple and realistic recipes (including play dough and fingerpaint) and the usual down-to-earth advice one would expect from Robin Barker.

Babies and Toddlers Good Food Cookbook, Australian Women's Weekly, ACP Publishing, Sydney, 1999.

It's laid out like a magazine with lots of colour photos and, more helpfully than most, has recipes grouped for suitable ages. Includes good food for mum and the family that the baby can share, and helpful hints on what you can freeze and for how long. Handy section on portable food and lunch boxes, parties and birthday cakes.

Cooking for Your Baby by Laraine Toms, Penguin, Ringwood, 1993.

One of those 'bible' type books that's been around for yonks. Written by someone called Laraine, so it's bound to be sensible. A large paperback the size of a novel with heaps of recipes, some simple, some with loads of ingredients, from first solids through to lunch box suggestions. *Good Food for Babies and Toddlers* by Laraine Toms, Penguin, Ringwood, 1994, is a condensed 'pocket' version.

GRIEF AND LOSS

It is rare, but some babies die in the last weeks of pregnancy and are induced stillborn. Some babies die soon after birth, or in the following weeks. Often the general baby books are no help to the grieving parents, and often you can't remember what you've been told by medical staff because of the shock and grief. During these terrible times there are lots of experts who may be able to offer you a great deal of help:

- ◎ midwives and doctors
- ◎ hospital social workers
- ◎ counsellors
- ◎ the SIDS and Kids organisation in your capital city, if relevant.

A friend or relative who can take notes of what is said by these people, and your options, can be invaluable.

There are support groups for parents and siblings affected by the death of a baby, or those trying to deal with a baby who has special needs. Ask your hospital to put you in touch with them. ▶

People react very differently to grief – some don't want to talk about it, and this can seem to others who grieve differently that they do not care as much. This is not the case. Grief counsellors can help a couple or a whole family, including brothers and sisters, understand what has happened. Your hospital or doctor should be able to help you find one who specialises in the loss of a baby (that's important). Or see contacts below.

Compassionate Friends

A support service for bereaved parents.
website: www.compassionate
friendsvictoria.org.au
NSW (02) 9290 2355
ACT (02) 6286 6134
Qld (07) 3254 2657
SA (08) 8351 0344
Tas (03) 6261 4250 *(Hobart)*
(03) 6344 4955 *(Launceston)*
Vic (03) 9888 4944
WA (08) 9486 8711

SIDS and Kids

The national SIDS organisation provides counselling and referrals in the case of a baby's death from any cause. Holds SIDS statistics, recommendations and research data. Call to find your local branch.
1300 308 307 *(24 hr)*
email: national@sidsandkids.org.au
website: www.sidsaustralia.org.au

Stillbirth and Neonatal Death Support (SANDS)

Telephone support and counselling service that can also direct you to support groups in your area.
ACT (02) 6287 4255
NSW (02) 9721 0124
Qld (07) 3254 3422
Freecall 1800 228 665 *(country)*
SA (08) 8277 0304
Tas (03) 9517 4470
Vic (03) 9899 0218
WA (08) 9474 3544
Freecall 1800 686 780

National Association for Loss and Grief (NALAG)

An educational, referral and networking organisation that can put you in touch with counsellors and support groups and services. Can provide contact numbers for other States and Territories.
PO Box 214
Essendon, Victoria 3040
(03) 9531 0358
Freecall 1800 100 023 *(country)*
email: info@nalagvic.org.au
website: www.nalagvic.org.au

VICTORIA

Bonnie Babes Foundation

Will put you in touch with your local office. Offers counselling for the loss of a baby during pregnancy or just after.

National office
PO Box 2220
Rowville 3178
(03) 9758 2800 *(24 hr, 7 days)*
email: enquiry@bbf.org.au
website: www.bbf.org.au

Centre for Grief Education

Bereaved people aged over 10 are eligible for up to eight sessions of free counselling.

McCulloch House
Monash Medical Centre
246 Clayton Rd
Clayton 3168
(03) 9545 6377
email: counselling@grief.org.au
website: www.grief.org.au

Recurrent Miscarriage Clinic

Royal Women's Hospital
132 Grattan St
Carlton 3053
(03) 9344 2709 *(clinic)*
(03) 9344 2000 *(hospital)*

When a Baby Suddenly Dies: Cot Death, the Impact and Effects by Janet Deveson Lord, Hill of Content, Melbourne, 1987.

A book for parents, siblings, relatives, friends and health workers about what happens after a sudden infant death.

Beginnings and Endings with Lifetimes in Between: A Beautiful Way to Explain Life and Death to Children by Bryan Mellonie and Robert Ingpen, Hill of Content, Melbourne, 1983.

A picture book for children.

Things About Zac, My Baby Brother by Nadia A. McComb, SIDS Research Foundation, Melbourne, 1996.

A book written by Zac's 7-year-old sister, which you can purchase through SIDS and Kids. Call (03) 9822 9611.

Cutting the Cord: Stories of Children, Love and Loss, edited by Debra Adelaide, Random House, Australia, 1998.

Personal stories from Australian writers including Roberta Sykes and Ruby Langford Ginibi, not only about death.

IMMUNISATION

The official Australian Government immunisation website will give the schedule in your area and explain the diseases and their vaccines. There's a long list of answers to frequently asked questions on this site.

Immunise Australia Program
Freecall 1800 671 811
website: http://immunise.gov.au

INFERTILITY

Counsellors are available at all infertility and IVF clinics and women's hospitals; or through any major hospital, which your doctor can refer you to. It's important to go to a counsellor specialising in infertility. They can best help you explore your options and also put you in touch with a support group.

ACCESS Infertility Network
Can supply information and suggest counsellors and support.
PO Box 959
Parramatta 2124

(02) 9670 2380
Freecall 1800 888 896 *(24 hr, 7 days)*
email: info@access.org.au
website: www.access.org.au

Battles with the Baby Gods by Amanda Hampson, Doubleday, Sydney, 1997.

A book of personal stories of women who have struggled with infertility.

Getting Pregnant: A Compassionate Resource to Overcoming Infertility by Professor Robert Jansen, Allen and Unwin, Sydney, 2003.

The author is a specialist in reproductive medicine who answers some common questions, and explains that it's quite normal to have difficulty in getting pregnant. A look at the medical tests and techniques available for diagnosis and treatment. Dr Jansen examines the reasons for lowered fertility, including environmental causes, endometriosis and other medical conditions, and the dramatic drop in fertility rates as women get older. The book is aimed at heterosexual couples.

MIDWIVES

Australian College of Midwives
National office
(02) 6230 7333
email: acmi@acmi.org.au
website: www.acmi.org.au

ACT PO Box 490
      Curtin 2605
NSW (Midwives Association)
      (02) 9281 9522
NT   PO Box 41781
      Casuarina 0811
Qld (07) 3358 6144
SA   (08) 8364 5729
Tas GPO Box 2022
      Hobart 7001
WA (08) 9340 1042
Vic (03) 9349 1110

NEW SOUTH WALES
**Australian Society for
Independent Midwives**
(02) 9888 7829

**Childbirth Education
Association**
PO Box 240
Sutherland 2232
(02) 8539 7188 (*9.30 a.m.–
2.30 p.m. Mon–Fri*)

VICTORIA
Midwives in Private Practice
(03) 9689 0255

MULTIPLE BIRTHS

Australian Multiple Birth Association (AMBA)
Contact for counselling and support, and to find your nearest club.
AMBA runs a pram hire service and provides a regular newsletter.
website: www.amba.org.au

Twins, Triplets and More: Their Nature, Development and Care by
Elizabeth Bryan, St Martin's Press, New York, 1998.
    The author is a paediatrician who specialises in multiple births.
More than One: Twins and Multiples and How to Survive Them by
Lindsay Simpson and Andiee Paviour, Simon and Schuster, Sydney, 1994.
    A book by mothers who've been there.

NATURAL HEALTH CARE

NEW SOUTH WALES
**National Herbalists Association
of Australia**
13 Breillat St
Annandale 2038
(02) 9555 8885 *(8 a.m.–3 p.m.
Mon–Fri)*
email: nhaa@nhaa.org.au
website: www.nhaa.org.au

QUEENSLAND
**Australian Natural Therapists
Association**
PO Box 657
Maroochydore 4558
(07) 5409 8222
Freecall 1800 817 577
email: anta1955@bigpond.com
website: www.anta.com.au
**Australian Acupuncture and
Chinese Medicine Association**
PO Box 5142
West End 4101
(07) 3846 5866
email: aacma@acupuncture.org.au
website: www.acupuncture.org.au

PARENT SERVICES

Parentline
Parentline can help parents cope
with their baby, or children, and
put them in touch with local agen-
cies for help in adjusting to their new
role. Has information on courses
and counselling on parenting issues
for dads as well as mums.

ACT	(02) 6287 3833
	(02) 6205 8800
NSW	13 2055
NT	1300 364 100
Qld	1300 301 300
SA	Freecall 1300 364 100
Tas	Freecall 1800 808 178 *(24 hr)*
Vic	13 2289 *(7 days)*
WA	(08) 9272 1466 *(24 hr)*

Relationships Australia
Call the number below for your
nearest local contact for help with
your adult relationships.
1300 364 277 *(Australia-wide)*
website: www.relationships.
com.au

AUSTRALIAN CAPITAL TERRITORY
**Queen Elizabeth II
Family Centre**
Specialises in postnatal advice and
help, day-stay and residential. For
referral to the centre, contact your doctor or local infant health centre nurse.
129 Carruthers St
Curtin 2605
(02) 6205 2333

NEW SOUTH WALES

Dial-a-Mum

A confidential ear supplied by trained volunteer mothers.

(02) 9477 6777 *(8 a.m. to midnight)*

Karitane

Contact for sleeping, crying, feeding and other problems. They provide 24-hour phone advice, live-in and day care, and can give you the number for your nearest unit.

Cnr Horsley Dve and Mitchell St
Carramar 2163
(02) 9794 1800
Care Line: (02) 9794 1852 *(24 hr)*
Freecall 1800 677 961 *(24 hr)*
email: karitane.online@swsahs.
nsw.gov.au
website: www.swsahs.nsw.gov.au/
karitane

Tresillian Family Care Centres

Contact for sleeping, crying, feeding and other problems. They provide live-in and day care, and can direct you to your nearest unit.

National office
McKenzie St
Belmore 2192
(02) 9787 0800
Parent Help Line:
(02) 9787 5255 *(24 hr)*
Freecall 1800 637 357 *(24 hr, country)*
email: tresillian@email.cs.nsw.gov.au
website: www.tresillian.net

NORTHERN TERRITORY

Children's Services Support Program

1st Floor, 25 Todd Mall Rd
Alice Springs 0870
(08) 8953 0785

Crisis Line

Help line for general counselling. Appointments for personal counselling during business hours can be made at any time. Extensive referral resources for the Northern Territory.

(08) 8981 9227 *(24 hr)*
Freecall 1800 019 116 *(24 hr)*

QUEENSLAND

Riverton Early Parenting Centre
58 Riverton St
Clayfield 4011
(07) 3860 7111
Child Health Lines:
(07) 3862 2333 *(24 hr, 7 days)*
Freecall 1800 177 279 *(24 hr, 7 days, country)*

SOUTH AUSTRALIA

Child and Youth Health

295 South Tce
Adelaide 5000
(08) 8303 1500
Parent Help Line:
1300 364 100 *(24 hr)*
website: www.cyh.com

Torrens House

(Provides live-in program to help with feeding, sleeping and management; by referral only.)
(08) 8303 1530
(08) 8303 1523 ▶

Crisis Care
13 1611 *(AH counselling, 4 p.m.–*
9 a.m. Mon–Fri, 24 hours weekends
and public holidays)
Helen Mayo House
PO Box 17
Eastwood 5063
(08) 8303 1183 *(24 hr, 7 days)*
(08) 8303 1425 *(24 hr, 7 days)*
Freecall 1800 182 232 *(country)*
website: www.wch.sa.gov.au

TASMANIA
Lady Gowrie Family Support Service
Provides counselling, referrals and parenting group contacts.
229 Campbell St
Hobart 7000
(03) 6230 6860
email: fss@gowrie-tas.com.au

Lady Gowrie Tasmania Resource Centre
Offers library service, printed information and videos.
PO Box 263
North Hobart 7002
(03) 6230 6824
Freecall 1800 675 416
Parenting Centres
Parent Information Telephone Assistance (PITAS)
Freecall 1800 808 178 *(24 hr)*

Hobart:
232 New Town Rd
New Town 7008
(03) 6233 2700
Launceston:
Walker House
17A Walkers Ave
Newnham 7248
(03) 6326 6188
Burnie:
34 Mace St
Burnie 7320
(03) 6434 6201

VICTORIA
Crisis Line
13 6169 *(24 hr)*
Caroline Chisholm Society
Can help with personal counselling, supported crisis accommodation, in-home family support services, post-natal depression support groups, parenting groups and courses.
PO Box 846
Moonee Ponds 3039
(03) 9370 3933 *(24 hr)*
Freecall 1800 134 863 *(24 hr, country)*
Lady Gowrie Child Centre
36 Newry St
North Carlton 3054
(03) 9347 6388
email: info@gowrie-melbourne.
com.au
website: www.gowrie-melbourne.
com.au
(Also offers children's programs for 0–5 years.)

Maternal and Child Health Line
For telephone counselling, advice and referral.
13 2229 *(24 hr)*
O'Connell Family Centre
(formerly Grey Sisters)
Provides counselling, information and support. Live-in and day-stay services available.
6 Mont Albert Rd
Canterbury 3126
(03) 9882 2326
Queen Elizabeth II Family Centre
Offers residential and day-stay help, home visits and educational programs.
53 Thomas St
Noble Park 3174
(03) 9549 2777
email: theqec@qec.org.au
website: www.qec.org.au
Tweddle Child and Family Health Service
Offers day visit and stay-over help with sleeping, crying, feeding, postnatal depression and parenting issues from 0 to 3 years.
53 Adelaide St
Footscray 3011
(03) 9689 1577
email: Tweddle@tweddle.org.au
website: www.tweddle.org.au

WESTERN AUSTRALIA
Family and Children Services
Parenting Line:
(08) 9272 1466 *(24 hr)*
Freecall 1800 654 432 *(24 hr, country)*
Family Help Line:
(08) 9221 2000 *(24 hr)*
Freecall 1800 643 000 *(24 hr)*
Ngala Family Resource Centre
9 George St
Kensington 6151
(08) 9368 9368
Freecall 1800 111 546 *(country)*
email: ngala@ngala.com.au
website: www.ngala.com.au

POSTNATAL DEPRESSION

See also Parent Services: any of the organisations listed there can help you. Ask your doctor to refer you to a specialist counsellor or centre, or you can contact your nearest women's hospital or major hospital for referral.

Thyroid Australia
For info and support groups nationwide: thyroid conditions can cause PND-type symptoms.
(03) 9888 2588
website: www.thyroid.org.au

Beyondblue
website: www.beyondblue.com.au/postnataldepression
Australian site on PND.

AUSTRALIAN CAPITAL TERRITORY
Queen Elizabeth II Family Centre
(02) 6205 2333 *(24 hr)*
(See Parent Services for full details.)

NEW SOUTH WALES
Karitane
(02) 9794 1852 *(24 hr)*
Freecall 1800 677 961 *(24 hr)*
(See Parent Services for full details.)

▶

Tresillian Parents Help Line
(02) 9787 5255 *(24 hr)*
Freecall 1800 637 357 *(24 hr, country)*
(See Parent Services for full details.)

QUEENSLAND
Brisbane Centre for Post-Natal Disorders
Belmont Private Hospital
1220 Creek Rd
Carina 4152
(07) 3398 0238 *(24 hr)*

SOUTH AUSTRALIA
Helen Mayo House
(08) 8303 1183 *(24 hr, 7 days)*
(08) 8303 1425 *(24 hr, 7 days)*
Freecall 1800 182 232 *(country)*
(See Parent Services for full details.)

TASMANIA
Parent Information Telephone Assistance (PITAS)
Freecall 1800 808 178 *(24 hr)*

VICTORIA
Post and Ante Natal Depression Association (PANDA)
Support Line:
(03) 9428 4600 *(Mon–Thurs)*
email: panda@vicnet.net.au
website: www.vicnet.net.au/~panda

WESTERN AUSTRALIA
PND Support Association (PNDSA)
(08) 9340 1622
email: pndsa@hotmail.com
PND Support Group
c/- Granny Spiers Community House
2 Albatross Crt
Heathridge 6027
(08) 9401 7021

Postnatal Depression: A Practical Guide for Australian Families by Lisa Fettling, IP Communications, Melbourne, 2002.
A mother of four with her own experience of PND offers advice on diagnosis, treatment and how to talk to doctors, and for male partners. She is co-author, with Belinda Tune, of *Women's Experience of Postnatal Depression: Kitchen Table Conversations*, IP Communications, 2005.

PREMATURE BABIES
Ask your obstetrician, midwife or hospital to put you in touch with a support group.
New South Wales Pregnancy and Newborn Services Network
Researches into the causes of premature birth and high-risk pregnancy.
(02) 9351 7318

SAFETY

These contacts provide a variety of services such as phone advice, display and sale of safety products and printed information. Most of the baby-care books and baby health centres also have lists of things you can do to make a home safe.

Kidsafe
(Child Accident Prevention Foundation of Australia)

ACT
Building 2
Pearce Community Centre
2 Collett Pl
Pearce 2607
(02) 6290 2244

NSW
Kidsafe House
Children's Hospital
Hainsworth St
Westmead 2145
(02) 9845 0890
email: kidsafe@chw.edu.au
and
(02) 4942 4488 *(Hunter Valley region)*

NT
Shop 20, Rapid Creek Shopping Centre
Trower Rd
Rapid Creek 0810
(08) 8985 1085
email: kidsafen@ozemail.com.au

Qld
50 Bramston Tce
Herston 4029
(07) 3854 1829

SA
Women's and Children's Hospital
72 King William Rd
North Adelaide 5006
(08) 8161 6318
email: sa@kidsafe.org.au

Tas
Abbotsfield Rd
Claremont 7011
(03) 6249 1933

WA
Princess Margaret Hospital for Children
Cnr Thomas St and Roberts Rd
Subiaco 6008
(08) 9340 8509

Vic
Safety Centre
Royal Children's Hospital
1st Fl, Flemington Rd
Parkville 3052
(03) 9345 6471 *(Kidsafe)*
(03) 9345 5085 *(Safety Centre)*

SINGLE PARENTS

AUSTRALIA-WIDE

Child Support Agency (CSA)

A government organisation which runs the collection of child maintenance payments by non-custodial parents.

131 272

Parents Without Partners

ACT	(02) 6248 6333
NSW	(02) 9853 3269
Qld	(07) 3275 3290
SA	(08) 8359 1552
Tas	(03) 6243 9225
Vic	(03) 9836 3211
WA	(08) 9389 8350

AUSTRALIAN CAPITAL TERRITORY

Canberra One Parent Family Support Service

Advice and referrals, home visits, organisation of housing, legal advice, emotional and financial support.

(02) 6247 4282

NEW SOUTH WALES

Single Parent Family Association

1300 300 496

SOUTH AUSTRALIA

SPARK Resource Centre

(08) 8226 2500

email: spark@sparkresourcecentre. org.au

TASMANIA

Family Support

(03) 6263 5464

email: fsbridgebrook@bigpond. com.au

VICTORIA

Council for Single Mothers and Their Children

Telephone support, information and referral for single mothers by single mothers. Lobby group for a better deal for sole parents.

Level 2, 54 Victoria St

Carlton South 3053

(03) 9654 0327 *(9.30 a.m.–3 p.m. Mon–Thurs)*

email: email@csmc.org.au

website: www.csmc.org.au

WESTERN AUSTRALIA

Lone Parent Family Support Service

Advice and referrals for single parents with children 0–16 years.

(08) 9389 8373 *(10 a.m.–3 p.m.)*

SLEEPING

If you're not getting enough sleep, you'll find everything else much more difficult. You may have a baby who won't nap during the day, or one who wakes up often at night, perhaps wanting to be fed every 2 hours even when a few months old. Many people now seek help with such problems from sleep seminars, clinics or residential (live-in for a few days) programs.

If you have private health insurance, check private hospitals near you to see if they have a day-visit or residential sleep program. Otherwise many public hospitals and specialist parenting centres run sleep clinics. See under Parent Services. Here are some books.

Settling Your Baby, published by the Child and Youth Health Department of South Australia.

A big pamphlet or small book compiled by a team of experts co-ordinated by the Torrens House residential care centre, this is a huge success story that has grown by word of mouth from an original print run of 2,000 to best-selling sales of more than 40,000. Available nationwide from many baby health nurses, hospitals and child-care centres, the National pharmacy chain in South Australia, or from the department itself for $5 plus postage and handling (usually no more than $1.50 within Australia). Telephone (08) 8303 1551 or write to Child and Youth Health, 295 South Terrace, Adelaide, 5000. Or order on its website: www.cyh.com.au

Sleep Tight, Sleep Right, published in 1998 by the Tweddle Child and Family Health Service, 53 Adelaide St, Footscray, Victoria 3011. For mail orders at $10 plus postage call (03) 9689 1577. There may be similar books from similar services near you.

The Baby Love Guide to Sleep by Robin Barker, Pan Macmillan, Sydney, 1998.

A pint-sized book starting from the baby's birth, which helps you to develop a routine and understand the sleep needs of a small baby. A condensed version of the sleep info in her book *Baby Love*.

Silent Nights: Overcoming Sleep Problems in Babies and Children by Brian Symon, Oxford University Press, Australia, 1998.

Written by an Australian doctor who has made sleep difficulties his specialty. An easy-to-get-into book that identifies lots of sleep problems and possible solutions, ranging from newborns and the first weeks through to toddlers and children. Covers special disruptive occasions such as daylight saving, moving house, relatives who sabotage your routine and first nightmares. ▶

Solve Your Child's Sleep Problems by Dr Richard Ferber, Dorling Kindersley, England, 1999.

Dr Ferber is the Big Cheese at the Boston Children's Hospital Center for Pediatric Sleep Disorders. His thesis is the basis for many of the sleep clinics run for mothers and babies in Australia, including his views on what children associate with sleep, and how to build up your periods of leaving a child crying and shutting the door behind you. Also covers night-time disturbances, the importance of a daily schedule to night-time sleeping, and how to stop night feeding.

TEENAGE AND YOUNG MUMS

Being pregnant as a teenager has special problems and special advantages. Having a baby is a big challenge if you're not yet fully an adult yourself, and like any pregnant woman, you need to know that all the services and help you will want are available.

The major hospitals in your State or Territory should have special information, classes and support groups for you, and you can find out about them from the maternity section or the social worker. They'll help you work out plans for your pregnancy and birth; how to look after the baby (or suggest organisations that will teach you) and plan for the future, such as getting back to school or into work; arrange financial help if your family is not being supportive; and they'll help you with any other worries you might have, speak to your parents if that's difficult for you, and even help you find accommodation.

It's really important for you and the baby to eat MORE than usual while you're pregnant. Don't eat less to try to look as if you're not pregnant: it's really dangerous to diet during pregnancy. You need more nutrients and calories (not junk food) than a pregnant woman who's older than you because while your baby is growing, you're still growing too.

Don't forget that doctors are required by law to keep secret anything you tell them – so if you're afraid of your family finding out, tell your doctor and they should put you in contact with a hospital youth worker or someone else who can help. It's important that you get medical care even if your family doesn't know.

Ring your closest women's hospital and ask to be put in contact with their clinic or staff member who looks after young mums. They will have books and videos you can borrow, as well as clinics and confidential advice.

NEW SOUTH WALES
Sydney's Westmead Hospital, (02) 9845 5555, and Royal Prince Alfred Hospital, (02) 9515 6111, have special services for young mums.

VICTORIA
Melbourne's Royal Women's Hospital has a special centre for young mums, the Young Women's Health Program.
(03) 9344 2189

WESTERN AUSTRALIA
King Edward Memorial Hospital for Women in Perth has an Adolescent Clinic.
(08) 9340 2222

Handbook for Young Pregnant and Parenting Women, developed by the Teenage Pregnancy Interest Group, Family Planning Victoria. Contact the Family Planning Victoria library on (03) 9257 0146 or your local community health centre.

WOMEN'S HEALTH CENTRES

AUSTRALIAN CAPITAL TERRITORY
Women's Centre for Health Matters
Bldg 1, Pearce Centre
Collett Place
Pearce 2607
(02) 6290 2166
email: admin@womenshealth
matters.org.au
Women's Health Service
Cnr Moore and Alinga Sts
Canberra City 2601
(02) 6205 1078
email: womens-health@apa.act.
gov.au

NEW SOUTH WALES
Women's Medical Centre
Rm 10, 2nd Fl
193 Macquarie St
Sydney 2000
(02) 9231 2366
Liverpool Women's Health Centre
26 Bathurst St
Liverpool 2170
(02) 9601 3555
email: lwhc@bigpond.com.au

NORTHERN TERRITORY
Royal Darwin Hospital
Rocklands Dve
Tiwi 0810
(08) 8922 8888 ▶

QUEENSLAND
**Women's Health
Queensland Wide**
165 Gregory Tce
Spring Hill 4000
(07) 3839 9962
Health Information Line:
(07) 3839 9988
Freecall 1800 017 676
TTY (07) 3831 5508
email: whcb@womhealth.org.au
website: www.womhealth.org.au

SOUTH AUSTRALIA
Women's Health Statewide
64 Pennington Tce
North Adelaide 5006
(08) 8239 9600
Freecall 1800 182 098
email: info@whs.sa.gov.au
website: www.whs.sa.gov.au

TASMANIA
Hobart Women's Health Centre
25 Lefroy St
North Hobart 7000
(03) 6231 3212
email: hwhc@trump.net.au
website:www.tased.edu.au/
tasonline/hwhc.htm

VICTORIA
Women's Health Victoria
Queen Victoria Women's Centre
Level 1, 123 Lonsdale St
Melbourne 3000
GPO Box 1160K
Melbourne 3001
(03) 9662 3755
email: whv@whv.org.au
website: www.whv.org.au
Health Information Lines
(9 a.m.–1 p.m. Mon–Fri):
(03) 9662 3742
Freecall 1800 133 321 *(country)*

WESTERN AUSTRALIA
Women's Healthcare House
100 Aberdeen St
Northbridge 6003
(08) 9227 8122
Freecall 1800 998 399
email: whch@iinet.net.au
website: www.womenshealthwa.
iinet.au

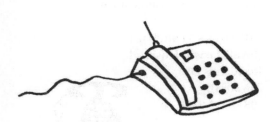

WOMEN'S HOSPITALS

AUSTRALIAN CAPITAL TERRITORY
Canberra Hospital
Yamba Dve
Garran 2605
(02) 6244 2222

NEW SOUTH WALES
Royal Hospital for Women
Prince of Wales Hospital
Barker St
Randwick 2031
(02) 9382 6111

NORTHERN TERRITORY
Royal Darwin Hospital
Rocklands Dve
Tiwi 0810
(08) 8922 8888
Alice Springs Hospital
Gap Rd
Alice Springs 0870
(08) 8951 7777

QUEENSLAND
Royal Brisbane and Women's Hospital
Cnr Bowen Bridge Rd and
Butterfield St
Herston 4006
(07) 3636 8111
Antenatal Clinic: (07) 3636 7182

SOUTH AUSTRALIA
Women's and Children's Hospital
72 King William Rd
North Adelaide 5006
(08) 8161 7000

TASMANIA
Royal Hobart Hospital
48 Liverpool St
Hobart 7000
(03) 6222 8308

VICTORIA
Royal Women's Hospital
132 Grattan St
Carlton 3053
(03) 9344 2000
Family Birth Centre:
(03) 9344 2388
Women's Health Information
Centre: (03) 9344 2007
Freecall 1800 344 207 *(country)*

WESTERN AUSTRALIA
King Edward Memorial Hospital for Women
Bagot Rd
Subiaco 6008
(08) 9340 2222

WOMEN'S INFORMATION SERVICES ————————

These wonderful services provide information and referral on a wide range of issues such as childbirth options, parenting, work, finances, health problems, legal matters, separation and custody. A good first stop to find a support group or other contacts in a specific area.

AUSTRALIAN CAPITAL TERRITORY
Women's Information and Referral Centre
Level 6, Eclipse House
197 London Circuit
Canberra City 2600
(02) 6205 1075
email: wirc@act.gov.au
website: www.wirc.act.gov.au

NEW SOUTH WALES
Women's Information and Referral Service
Level 4, Stockland House
175–183 Castlereagh St
Sydney 2000
(02) 9334 1160
Freecall 1800 817 227
TTY 1800 673 304
email: dfw@women.nsw.gov.au
website: www.women.nsw.gov.au

NORTHERN TERRITORY
Women's Information Centre
Eurilpa House
PO Box 721
Alice Springs 0871
(08) 8951 5880

QUEENSLAND
Women's Infolink
56 Mary St
Brisbane 4000
(07) 3224 2211
Freecall 1800 177 577
TTY 1800 677 577
email:
infolink@premiers.qld.gov.au
Women's Information and Referral Centre
230 Mulgrave Rd
Cairns 4870
(07) 4051 9366
email: wirc@wirc.org.au

SOUTH AUSTRALIA
Women's Information Service
Station Arcade
136 North Tce
Adelaide 5000
(08) 8303 0590
Freecall 1800 188 158
TTY (08) 8303 0590
email: info@wis.sa.gov.au
website: www.wis.sa.gov.au

TASMANIA
Information and Referral Service
Women Tasmania
Franklin Square
104 Macquarie St
London Chamber
Hobart 7000
(03) 6233 2208
Freecall 1800 001 377
email: wt.admin@dpac.tas.gov.au
website: www.women.tas.gov.au

VICTORIA
Wire Women's Information
1st Fl, 247 Flinders Lane
Melbourne 3000
1300 134 130
email: inforequests@wire.org.au
website: www.wire.org.au

WESTERN AUSTRALIA
Women's Information Service
Office for Women's Policy
1st Fl, Westralia Square
141 St George's Tce
Perth 6000
(08) 9264 1900
Freecall 1800 199 174
email: wpo@dcd.wa.gov.au
website:
www.women.wa.community
development.wa.gov.au

WORK: GOING BACK

Find out if your company has any programs that might suit you – job sharing or part-time. Check what this means for entitlements such as sick pay and holiday pay.

See if your State or Territory government, or the federal government, has any schemes, retraining programs or subsidies that might help you ease back into the workforce if you've been out of it for a long while. Check the White Pages under Department of Employment and Training, or Centrelink, but these names can vary or change.

WORLD WIDE WEB

If you have access to the Internet, you can contact heaps of websites about all aspects of pregnancy and parenthood. It's best to use your search engine, rather than getting a whole list of them here, because websites come and go. (Beware of those pesky porn sites that pop up when you're looking for pregnancy information. And any site that seems to be pushing sponsors' products or trying to get your details on a mailing list. Websites can vary from large community sites with chatrooms to individual obstetricians' sites with articles about pregnancy.

NEW ZEALAND CONTACTS ————————

Here are three places to give you a starting point.

NZ Family Planning Association
Can give you contact details for the office closest to you.
National office
PO Box 11515
Wellington
(04) 384 4349
email: fpa@fpanz.org.nz

New Zealand College of Midwives
PO Box 21106
Christchurch
(03) 377 2732
email: nzcom@nzcom.org.nz
website: www.midwife.org.nz

National Women's Hospital
Claude Rd
Epsom
Auckland
(09) 638 9919

acknowledgements

Thanks are due to many people who went so far out of their way to help with this book they needed a cut lunch and some travel insurance.

The unbelievably fabulous Dr Maria Dziardek, developmental biologist at the Department of Anatomy and Cell Biology at Melbourne University, almost drowned under a mountain of faxes, and read and corrected an early draft of each and every What's Going On section.

Manuscript readers and fact-checkers included Ruth Trickey of the Clifton Hill Natural Health Centre, who provided constant assistance with medical and herbal matters; Melanie Pitts, midwife and childbirth educator from Masada Hospital, Melbourne; and Dr Ann Olsson, obstetrician and gynaecologist, Adelaide, who made many useful suggestions. Independent midwife Annie Sprague answered almost endless queries.

I couldn't be more grateful to Dr Len Kliman, obstetrician and gynaecologist, to whom I entrusted my life and my baby's life, and the first draft of the manuscript. We were all in safe hands.

Research for all the special topics was meticulously compiled originally by Fiona Wood, with some assistance from Aimee Said.

Without exception, staff from the Royal Women's Hospital in Melbourne who were approached gave immediate and remarkably generous help with reading bits of the manuscript, checking facts or providing information. Dietitian Elizabeth Gasparini from the Department of Nutrition and Dietetics contributed to and checked relevant parts of the manuscript, as did Sue Fawcett, an associate genetic counsellor from the Genetic Counselling Service. Thanks also to Kay Oke, an infertility counsellor in the Reproductive Biology Unit, and Kym Davey from the Young Mothers' Clinic.

Thanks are also due to Dr Mike Paech, specialist anaesthetist at the King Edward Memorial Hospital for Women, in Perth, for his information on pain relief during labour and delivery; Deb Withers and Jo Durst from the SIDS Research Foundation; Michelle Mason from the Masada Hospital Day Stay Program for Mothers and Babies in Melbourne; the Monash Medical Centre IVF program's Professor David de Kretzer, who discussed with me how long people should 'try' before seeking help; Dr Tony Holmes, director of the Craniofacial Unit at the Royal Children's Hospital in Melbourne, and Dr David David, head of the Australian Craniofacial Unit in Adelaide, for advising on baby head shapes and sleeping positions; and Dr Henrietta Williams of the Family Planning

Association. Independent lactation consultant Margaret Callaghan gave the bosom bits a once-over.

For help with the bibliography and the generous donation of pregnancy and baby books to the Young Mothers' Clinic at the Royal Women's Hospital, thanks to J. G., Imogen Cook and Gab Connellan at Penguin Books, the publicity staff at Random House, Catherine Proctor of Pan Macmillan, Roberta Marcroft at HarperCollins, Michelle Hurley at Allen and Unwin, Stephanie van den Broek and Nicki Robilliard at Dorling Kindersley, Dimity Barber at Oxford University Press, Fiona Robinson at Simon and Schuster, and Rosey Cummings at Tweddle Child and Family Health Service.

I never understood why authors bang on about how their editor did so much work and saved them from making terrible mistakes. Oo-er. Now I get it. Thank you Lesley Dunt.

Thanks as well to Sandy Cull and Leonie Stott for their collaboration and hard work on the design. And a very big hurrah to the Executive Publisher at Penguin Books, Julie Gibbs – every author should have one.

I'd like to thank also all the Lorraines, especially Jane Drury and Katie Purvis for their proofreading and editorial help, and Sandra Jackson.

More personally, I understand now more of what my own mother, Linda Cooke, must have been through, and I owe her great thanks. Anna Daffy did a lot of brilliant Oofty Goofty wrangling. And for blazing the trail I thank especially Philippa Hawker, Gina Riley and Jen Saunders. For constancy of friendship, I salute Judith Lucy and Libbi Herries. For her kindness, I'd like to thank Lily Brett.

The largest thanks of all must go to the remarkable Geoffrey Leonard.

Lest we forget: we need to support the politicians who promise and deliver the upgrading of facilities, research and the public programs of our women's and children's hospitals, and local child-care and maternal and child health services, rather than the ones who just faff on vaguely about the importance of 'family values'.

By its nature this book is subjective, as well as including about a gerzillion facts. Those acknowledged here are not responsible for errors, or for current fashionable advice and accepted statistics that may change in an inkling. Nor are they responsible for any of the author's own, damned flighty opinions.

And just one final point. When authors compare producing a book to having a baby, they need a damned good slapping.

index

Kaz Cooke is an author, magazine columnist, cartoonist and mother. She does not live in a rustic French farmhouse with a frightfully artistic husband, and what's more there appears to be some mashed banana in her hair.

Now you've got the baby, what on earth are you going to do with it?

Read Kaz's reassuring and authoritative sequel to *Up the Duff*

Kidwrangling
delivers all the up-to-date, reliable info on:

BABIES ★ getting through the first weeks ★ bosoms ★ bottles ★ sleeping ★ crying ★ coping ★ new mum & newborn health ★ bonding ★ the blues ★ mum's post-baby body ★ equipment ★ first food ★ teething ★ dummies
TODDLERS and **PRESCHOOLERS** ★ using the loo ★ teaching kids how to behave ★ dealing with common illnesses ★ family food ★ child care ★ exercise ★ getting ready for school
PLUS emotional & physical development 0 to 5 ★ immunisation ★ games, toys & activities ★ safety ★ what dads need to know ★ birthday parties & presents ★ being at home ★ paid work ★ travel ★ best-ever lists of where to go for extra help ★ & much more.

'*An impressive, meticulously researched, wide-ranging 770 pages of support and confidence-building for new parents*'
AUSTRALIAN DOCTOR

'*An absolute essential for everyone, whether you're a first-timer or an old hand at the parenting adventure. Heaps of advice to reassure you on every concern*'
WOMAN'S DAY